LET GOD USE YOU TO SOLVE YOUR PROBLEMS

God Will Instruct You
and Teach You In the
Way You Should Go

EDWARD D. ANDREWS

LET GOD USE YOU TO SOLVE YOUR PROBLEMS

God Will Instruct You and Teach You In the Way You Should Go

Edward D. Andrews

Christian Publishing House

Cambridge, Ohio

CHRISTIAN
PUBLISHING
HOUSE

FOUNDED 2005

Unless otherwise stated, Scripture quotations are from Updated American Standard Version (UASV) Copyright © 2022 by Christian Publishing House

LET GOD USE YOU TO SOLVE YOUR PROBLEMS: God Will Instruct You and Teach You In the Way You Should Go by Edward D. Andrews

ISBN-10: 1945757868

ISBN-13: 978-1945757860

Table of Contents

Book Description

In a world fraught with challenges and uncertainty, faith remains our most enduring beacon of hope. "Let God Use You to Solve Your Problems: God Will Instruct You and Teach You in the Way You Should Go" offers a unique exploration of how a steadfast reliance on God's wisdom, coupled with an active role in our own spiritual development, can serve as a roadmap to navigating life's complexities.

This book provides an enlightening journey into a deeper understanding of God's role in our lives, not as a miracle worker performing supernatural acts on demand, but as a divine guide illuminating our path through the teachings of Scripture and personal experiences. It shows how, by letting go and trusting in God, we can find the strength, courage, and wisdom to confront and overcome our problems.

The author, a conservative Bible scholar, encourages readers to actively engage with their faith, teaching how God instructs us through His Word, life experiences, and our own spiritual growth. Throughout the chapters, readers will learn the art of biblical discernment, nurturing spiritual growth, embracing patience in God's timing, and turning trials into triumphs through God's guidance.

This book ultimately underscores the importance of personal responsibility in a faithful Christian life. It provides a nuanced and balanced understanding of faith that inspires action and involvement in our communities, allowing us to serve God and others while becoming reflections of God's love.

"Let God Use You to Solve Your Problems" is more than a book; it's a spiritual guide for those seeking to blend trust in divine wisdom with personal initiative, creating a life that is not just endured but lived fully and meaningfully in God's light.

Preface

As I sit down to pen these words, I am mindful of the many moments in my own life when the still, small voice of God provided direction in times of uncertainty and solace during periods of distress. His teachings, present in the Bible and the world around us, served as my guide, my compass pointing me toward the right path. Yet, I was also acutely aware of my own agency in this journey, my own responsibility to act upon His guidance and participate actively in His plans for me.

This realization forms the heart of this book, "Let God Use You to Solve Your Problems: God Will Instruct You and Teach You in the Way You Should Go". It is written with the intention of sharing with you, dear reader, the understanding that our relationship with God is not one of passive reliance but of active engagement. It is a partnership where we embrace His teachings, internalize His wisdom, and use these lessons to navigate our life's challenges.

This is not a book about waiting for miracles. Rather, it is about finding the miraculous in the mundane, seeing God's hand in every aspect of our lives and recognizing that His greatest miracles often occur within us - in the transformation of our hearts and minds as we grow in His wisdom.

The chapters you will encounter are a distillation of a lifelong journey of faith, study, and experience. They represent a thoughtful, balanced perspective that aligns with conservative Biblical teachings and eschews the misinterpretation of God's role in our lives. This book is an invitation to step out of passivity and embrace the active role God has intended for us in our spiritual growth and problem-solving.

As you journey through these pages, my hope is that you will gain a renewed understanding of how to let God use you to solve your problems. But more than that, I hope it ignites in you a deeper connection with God and empowers you to become a more active participant in your own life, all while staying firmly rooted in His teachings.

May you find guidance, comfort, and inspiration in these pages, and may they illuminate your path just as God's Word has illuminated mine.

Edward D. Andrews

Author of 220+ books

Introduction

Welcome, dear reader, as we embark on a journey of discovery and transformation together. This book is more than just words on a page; it's an exploration of our relationship with God and the role He plays in helping us address the challenges that life invariably brings.

Too often, we view our faith as a passive thing—a belief system we adhere to, but one that asks little of us beyond ritual observance. We find ourselves praying for miracles, hoping for divine intervention, and waiting for God to solve our problems. But is that the true nature of our relationship with our Creator? Is it possible that God is calling us to a more active role, encouraging us to use the wisdom He provides us to solve our own problems? I believe the answer is a resounding "Yes."

Within this book, we will delve into what it truly means to allow God to use us. To do this, we need to grasp that God is more than an external force; He seeks to guide us, instruct us, and teach us in the way we should go. His Word and the world around us are filled with lessons waiting to be learned, wisdom waiting to be gleaned, and guidance waiting to be followed.

We will explore biblical principles and life experiences that encourage us to become active participants in our spiritual journey, not mere spectators. The journey may not always be comfortable, as it will call for us to examine our attitudes, our actions, and our very hearts. But it will be rewarding, because it is within this active participation that we experience growth, transformation, and true spiritual fulfillment.

This book, then, is not a call to simply believe, but to act on that belief. To step into the complexities of life with faith in one hand and responsibility in the other, knowing that God will guide us, and that we have the ability and the duty to act on His guidance.

I invite you to journey with me, with an open mind and an open heart. Let's learn together, grow together, and discover the powerful transformation that occurs when we let God instruct us and teach us in the way we should go.

CHAPTER 1 Understanding God's Role in Our Lives: A Biblical Perspective

Introduction: Understanding the Importance of God's Role

From the onset, it is essential to appreciate the central role that God plays in our lives. His relevance isn't limited to just spiritual matters; instead, He intricately involves Himself in all aspects of our existence. As we delve into this chapter, we shall navigate the biblical scriptures to uncover how God's role is articulated in the pages of both the Old and New Testaments.

The Creator and Sustainer of Life

Our first encounter with God in the Bible is as the Creator. Genesis 1:1 states, "In the beginning, God created the heavens and the earth." It is by His power and will that everything exists. From the expanse of the universe to the complexity of every living being, every aspect of creation testifies to God's power, wisdom, and creativity.

But God's role doesn't end with creation. Nehemiah 9:6 (ASV) asserts, "Thou art Jehovah, even thou alone; thou hast made heaven, the heaven of heavens, with all their host, the earth and all things that are thereon, the seas and all that is in them, and thou preservest them all; and the host of heaven worshippeth thee." Hence, God is not only our Creator but also the sustainer of all life.

The Source of Guidance and Wisdom

God's role in our lives also includes guiding our paths and granting wisdom. Psalm 32:8 (ASV) reads, "I will instruct thee and teach thee in the way which thou shalt go: I will counsel thee with mine eye upon thee." This verse exemplifies how God actively involves Himself in our lives, guiding us and providing wisdom in our decision-making.

The New Testament reinforces this perspective. In James 1:5 (ESV), we read, "If any of you lacks wisdom, let him ask God, who gives generously to all without reproach, and it will be given him." This generous offer of divine wisdom testifies to God's active involvement in our daily lives.

The Provider and Protector

God's role also extends to being our provider and protector. In the Old Testament, God's people understood Him to be their "Jehovah Jireh" – the Lord who provides, as in Genesis 22:14 (ASV). This concept is also seen in the New Testament, where Philippians 4:19 (ESV) assures us, "And my God will supply every need of yours according to his riches in glory in Christ Jesus."

As our protector, we find comfort in scriptures like Psalm 121:7-8 (ASV): "Jehovah will keep thee from all evil; He will keep thy soul. Jehovah will keep thy going out and thy coming in From this time forth and for evermore."

The Ultimate Judge

Lastly, but certainly not least, God serves as the ultimate judge. In Genesis 18:25 (ASV), Abraham recognized God as "the judge of all the earth." The New Testament further amplifies this role in 2 Corinthians 5:10 (ESV), "For we must all appear before the judgment seat of Christ, so that each one may receive what is due for what he has done in the body, whether good or evil."

This role underscores the moral and ethical dimensions of God's involvement in our lives. He sets the moral standards (Ten Commandments), holds us accountable, and will ultimately judge each person's life.

Conclusion: Recognizing God's Pervasive Presence

In sum, understanding God's role in our lives as our Creator, Sustainer, Guide, Provider, Protector, and Judge allows us to appreciate His pervasive presence in our daily lives. As we journey through life, this realization helps us trust God more, lean on His wisdom, seek His protection, rely on His provision, and live in a manner befitting of His eventual judgment. As we grow in this understanding, we move closer to fulfilling the purpose for which we were created—to glorify God and enjoy Him forever.

God's Role as Our Creator: The Genesis of Our Relationship

The Majesty of Creation

From the very onset of the Bible, we encounter God as the Creator. The book of Genesis opens with a simple yet profound statement, "In the beginning, God created the heavens and the earth" (Genesis 1:1 ASV). These opening words depict God as the architect of the universe, the originator of life, and the designer of all reality.

The Genesis account proceeds to narrate how God, in His wisdom and power, formed the universe in six days. He created the sun, moon, and stars; separated the waters from the dry land; brought forth plants and animals; and finally, fashioned mankind in His own image. Genesis 1:27 (ASV) says, "And God created man in his own image, in the image of God created he him; male and female created he them."

Created in God's Image

Being created in God's image underscores our unique relationship with Him. We bear the imprint of our Creator, setting us apart from all other creatures. We possess characteristics reflective of God—such as the capacity for love, justice, creativity, wisdom, and moral discernment—which equip us for a relationship with Him.

This divine image places upon us a significant responsibility. Genesis 1:28 (ASV) instructs, "And God blessed them: and God said unto them, Be fruitful, and multiply, and replenish the earth, and subdue it; and have dominion over the fish of the sea, and over the birds of the heavens, and over every living thing that moveth upon the earth." As bearers of God's image, we are entrusted to steward His creation responsibly and to reflect His character in our interactions with others and the world around us.

Our Relationship with the Creator

From our origin, we are intimately connected with God. This relationship is a vital aspect of our being and purpose. As the prophet Isaiah declares, "But now, O Lord, thou art our Father; we are the clay, and thou our potter; and we all are the work of thy hand" (Isaiah 64:8 ASV). This analogy describes a relationship of dependence and trust. We rely on our Creator for our being, purpose, and sustenance, just as a clay pot relies on the potter.

Our relationship with God, our Creator, is not merely transactional or functional; it's relational and covenantal. God is not a distant deity, uninvolved and unconcerned with His creation. Instead, He is a relational God who desires to be involved in our lives. As Jeremiah 29:11 (ESV) reminds us, "For I know the plans I have for you, declares the Lord, plans for welfare and not for evil, to give you a future and a hope."

Conclusion: A Creator Worthy of Worship

Understanding God as our Creator shapes our perception of Him and our place in His creation. It gives us a deep sense of belonging and purpose. Knowing that we are not products of chance but are intentionally fashioned by God imparts value to our existence.

Therefore, our response to God's role as our Creator should be one of humility, gratitude, and worship. As Psalm 95:6 (ASV) invites us, "Oh come, let us worship and bow down; Let us kneel before Jehovah our Maker."

As we proceed in the subsequent chapters, we will explore other facets of God's role in our lives. But it's here, at the foundation of our existence, where our relationship with God begins—as our Creator. Understanding this role is fundamental in grasping the other dimensions of His involvement in our lives.

God as Our Sustainer: The Provider of Life and Blessings

The Source of All Life

In the biblical narrative, God's role extends far beyond our creation. He remains actively involved in the sustenance of our lives and the entire universe. God is presented as the source of life, the one who "giveth to all life, and breath, and all things" (Acts 17:25 ASV).

This understanding of God as the sustainer of life reaffirms the notion of our reliance on Him. Just as we owe our creation to God, we owe our ongoing existence to His continued care and providence. We are not independent entities, autonomous and self-sufficient. We are part of God's creation, dependent on His sustaining grace.

The Provider of Daily Needs

God's sustenance is not confined only to our life and breath; it extends to our daily needs as well. He is our provider, the source of our physical necessities. We see this in Matthew 6:31-33 (ESV), where Jesus instructs His followers not to worry about what they will eat or drink or wear, saying, "But seek first the kingdom of God and his righteousness, and all these things will be added to you."

The Psalmist also reflects this understanding when he declares, "I have been young, and now am old; Yet have I not seen the righteous forsaken, Nor his seed begging bread" (Psalm 37:25 ASV). God, as our sustainer, does not abandon us to fend for ourselves but graciously provides for our needs.

The Bestower of Blessings

God's role as our sustainer also encompasses the spiritual blessings He bestows upon us. These blessings include love, peace, joy, patience, kindness, goodness, faithfulness, gentleness, and self-control (Galatians 5:22-23 ESV)—the fruit of the Spirit. Such qualities are not merely human traits; they are divine blessings, gifts from our Sustainer, intended to enrich our lives and reflect His character.

A Personal and Loving Sustainer

What's remarkable about God as our Sustainer is the personal and caring nature of His provision. He doesn't simply sustain us out of obligation or necessity. Instead, God's sustenance is a manifestation of His love for us. As the Apostle Paul affirms, "He who did not spare his own Son but gave him up for us all, how will he not also with him graciously give us all things?" (Romans 8:32 ESV). God's ultimate act of provision—the giving of His Son, Jesus Christ—demonstrates His boundless love and the extent of His care for us.

Conclusion: Responding to Our Sustainer

Recognizing God as our Sustainer should elicit a response of gratitude, trust, and surrender. Gratitude for His constant provision, trust in His ability to provide for our needs, and surrender to His sustaining power in our lives. It's a humbling reality that prompts us to declare, along with the Psalmist, "My soul, wait thou in silence for God only; For my expectation is from him" (Psalm 62:5 ASV).

Indeed, God is more than just our Creator; He is our Sustainer. He not only brought us into existence, but He continuously provides for us, blesses us, and upholds us. Our acknowledgment of this role strengthens our relationship with Him and intensifies our appreciation for His loving involvement in our lives.

God as Our Guide: Divine Wisdom in the Scriptures

Scripture: The Fountain of Divine Wisdom

In addition to being our Creator and Sustainer, God also takes on the role of our Guide. His guidance is found primarily in the Holy Scriptures, the Bible, which are a treasure trove of divine wisdom. The Apostle Paul, in his second letter to Timothy, confirms this when he says, "All Scripture is breathed out by God and profitable for teaching, for reproof, for correction, and for training in righteousness" (2 Timothy 3:16 ESV).

The Scriptures are not merely human writings. They are divinely inspired, the very breath of God, providing us with knowledge and wisdom about Him, His character, and His will. When we immerse ourselves in the Scriptures, we allow God to guide us through His revealed word.

Wisdom for Life's Decisions

The Scriptures offer wisdom for all of life's decisions. They equip us to make choices that align with God's will and that promote justice, righteousness, and love. As the Psalmist states, "Thy word is a lamp unto my feet, And light unto my path" (Psalm 119:105 ASV). Just as a lamp illuminates a dark path, making it safer and easier to travel, the Scriptures enlighten our life's path, guiding us in the right direction.

This wisdom for life's decisions isn't limited to the big, life-altering ones. It applies to the day-to-day choices we make as well. Whether it's how we interact with others, manage our resources, or respond to challenges, God's guidance is available to us through His Word.

Correcting and Shaping our Path

Not only do the Scriptures guide us toward making the right decisions, but they also correct us when we stray from the path. They serve as a mirror, revealing our shortcomings and errors (James 1:23-

25 ESV), prompting us to repent and return to the path of righteousness. As mentioned in Hebrews 4:12 ESV, "For the word of God is living and active, sharper than any two-edged sword, piercing to the division of soul and of spirit, of joints and of marrow, and discerning the thoughts and intentions of the heart."

The Role of the Holy Spirit

Understanding and applying God's wisdom in the Scriptures is made possible by the Holy Spirit. As Jesus promised, the Holy Spirit "will guide you into all the truth" (John 16:13 ESV). This guidance is not an esoteric, mystical process, but rather a matter of enlightening our understanding of God's Word and helping us apply it appropriately in our lives.

Conclusion: Embracing God's Guidance

To accept God as our guide means to immerse ourselves in the Scriptures, to let His wisdom shape our lives and decisions. It involves a humble acknowledgment that we don't have all the answers and a desire to seek God's wisdom above our own. As Proverbs 3:5-6 ASV exhorts us, "Trust in Jehovah with all thy heart, And lean not upon thine own understanding: In all thy ways acknowledge him, And he will direct thy paths."

Embracing God's guidance means allowing His Word to illuminate our path, correct our course, and shape our character. It's a transformative process, one that brings us into a deeper relationship with God and molds us into the likeness of His Son, Jesus Christ. Ultimately, recognizing God as our Guide ensures that we walk the path He has laid out for us—a path that leads to life, peace, and eternal communion with Him.

God as Our Teacher: Life Lessons from Biblical Stories

Biblical Narratives: A Tool for Instruction

The Bible is rich with narratives that provide more than just historical accounts. These stories are a powerful tool in God's hand to teach us life lessons. The Apostle Paul stated that "whatever was written in former days was written for our instruction, that through endurance and through the encouragement of the Scriptures we might have hope" (Romans 15:4 ESV).

The narratives in the Bible present us with a mirror into human nature, our inclinations, potential, failures, and successes. They show God's faithfulness, justice, and mercy in dealing with humanity. Through these narratives, God assumes the role of a teacher, providing us with lessons that have stood the test of time.

Life Lessons from the Story of Abraham

Consider the life of Abraham, often called the "father of faith." In Genesis 12:1-2 ASV, God said to Abram, "Get thee out of thy country, and from thy kindred, and from thy father's house, unto the land that I will show thee: and I will make of thee a great nation." From Abraham's life, we learn about the virtue of faith and trust in God's promises, even when circumstances seem impossible. Abraham's life teaches us about the blessings that come with obedience and the consequences of making decisions based on our understanding.

The Story of Joseph: Perseverance Amid Trials

The life of Joseph is another powerful narrative filled with valuable lessons. Despite being sold into slavery by his brothers, wrongfully accused, and forgotten in prison, Joseph remained faithful to God. In the end, God elevated him to a position of authority in Egypt. Joseph's life story teaches us about maintaining integrity and faith in God amidst trials, the rewards of patience, and the power of forgiveness. (Genesis 37-50).

The Life of David: Repentance and Mercy

David, the shepherd boy who became king, also offers an array of life lessons. He is described as a "man after God's own heart" (1 Samuel 13:14 ESV). David's story teaches us about the importance of a heart fully committed to God, the dangers of succumbing to temptation as seen in the incident with Bathsheba (2 Samuel 11), and the beauty of sincere repentance as reflected in Psalm 51. David's life is also a testament to God's mercy and forgiveness.

Jesus Christ: The Perfect Teacher

Above all, the life, teachings, death, and resurrection of Jesus Christ provide us with the most profound lessons. He is the perfect teacher, providing us with lessons on love, forgiveness, humility, sacrifice, and so much more. His teachings, parables, and interactions with people are rich sources of divine wisdom.

Conclusion: Embracing God as Our Teacher

To understand God as our teacher, we must approach the Bible with a humble and teachable spirit, recognizing that the stories it contains are more than historical narratives. They are divinely inspired lessons about life, faith, and the character of God.

As we explore these narratives, it's crucial to pray for understanding and for the Holy Spirit to illuminate the truths contained in these stories. After all, the goal is not just to learn about these characters but to be transformed by the life lessons they offer. To quote James 1:22 ESV, "But be doers of the word, and not hearers only, deceiving yourselves."

The Bible as God's teaching tool is transformative, providing us with guidance and wisdom. Let's embrace God as our teacher, allowing the life lessons from biblical stories to mold us into Christ-like beings, equipped to navigate life in a way that brings glory to God.

The Misconceptions: Separating Fact from Fiction

Misconception 1: God's Role is Merely as a Distant Watcher

The Deistic notion, commonly held by many, that God is a distant watcher who set the world in motion and then stepped back to observe, is contrary to the biblical presentation of God. Scripture shows that God is intimately involved in the world He created, actively sustaining, guiding, and governing all things. In Colossians 1:17 ESV, it says, "And he [Jesus] is before all things, and in him, all things hold together."

God is not just a distant observer but a personal, relational being who seeks to guide His children according to His perfect wisdom and love.

Misconception 2: God's Role is to Fulfill Our Desires

Another widespread misconception is the idea that God exists to fulfill our desires, much like a divine genie. This view reduces God to a service provider, who we call upon only when we need something. However, this is a misrepresentation of the biblical God who is our loving Father.

While it's true that God cares for us and wants to bless us (Matthew 7:11 ESV), His primary desire is for us to grow in the knowledge and likeness of Christ, which often involves experiencing challenges and trials (Romans 5:3-5 ESV).

Misconception 3: God is a Vengeful and Angry God

A common misinterpretation in understanding God's character is viewing Him as a vengeful and angry God, always waiting to punish us for our mistakes. It's true that God is holy and just, and He hates sin (Psalm 5:4 ASV). However, this does not negate His attributes of mercy, compassion, and love.

In the biblical narrative, God continually reaches out to His fallen creation, offering redemption and reconciliation through Jesus Christ (Romans 5:8 ESV).

Misconception 4: God Does Not Care About Our Everyday Lives

Some people believe that God is only interested in "big" issues or religious activities. However, the Bible assures us that God cares about every detail of our lives. As noted in Matthew 10:30 ESV, "But even the hairs of your head are all numbered." God is deeply invested in our lives and cares for even our mundane affairs.

Misconception 5: God Will Not Allow Suffering for His People

There is a widely held view that being a Christian exempts one from suffering. However, the Bible does not promise a life free from trials. In fact, Christ told His followers, "In the world, you will have tribulation" (John 16:33 ESV).

Suffering can serve a purpose in God's plan, often leading to spiritual growth, character development, and a deeper dependence on God (James 1:2-4 ESV).

Conclusion: Separating Fact from Fiction

As we seek to understand God's role in our lives, it's essential to separate fact from fiction. The most reliable source of truth about God is the Bible. The inspired, inerrant Word of God, moved by the Holy Spirit, reveals who God is and how He operates.

Let's commit to a diligent study of the scriptures, seeking to understand God's role as it truly is, and not as it is often misrepresented. Remember, Proverbs 2:6 ESV states, "For the LORD gives wisdom; from his mouth come knowledge and understanding." Let us pray for wisdom and discernment to avoid misconceptions and comprehend God's role in our lives accurately.

Beyond Miracles: Seeing God's Work in Everyday Life

The Limitation of Focusing Solely on Miracles

A miracle, in a religious context, is often understood as an extraordinary event, defying natural laws, attributed to divine intervention. While miracles indeed demonstrate God's power and glory, focusing solely on these extraordinary acts can limit our understanding and appreciation of God's constant activity in our lives.

Miracles, as recorded in the Bible, are exceptions rather than norms, employed by God to authenticate His message or messenger (Hebrews 2:3-4 ESV). While it's beneficial to appreciate and celebrate these miracles, we should not overlook God's continuous work in our everyday lives.

Seeing God's Work in the Ordinary

God's work is not confined to miraculous events. It extends to the ordinary, mundane aspects of our daily lives. The Bible states in Acts 17:28 ESV, "For 'In him we live and move and have our being.'" This verse emphasizes God's constant presence and activity in our lives.

From the gift of life we receive each morning (Lamentations 3:22-23 ESV) to the divine guidance we experience daily (Psalm 32:8 ASV), God is consistently at work, shaping our lives and drawing us closer to Him. Recognizing God's hand in these everyday moments can deepen our faith and appreciation for His constant care.

Divine Providence: God's Guiding Hand in Our Lives

Divine Providence refers to God's sovereign control over all events, circumstances, and outcomes in the universe. It is God's invisible hand at work, ordering everything to serve His purpose. The Apostle Paul reiterates this in Romans 8:28 ESV, "And we know that for those who love God all things work together for good, for those who are called according to his purpose."

Understanding Divine Providence allows us to see beyond the apparent randomness of life's events. Even when things seem chaotic or don't make sense, we can trust that God is at work, orchestrating everything for our good and His glory.

Witnessing God's Work in Character Transformation

One of the most profound ways God works in our lives is through the transformation of our character. As we submit to God and His Word, we gradually reflect more of Christ's character. The Apostle Paul refers to this process as being transformed into Christ's image (2 Corinthians 3:18 ESV).

This transformation may not be as dramatic as a miracle, but it's a powerful testament to God's ongoing work in our lives. Witnessing the fruit of the Spirit (Galatians 5:22-23 ESV) growing in our lives affirms God's active role in shaping us.

Conclusion: Seeing God's Work Beyond Miracles

The expectation of miraculous interventions can sometimes blind us to the multitude of ways God works in our everyday lives. Let us not overlook the miracle of life, the blessing of each day, the wisdom gained from the scriptures, the lessons learned through trials, and the growth experienced in our character.

God is indeed a miracle-working God, but He is also the sustainer of life, the giver of blessings, the author of wisdom, and the master teacher. It is in these often overlooked aspects of our lives that we can truly appreciate God's active involvement, realizing that His work goes far beyond miracles.

Our Active Participation: Responding to God's Guidance

God's Guidance: An Invitation to Act

Understanding God's guidance involves recognizing that His divine instruction is not a passive gift but an active invitation. It is a call to us to respond with faith, obedience, and action. In the Book of James, we're reminded that faith without works is dead (James 2:17 ESV), meaning that our belief in God and His guidance should motivate our actions.

Responding to God's Guidance with Obedience

Obedience is a fundamental response to God's guidance. From the beginning, God's instructions to humanity necessitated obedience. God commanded Adam and Eve in the Garden of Eden (Genesis 2:16-17 ASV), and their disobedience led to severe consequences.

On the contrary, the obedience of Noah saved his family (Genesis 6-9 ASV), and Abraham's obedience made him the father of many nations (Genesis 12:1-4 ASV). These examples underscore the importance of obedience in responding to God's guidance.

Responding with Prayer and Discernment

Another crucial aspect of our active participation in God's guidance is prayer and discernment. Prayer is a powerful tool for understanding God's will and seeking His guidance. It connects us with God on a deeper level, opening our hearts and minds to His wisdom and direction.

Discernment, on the other hand, helps us distinguish between God's voice and other competing voices. As Christians, we must develop a discerning heart, guided by the Holy Spirit and the Word of God, to accurately perceive and follow God's guidance.

Acting on God's Guidance: Taking Steps of Faith

Merely recognizing God's guidance is not sufficient. We are called to act on it. Whether it's a call to serve, a prompting to forgive, or a command to trust, our active response is crucial.

When Moses was called to lead the Israelites out of Egypt, he initially doubted his ability (Exodus 3:11 ESV). Yet, he ultimately acted on God's guidance and fulfilled his God-given mission. His story reminds us that responding to God's guidance often requires courage and faith.

Conclusion: The Partnership of Divine Guidance and Human Action

In sum, understanding God's role in our lives demands that we not only receive His guidance but also actively respond to it. This relationship between divine guidance and human action is a sacred partnership, which requires our obedience, prayerful discernment, and faithful action.

Just as a ship needs a wind to move but also requires a rudder to steer, so our lives need both God's guidance and our active response. May we be attentive to God's guidance and willing to act on it, knowing that this partnership aligns us with God's will and enables us to fulfill His purposes for our lives.

Embracing the True Role of God in Our Lives

God's Role: Our Father, Sustainer, Guide, and Teacher

Understanding and embracing the role of God in our lives is paramount in developing a strong, faith-filled Christian walk. To comprehend this, we must first recognize God as our Father, Sustainer, Guide, and Teacher.

In the Scriptures, God is depicted as our Heavenly Father. Jesus teaches us to pray, addressing God as "Our Father in heaven" (Matthew 6:9 ESV). As a loving Father, God nurtures us, disciplines us, and looks after our well-being.

God is also our Sustainer, the Provider of life and blessings. As expressed in Acts 17:28 ESV, "In him we live and move and have our being." He provides for our physical and spiritual needs, ensuring that we lack nothing as we walk with Him.

Furthermore, God is our Guide, leading us in paths of righteousness. The Psalms beautifully illustrate this, with the psalmist proclaiming, "He leads me in paths of righteousness for his name's sake" (Psalm 23:3 ESV).

Lastly, God serves as our Teacher, instructing us through His Word and the lessons of life. The Bible is full of life's instructions, as it is "useful for teaching, rebuking, correcting and training in righteousness" (2 Timothy 3:16 ESV).

The Misconceptions: Clearing the Air

Embracing the true role of God also means clearing away misconceptions. Contrary to some beliefs, God is not a genie that grants every wish nor a cosmic force detached from human experience. He is a personal God who wants a relationship with us.

God is not exclusively responsible for solving all our problems while we passively observe. Instead, He invites us to work with Him, guiding and enabling us, but also expecting our active participation in the process.

Similarly, we should dispel the misconception that God only works through miraculous events. He indeed performs miracles, but He also works in the ordinary, everyday moments of life. God's work is often seen in acts of love, kindness, forgiveness, and justice that we witness or partake in daily.

Our Active Participation: Working with God

Embracing the role of God in our lives means understanding that God desires our cooperation in His work. We are not passive observers but active participants in God's plan.

We are to respond to His guidance with obedience, discernment, and action, acting on His guidance and making decisions in line with His Word. This doesn't mean that we won't face challenges or confusion, but through prayer and persistent faith, we can stay in tune with God's guidance.

Conclusion: A Deeper Relationship with God

Embracing the true role of God in our lives is about fostering a deeper relationship with Him. It involves understanding His character, clearing away misconceptions, and cooperating with Him in our lives. When we do this, we position ourselves to receive His instruction, blessings, and the fullness of His love. It leads us to a richer, more fulfilling Christian journey that resonates with God's ultimate plan for us.

CHAPTER 2 Letting Go and Letting God: Embracing Trust in the Lord

Introduction: The Concept of Letting Go and Letting God

The saying "let go and let God" is often spoken among Christians as a symbol of surrender, a recognition that human effort can only go so far and that ultimately, we must trust God's will. However, it's important to understand that this phrase doesn't appear in the Bible as is. What does exist is a deeply embedded biblical principle reflecting the message of the phrase. This chapter will take you through the biblical understanding of "letting go and letting God" and how to adopt it into your daily life.

The Biblical Interpretation

The principle of "letting go and letting God" aligns with numerous biblical passages. Proverbs 3:5-6 instructs, "Trust in the LORD with all your heart, and do not lean on your own understanding. In all your ways acknowledge him, and he will make straight your paths" (ESV). Here, the focus is on trusting God and acknowledging Him in every part of our life. When we do this, God promises to guide us.

However, trusting God and acknowledging Him in all our ways requires a level of surrender and submission, a concept that is embedded within the idea of "letting go and letting God". This doesn't mean we should sit idly and wait for miracles to happen. Instead, it implies active faith - a deep and abiding trust in God's wisdom, love, and sovereignty.

35

Active Faith: The Practical Aspect of Letting Go and Letting God

Active faith is demonstrated when we give up control and cease our efforts to manipulate outcomes, trusting instead in God's perfect will. However, letting go of control doesn't imply a passive or lazy faith. The Bible encourages action and diligence. James 2:26 in the New Testament asserts, "For as the body apart from the spirit is dead, so also faith apart from works is dead" (ESV). Here, the Apostle James emphasizes that a genuine faith in God is expressed in our deeds. The act of "letting go and letting God" is an active one, involving both the surrender of our will to God and the pursuit of actions that align with His commandments and will.

The Power of Trusting in God

When we are faced with trials and tribulations, our first instinct is often to rely on our understanding and strength. Yet, according to the scriptures, we are called to put our trust in God. The prophet Isaiah wrote, "but they who wait for the LORD shall renew their strength; they shall mount up with wings like eagles; they shall run and not be weary; they shall walk and not faint" (ESV, Isaiah 40:31). This verse beautifully illustrates the rewards of trusting in the Lord. Letting go and allowing God to lead us gives us strength and endurance beyond our natural capabilities. This is not a passive waiting but an active trust in God's sovereignty and goodness.

Letting Go and Letting God in the Everyday

What does this principle look like in practical, day-to-day life? Consider the example of King David, who often found himself in situations beyond his control. Yet, his response was often one of trust and submission to God. In Psalm 55:22, he encourages others, "Cast your burden on the LORD, and he will sustain you; he will never permit the righteous to be moved" (ESV). This scripture paints a vivid picture of what it means to "let go and let God". It's about casting our anxieties and concerns onto God and trusting Him to provide for us and guide us through the difficult situations we face.

The Biblical Basis of Trust: Foundational Scriptures

Trusting in God is a central theme in both the Old and New Testaments of the Bible. The scriptures provide multiple instances where trust in God is not only encouraged but is portrayed as a bedrock of our relationship with Him. By examining these foundational scriptures, we can form a deeper understanding of what it means to trust God.

Trust in the Old Testament: An Active Faith

Trust in God, as expressed in the Old Testament, is often depicted as an active faith, a relationship requiring both belief in God and obedience to His laws. A perfect illustration of this active faith is found in the life of Abraham. God promised Abraham that he would be the father of many nations (Genesis 17:4, ASV). Despite his old age and the seeming impossibility of this promise, Abraham trusted God. He did not merely believe in God's existence, but he trusted in God's promise and was obedient to His commands. This is an active faith, a faith that trusts in God's promises and responds with obedience.

Another key verse in the Old Testament that underscores this concept is Proverbs 3:5-6, which states, "Trust in Jehovah with all thy heart, and lean not upon thine own understanding: In all thy ways acknowledge him, and he will direct thy paths" (ASV). This scripture demonstrates that trust involves a complete reliance on God instead of our understanding. It calls us to acknowledge God in every aspect of our lives, and in doing so, God will guide our paths.

Trust in the New Testament: A Deepened Understanding

In the New Testament, trust in God deepens into a personal, intimate relationship with Jesus Christ. This trust involves putting our faith in Jesus as our Savior, as outlined in John 3:16, which states, "For God so loved the world, that he gave his only Son, that whoever believes in him should not perish but have eternal life" (ESV). Here, trust is equated with believing in Jesus and results in eternal life.

The Apostle Paul further emphasizes this idea in his letter to the Philippians. In Philippians 4:6-7, he writes, "do not be anxious about anything, but in everything by prayer and supplication with thanksgiving let your requests be made known to God. And the peace of God, which surpasses all understanding, will guard your hearts and your minds in Christ Jesus" (ESV). Paul encourages us to place our trust in God by turning our anxieties into prayers. He assures us that, in doing so, we will experience the peace of God, which is beyond our understanding.

Practical Application of Trust

Trusting in God is not merely a mental assent but a practical action that should impact our everyday lives. It involves surrendering our control and relying on God's guidance. This principle is succinctly expressed in Psalm 37:5, which instructs, "Commit thy way unto Jehovah; Trust also in him, and he will bring it to pass" (ASV).

Trust, therefore, involves a commitment to God's way, an unwavering confidence in His promises, and a firm belief in His power. It's not about expecting God to perform supernatural miracles without our participation. Instead, it's about aligning our lives to God's word, seeking His will in prayer, and expecting Him to act in accordance with His promises.

In conclusion, trust is a foundational principle in the Bible, encompassing an active faith that believes in God's promises, commits to His way, and relies on His guidance. It involves a surrender of our control, an acknowledgement of God's sovereignty, and a commitment to obey His commands. It's an active faith that engages with God and anticipates His faithful response. So, in our journey of faith, let us embrace this biblical trust, letting go of our ways, and letting God guide us according to His perfect will.

Understanding True Surrender: Not Abandonment but Partnership

A misconception often associated with the concept of "letting go and letting God" is the idea that surrender to God implies a form of spiritual abandonment, where one does nothing and merely awaits divine intervention. However, a careful examination of biblical scriptures reveals a more complex picture of surrender as an active partnership with God rather than a passive abandonment.

Surrender in the Old Testament: Active Trust and Obedience

Surrender, as described in the Old Testament, is less about passivity and more about active trust and obedience to God's laws. For instance, when God commanded Noah to build an ark in preparation for a great flood, Noah didn't simply sit back and expect God to do everything. Instead, Noah actively partnered with God by obeying His command and building the ark. Genesis 6:22 (ASV) encapsulates this active obedience: "Thus did Noah; according to all that God commanded him, so did he."

Surrender in the New Testament: Faith Expressed through Works

The New Testament further refines our understanding of surrender. It is not depicted as a hands-off approach but a faith that is expressed through works. James 2:17 (ESV) states, "So also faith by itself, if it does not have works, is dead." Here, James is saying that faith, if it doesn't result in action (works), is not genuine faith.

Surrendering to God, therefore, implies an active faith that expresses itself in deeds aligned with God's will.

The Nature of Partnership with God

The story of Paul and Silas in Acts provides a beautiful illustration of this partnership. After being beaten and imprisoned, they did not simply wait for God to save them. Instead, they engaged in active prayer and worship (Acts 16:25, ESV). Consequently, an earthquake occurred, freeing them from their chains. However, even then, they did not just leave. They stayed and used the opportunity to share the Gospel with the jailer and his family.

This story shows us that surrendering to God is not passive; it requires us to actively partner with God, involving us in constant prayer, worship, and engagement in actions that reflect God's will.

Practical Application: How to Surrender Actively to God

In practical terms, surrendering to God means entrusting our worries, plans, and desires to Him, actively seeking His will through prayer and Bible study, and obediently acting according to His guidance. It's about echoing the prayer of Jesus in the Garden of Gethsemane, "not as I will, but as you will" (Matthew 26:39, ESV).

Yet, as we submit our will to God, we are not left inactive. We are called to engage in good works, love others, and spread the Gospel – actions that reflect our trust in God and our submission to His will. This is not a process of spiritual abandonment but an active partnership with God, where we work together with Him in faith.

In conclusion, the biblical concept of surrender is not about sitting back and expecting God to do everything. It's about actively partnering with God in a relationship of trust and obedience. It's about letting go of our ways, submitting to God's will, and taking active steps in faith and obedience. This understanding of surrender offers a more empowering and active perspective on what it means to "let go and let God."

Letting Go of Control: The Challenge of Human Nature

The biblical call to trust in the Lord often necessitates letting go of our inherent desire for control. This relinquishment of control poses a significant challenge, largely due to our human nature, which often inclines us towards self-reliance and autonomy. A thorough understanding of the complexities of human nature as depicted in the Bible helps us understand this challenge and guides us towards embracing a true trust in God.

Human Nature and the Desire for Control

From a biblical perspective, our desire for control is rooted in our human nature, the fallen condition we inherited due to the sin of Adam and Eve. When they chose to eat the forbidden fruit in the Garden of Eden, it was an assertion of their will over God's, a desire to be like God knowing good and evil (Genesis 3:5, ASV).

This disposition towards self-reliance continues to manifest in our lives. We often seek to control our circumstances, relying on our understanding and abilities, a tendency succinctly captured by the wisdom of Proverbs 3:5, "Trust in Jehovah with all thy heart, And lean not upon thine own understanding" (ASV).

The Challenge of Letting Go

Letting go of this ingrained desire for control is no easy feat. Jesus' interaction with the rich young ruler in Mark 10:17-22 (ESV) illustrates this challenge. Despite his obedience to the commandments, the ruler's attachment to his wealth prevented him from surrendering control and following Jesus. His case serves as a stark reminder of the difficulties associated with renouncing our human tendencies for self-reliance and control.

Trust and Surrender as a Counter to the Desire for Control

Despite the challenge, the Bible repeatedly encourages us to overcome our desire for control through trust and surrender to God. In Jeremiah 17:7-8 (ASV), we read, "Blessed is the man that trusteth in Jehovah, and whose trust Jehovah is." This passage suggests a life of flourishing and fruitfulness associated with placing trust in God, rather than relying on oneself.

The New Testament also underscores this principle. The Apostle Paul, in Philippians 4:6-7 (ESV), writes, "Do not be anxious about anything, but in everything by prayer and supplication with thanksgiving let your requests be made known to God. And the peace of God, which surpasses all understanding, will guard your hearts and your minds in Christ Jesus." Paul's exhortation encourages a surrender of control, an antidote to anxiety, providing a path to experience God's peace that surpasses human comprehension.

Practical Steps Towards Letting Go

Letting go of control starts with acknowledging our human tendency towards self-reliance and confessing it to God. It involves a daily decision to surrender our will to God, seeking His guidance through prayer and meditation on His Word.

Moreover, it entails embracing a perspective shift – viewing circumstances not as things to be controlled but opportunities to rely on God. This shift is not a denial of responsibility or effort but a recognition of God's sovereignty and an invitation for His involvement in our lives.

In conclusion, letting go of control to trust God is a challenging but critical aspect of the Christian faith. The challenge is deeply rooted in our human nature and our desire for self-reliance. However, through the biblical principles of trust and surrender, we can counter this desire and open ourselves to the peace and guidance that come from letting go and letting God.

Embracing Trust: The Heart of a Faithful Christian

At the heart of being a faithful Christian is the embrace of a profound trust in God. Trust, in this context, is not just a passive belief but an active reliance on God's character, His promises, and His providence. This form of trust goes beyond intellectual assent to God's existence; it shapes our thoughts, our actions, and our responses to life's challenges.

The Biblical Call to Trust

The Bible is replete with calls to trust in God. In the Old Testament, we find the exhortation in Proverbs 3:5 (ASV), "Trust in Jehovah with all thy heart, And lean not upon thine own understanding." This verse not only encourages us to trust in God but also warns against the dangers of self-reliance. It emphasizes the need to depend wholly on God rather than our wisdom or understanding.

The New Testament also extols the virtue of trust in God. Jesus, in Matthew 6:25-34 (ESV), teaches about the futility of worry, encouraging trust in God who cares for the lilies of the field and the birds of the air. Jesus' words point to a Fatherly God who is not only aware of our needs but also committed to providing for them.

The Outworking of Trust

Embracing trust in God has far-reaching implications for the Christian life. Trust affects our perspectives, our decisions, and our actions.

A heart of trust allows us to see our circumstances through the lens of God's sovereignty and goodness. We begin to realize that even in the midst of trials, God is at work for our good and His glory (Romans 8:28, ESV).

Trust also impacts our decisions. Proverbs 16:3 (ASV) says, "Commit thy works unto Jehovah, And thy purposes shall be established." Here, trust is equated with committing our works to God, indicating that our decisions and actions should be guided by our confidence in God.

Lastly, trust influences our actions. James 2:26 (ESV) states, "For as the body apart from the spirit is dead, so also faith apart from works is dead." Genuine trust in God is not idle; it spurs us into action, producing works that testify to our faith.

The Journey of Trust

Embracing trust in God is a journey, not a one-time event. It begins with a recognition of God's character and promises, as revealed in His Word. It grows as we experience God's faithfulness in our lives and as we choose to rely on Him in the face of life's challenges.

This journey also involves periods of struggle and doubt. In Mark 9:24 (ESV), the father of a possessed boy cries out to Jesus, "I believe; help my unbelief!" His honest admission reflects the struggle we often face in fully trusting God. Yet, it also reveals the path to deepening trust – a humble acknowledgement of our doubts and a heartfelt plea for God's help to overcome them.

In conclusion, embracing trust in God is at the heart of a faithful Christian life. It's a journey that transforms our perspectives, guides our decisions, and fuels our actions. It's a journey marked by both assurance and struggle, by moments of confident reliance on God and honest admissions of doubt. Yet, in every step of this journey, we are drawn closer to the heart of God, learning to let go of our ways and to let God be God in our lives. Through this journey of trust, we truly learn what it means to "let go and let God."

God's Faithfulness: Unchanging and Unending

Trust in Practice: Examples from Biblical Figures

The Bible is rich with narratives of individuals who exemplified trust in God in their life's journey. These accounts serve as a source of inspiration and instruction for us as we navigate our own path of faith, demonstrating the practical implications of trusting in God. Let's explore the lives of three biblical figures - Abraham, David, and Paul - and observe how they embodied a life of trust in God.

Abraham: Trust in God's Promises

Abraham, originally Abram, stands as a monumental figure in the Old Testament, often referred to as the father of faith. His trust in God was rooted in God's promises and was tested in dramatic ways. In Genesis 12, God promised to make Abram into a great nation, despite his old age and his wife's barrenness. Abram's response, as recorded in Genesis 15:6 (ASV), was to "believe in Jehovah; and he reckoned it to him for righteousness."

This trust in God's promise was profoundly tested when God asked Abraham to sacrifice his son Isaac, the very son through whom God's promises were to be fulfilled. In Genesis 22, Abraham's willingness to obey, even in this, demonstrates an unwavering trust in God's character and promises. Abraham's life serves as a compelling example of trust in God's promises, even in the face of seemingly impossible circumstances.

David: Trust in God's Protection

David, the shepherd boy who became a king, provides another profound example of trust in God. His life was riddled with challenges, from facing the giant Goliath to evading King Saul's murderous pursuits. Yet, in each instance, David's trust in God's protection is evident.

In 1 Samuel 17 (ASV), as David faces Goliath, he declares, "Jehovah saveth not with sword and spear; for the battle is Jehovah's."

David's trust in God's protection and deliverance was not based on human strength or strategy but on God's power and faithfulness. This trust carried David through many trials and enabled him to praise God amidst adversity, as seen throughout the Psalms.

Paul: Trust in God's Purpose

The apostle Paul is a New Testament figure who remarkably illustrates trust in God's purpose. His dramatic conversion in Acts 9 (ESV) transformed him from a zealous persecutor of Christians into a fervent apostle for Christ. Paul's life was marked by suffering for the sake of the Gospel, including imprisonments, beatings, and shipwrecks.

Yet, Paul maintained a steadfast trust in God's purpose throughout his trials. In Philippians 1:12-14 (ESV), Paul writes from prison, "I want you to know, brothers, that what has happened to me has really served to advance the gospel." Paul's trust in God's purpose enabled him to see his sufferings as means for advancing God's work, a perspective that sustained him amidst severe trials.

In conclusion, the lives of Abraham, David, and Paul provide tangible illustrations of trust in God's promises, protection, and purpose. Their stories invite us to move beyond a theoretical understanding of trust to a lived expression of it. They remind us that trust is not merely a passive state but an active posture that influences our perspective, shapes our decisions, and fuels our actions. As we navigate our journey of faith, may we learn from these biblical figures, letting go of our control and letting God lead us in His ways.

Navigating Doubt: Strengthening Trust in Difficult Times

Living a life of trust in God does not imply a journey free of challenges or doubts. In fact, doubt is a common human experience, even for the most faithful servants of God. However, it's crucial to understand that doubt doesn't necessarily mean a lack of faith or trust. Instead, it could be a stepping stone towards a deeper, more mature trust in God. The key lies in how we navigate these seasons of doubt and uncertainty.

Understanding Doubt

It's important to distinguish doubt from unbelief. Doubt often represents a struggle with belief, a seeking for understanding amidst uncertainty, while unbelief is a willful rejection of God's truth. Doubt can be a part of our journey of faith, a wrestling that can lead to deeper trust if navigated rightly.

Notably, the Bible does not shy away from expressing doubt. The Psalms, in particular, are filled with heartfelt laments and questions. In Psalm 13 (ASV), David begins with the agonizing question, "How long, O Jehovah? Wilt thou forget me forever?" Yet, by the end of the psalm, he declares his trust in God's steadfast love and salvation. David's psalm demonstrates that expressing doubt does not mean forsaking faith. Instead, it is an honest dialogue with God, a part of the process of wrestling with uncertainties while remaining anchored in God's character.

Navigating Doubt through Trust

So how can we navigate doubt in a way that strengthens our trust in God? There are three key strategies: grounding ourselves in God's Word, relying on the Christian community, and maintaining a prayerful life.

Firstly, grounding ourselves in God's Word is vital. God's Word is the definitive source of truth, an anchor in the stormy sea of doubt. As we read and meditate on Scripture, we're reminded of God's character and His promises. This can help realign our focus and perspective, even in times of doubt.

Secondly, leaning on the Christian community can be tremendously beneficial. Sharing our doubts with trusted brothers and sisters in Christ allows us to receive encouragement, perspective, and guidance. The New Testament continually emphasizes the importance of mutual edification within the body of Christ, as seen in passages like

Hebrews 10:24-25 (ESV): "And let us consider how to stir up one another to love and good works, not neglecting to meet together..."

Lastly, maintaining a prayerful life is essential. Like the Psalms, our prayers can be honest and raw before God, expressing our doubts, fears, and questions. God is not threatened by our doubts; rather, He invites us to cast all our anxieties on Him (1 Peter 5:7, ESV). Prayer is not only a means of expressing our doubts but also a channel of receiving God's comfort, guidance, and peace.

In conclusion, doubt is not the opposite of trust; it can be a stepping stone toward a deeper, more mature trust in God. By grounding ourselves in God's Word, leaning on the Christian community, and maintaining a prayerful life, we can navigate seasons of doubt in a way that strengthens our trust in God. Even in the most challenging times, we can echo the words of the father in Mark 9:24 (ESV), who said to Jesus amidst his doubt, "I believe; help my unbelief!" The journey of trust involves wrestling with doubt, yet always holding fast to the steadfast character of our God. Let us let go and let God guide us in His wisdom and love, even in the face of our most daunting doubts.

The Balance: Trusting God and Taking Personal Responsibility

"Letting go and letting God" is a principle of trust in divine providence. However, it should not be misunderstood as a call to passivity or an abdication of personal responsibility. The Christian life is one of active engagement in the world, guided by a deep trust in God. Trusting God and taking personal responsibility are not mutually exclusive; instead, they exist in a balanced interplay, with each aspect informing and strengthening the other.

Understanding Biblical Trust

Biblical trust is not synonymous with passivity or inaction. Instead, it implies a restful reliance on God, recognizing that our efforts are not self-sufficient but are reliant on His grace and providence. In Proverbs 3:5-6 (ASV), we are admonished, "Trust in Jehovah with all thy heart, And lean not upon thine own understanding: In all thy ways acknowledge him, And he will direct thy paths." Here, trusting God does not negate our need for action; rather, it frames our action within God's sovereignty.

Understanding Personal Responsibility

Scripture emphasizes personal responsibility, portraying it as an essential aspect of Christian life. For instance, Galatians 6:5 (ESV) asserts, "For each will have to bear his own load." This verse underscores the role of individual accountability in the Christian journey. It does not contradict the principle of trusting in God. Instead, it supplements it, demonstrating that personal effort and divine trust can coexist harmoniously.

The Balance in Practice

Balancing trust in God and personal responsibility may look different in various life contexts, but there are common principles that can guide us. One such principle is that our trust in God should motivate, not hinder, our personal efforts.

In the realm of work, for example, the Apostle Paul writes in Colossians 3:23 (ESV), "Whatever you do, work heartily, as for the Lord and not for men." This passage calls for diligent effort, not lackadaisical passivity. However, the motivation for such effort is fundamentally a trust in God, as our ultimate "employer" is the Lord.

In terms of moral responsibility, we are called to "work out [our] own salvation with fear and trembling" (Philippians 2:12, ESV). Again, personal responsibility is evident. Yet, the very next verse (Philippians 2:13, ESV) declares, "for it is God who works in you, both to will and to work for his good pleasure." This beautiful tension encapsulates the balance between human effort and divine trust.

Balancing trust in God with personal responsibility is an essential aspect of the Christian life. Trusting in God should not lead to passive inaction, but rather motivate dedicated, diligent effort. Our personal responsibility, in turn, is framed by a deep reliance on God's sovereignty and grace.

Through this balance, we can fully live out the Christian call to be active agents in the world, grounded in an unwavering trust in God. In doing so, we can echo the words of the Apostle Paul in 1 Corinthians 15:10 (ESV), "But by the grace of God I am what I am, and his grace toward me was not in vain. On the contrary, I worked harder than any of them, though it was not I, but the grace of God that is with me."

In conclusion, "letting go and letting God" is not about passivity, but about harmonizing our active participation with divine guidance. This balance between trusting God and taking personal responsibility forms the heart of a robust, active, and authentic Christian faith. As we grow in understanding and practicing this balance, we can be assured of being able to navigate any challenges that life throws at us, for we know that our trust is in God and that He works in and through us.

The Freedom in Surrender and Trust

When we speak of surrender and trust, it might instinctively feel like a loss, like giving up control. But within the Christian paradigm, surrender and trust yield not bondage but freedom. This freedom is rooted in the knowledge and experience of God's sovereignty, goodness, and faithfulness. Understanding this truth and its implications, we find that "letting go and letting God" ushers in a profound spiritual freedom that enriches every facet of our lives.

Biblical Surrender: Embracing God's Will

The concept of surrender permeates the Bible, consistently depicted not as a sign of defeat, but as a willing submission to God's will. Christ Himself provides the most poignant example of surrender in the Garden of Gethsemane, praying, "Father, if you are willing, remove this cup from me. Nevertheless, not my will, but yours, be done" (Luke 22:42, ESV). This surrender did not lead to His downfall but paved the way for the world's redemption.

In surrender, we yield our will to God's will, our plans to His plans, acknowledging His omniscience and wisdom. This is not a resignation to fate but an active alignment with God's purposes. Surrendering to God implies a conscious decision to set aside our desires and preferences, letting God's will guide our paths.

Biblical Trust: Relying on God's Faithfulness

Trust is an integral part of the Christian faith, grounded in the character and promises of God. The Bible encourages us to trust in God, stating, "It is better to take refuge in the Lord than to trust in man" (Psalm 118:8, ASV). Trusting God means depending on Him for our needs, guidance, and deliverance, regardless of our circumstances.

Such trust recognizes God's sovereignty and faithfulness. It acknowledges His ability to do "far more abundantly than all that we ask or think" (Ephesians 3:20, ESV). Biblical trust goes beyond mere intellectual assent to God's reliability; it involves leaning on God's promises and believing that He will fulfil His word.

The Freedom in Surrender and Trust

The act of surrendering to God and trusting Him leads to a profound sense of freedom. It frees us from the burden of self-reliance, the anxiety of uncertainty, and the weight of sin.

This freedom is not merely a psychological relief; it is rooted in our restored relationship with God. Paul writes, "For freedom Christ has set us free; stand firm therefore, and do not submit again to a yoke of slavery" (Galatians 5:1, ESV). The freedom that comes from surrender and trust is a manifestation of this liberation that Christ procured for us.

By surrendering our lives to God, we are not surrendering to a capricious deity, but to a loving Father who has our best interests at heart. In trusting Him, we are not putting our faith in an unreliable source, but in the Creator of the universe, who is faithful to His promises. In this, we find a freedom that transcends our circumstances, one that enables us to live in peace and joy, even in the midst of trials and tribulations.

Conclusion

Surrendering to God and trusting Him might seem counterintuitive in a world that values self-reliance and control. However, in the Kingdom of God, surrender and trust are the gateways to true freedom. As we learn to surrender our will to God's and trust in His unwavering faithfulness, we experience a profound freedom that the world cannot offer.

This freedom does not mean that we become passive in our faith journey. On the contrary, it enables us to actively participate in God's work, free from the crippling effects of sin, fear, and anxiety. It empowers us to live fulfilling, purposeful lives, secure in the knowledge that our loving God is in control.

In this freedom, we discover the joy of "letting go and letting God," living each day in reliance on Him, confident in His promises, and secure in His love. The freedom we find in surrender and trust is truly a treasure, a profound blessing that enriches our walk with God, making our faith journey a vibrant and joyous adventure.

CHAPTER 3 Guided by Scripture: How God Instructs Us Through His Word

Introduction: The Importance of Scripture in Christian Life

There is no greater resource for Christian living than the Scriptures. The Bible is God's revelation of Himself to humanity, His recorded interactions with our ancestors, His principles, His promises, and His prophetic utterances. It is the definitive guidebook for the Christian journey and our primary source of knowledge about God and His plan for our lives.

The Scriptures are described in 2 Timothy 3:16-17 (ESV) as follows: "All Scripture is breathed out by God and profitable for teaching, for reproof, for correction, and for training in righteousness, that the man of God may be complete, equipped for every good work." This passage underscores the profound significance of Scripture in the Christian life.

A Guide for Teaching and Doctrine

The Bible serves as a fundamental source of teaching and doctrine. It reveals who God is, His nature, attributes, and works. It introduces us to Jesus Christ, the Son of God, elucidating His birth, life, teachings, miracles, death, and resurrection. The Scriptures elucidate the path to salvation, the meaning and significance of faith, grace, and righteousness, among other core doctrines of the Christian faith.

The Old Testament, or the Hebrew Scriptures, captures the history of the Israelites, God's chosen people, their relationship with

53

God, their trials, triumphs, failures, and faith. It features numerous prophecies, many of which are fulfilled in the New Testament.

The New Testament begins with the life of Jesus Christ, as captured in the Gospels, followed by the Acts of the Apostles, which chronicle the early Church's journey. The letters or epistles offer practical advice and deep theological insights to different individuals and churches. The Book of Revelation provides a prophetic vision of end times, offering hope and solace to Christians about God's ultimate victory.

A Resource for Correction and Reproof

The Bible is not merely a compilation of lofty principles and historical accounts; it is also a tool for correction and reproof. It challenges our biases, confronts our sins, and urges us to change our ways. It serves as a moral and spiritual compass, guiding us in our daily lives, helping us differentiate right from wrong, and encouraging us to live in a manner that glorifies God.

Proverbs 3:11-12 (ASV) affirms this, "My son, despise not the chastening of Jehovah; Neither be weary of his reproof: For whom Jehovah loveth he reproveth, Even as a father the son in whom he delighteth." The Scriptures rebuke, exhort, and shape us, molding us into the likeness of Christ.

A Training Tool for Righteousness

In addition to teaching and correcting, the Bible serves as a training tool for righteousness. It equips us to live a godly life, providing practical instructions and examples. From accounts of great faith like Abraham and Esther to admonitions on love and forgiveness in the epistles, the Scriptures offer ample guidance for righteous living.

In conclusion, the Bible is an essential guide in the Christian journey. As the inspired, inerrant Word of God, it is a repository of divine wisdom, a mirror that reveals our true self, and a lamp that lights our path. Recognizing and appreciating its importance is the first step in being guided by Scripture, allowing it to inform our beliefs, shape our character, and direct our actions.

The Bible: God's Living Word and Primary Communication

The Bible, being the inspired and inerrant Word of God, serves as His primary mode of communication with mankind. It is more than just an ancient text with historical and cultural significance; it is the living Word of God, active and potent, transcending time and space, relevant to every generation and culture.

The author of Hebrews poignantly captures this truth in Hebrews 4:12 (ESV): "For the word of God is living and active, sharper than any two-edged sword, piercing to the division of soul and of spirit, of joints and of marrow, and discerning the thoughts and intentions of the heart." This divine text is not static but dynamic, deeply personal and life-changing, with the capacity to impact every facet of our lives.

Understanding the Inspiration of the Bible

To understand the Bible as God's living Word and primary means of communication, we must first grasp the concept of inspiration. As previously mentioned, the Bible is the inspired Word of God, which means it originates from Him and was communicated through human authors moved by the Holy Spirit.

This concept is highlighted in 2 Peter 1:21 (ESV), "For no prophecy was ever produced by the will of man, but men spoke from God as they were carried along by the Holy Spirit." The inspiration of the Bible is therefore a divinely-guided process, ensuring the words written reflect God's will, wisdom, and commands.

The Bible as God's Living Word

The Bible being described as 'living' emphasizes its enduring relevance and its ability to communicate God's eternal truths to us. It is not merely a record of what God said or did in the past; rather, it speaks to the reader in the present, offering divine guidance, wisdom, correction, and comfort. God's Word, as found in the Scriptures, is actively involved in the lives of believers, shaping their beliefs, influencing their decisions, and molding their character.

One of the great examples is Psalm 119, which is a lengthy meditation on the value of God's law and commands. Verse 105 (ASV) says, "Thy word is a lamp unto my feet, And light unto my path." This depicts God's Word as a guiding light, providing direction and clarity in life's journey, demonstrating its active and living nature.

The Bible as God's Primary Communication

God has, throughout history, communicated with humanity in various ways, such as through dreams, visions, and prophets. However, the primary and most comprehensive method God has chosen to communicate His character, will, and plan is through the Scriptures. The Bible is His authoritative declaration, containing everything we need for salvation and godly living.

Paul makes this clear in his second letter to Timothy, "All Scripture is breathed out by God and profitable for teaching, for reproof, for correction, and for training in righteousness," (2 Timothy 3:16, ESV). This verse underscores the Bible's divine origin and its practical function in the believer's life.

Therefore, as believers desiring to know God and His will, we should prioritize interacting with the Scriptures, for it is the primary means through which God speaks. As we study and meditate on the Bible, aided by the illuminating work of the Holy Spirit, we can expect to hear from God, understand His will, and be transformed by His truths.

In conclusion, the Bible is God's living Word, a vibrant and dynamic text that speaks directly into our lives. It is His primary mode of communication, a treasury of divine wisdom and guidance. As such, it warrants our careful study, earnest meditation, and unwavering obedience, for it is through the Scriptures that God instructs, corrects, and nourishes us on our Christian journey.

How God Instructs: The Nature of Biblical Teachings

The Bible, the inspired and inerrant Word of God, is a remarkable tapestry of divine teachings. It encompasses a myriad of literary styles including narratives, laws, poetry, prophecy, wisdom literature, gospel accounts, epistles, and apocalyptic writings. Each of these genres, under the divine guidance of the Holy Spirit, uniquely contributes to the overall message of the Bible and provides a wealth of spiritual instruction to the reader.

Diverse Literary Styles, Unified Message

The Bible is a compilation of 66 books, authored by approximately 40 different writers from diverse backgrounds over a span of approximately 1,500 years. Despite the diversity of its human authors and the range of their historical, cultural, and personal contexts, the Bible carries a unified message about God, His character, His relationship with humanity, and His grand plan for creation. This unity amid diversity demonstrates the divine hand guiding its composition.

Each literary style employed in the Bible has its unique characteristics, and understanding these can enhance our interpretation and application of biblical teachings. For instance, the laws found in the books of Exodus, Leviticus, and Deuteronomy have a specific context in the history of Israel, yet they also reveal broader principles about God's holiness and standards of justice. Similarly, the prophetic writings frequently used symbolic language to convey God's messages of judgment and restoration, while the gospels provide historical accounts of Jesus' life and teachings, offering insights into God's incarnate revelation of Himself.

Biblical Teachings and Their Application

The Bible provides a variety of teachings to guide us in our Christian journey. It offers moral and ethical instructions, doctrinal teachings, practical wisdom for daily living, and prophetic insights about God's kingdom.

The moral and ethical teachings, often found in the laws and epistles, instruct us on God's standards for righteous living. These teachings, grounded in God's character, provide guidance for our behavior and decision-making, helping us to reflect His character in our lives.

Doctrinal teachings, which give systematic insights about God, humanity, salvation, and other theological concepts, are spread throughout the Scriptures. They are especially prominent in the epistles of the New Testament, which were written to address specific theological issues within the early Christian communities. These teachings help us understand and articulate our faith more accurately.

Wisdom literature, such as Proverbs and Ecclesiastes, provide practical wisdom for daily living. They touch upon diverse topics like relationships, work, wealth, speech, and character, offering timeless principles for navigating life's complexities.

Lastly, the prophetic and apocalyptic writings provide a future-oriented perspective, offering hope and encouragement for believers living in challenging times. They remind us of God's ultimate victory and our future inheritance in His kingdom, enabling us to persevere in our faith.

The Holy Spirit's Role in Instruction

Understanding and applying the Bible's teachings is not a purely intellectual exercise. It requires the illuminating work of the Holy Spirit, who opens our minds to understand the Scriptures and applies God's Word to our hearts. In John 14:26 (ESV), Jesus promises, "But the Helper, the Holy Spirit, whom the Father will send in my name, he will teach you all things and bring to your remembrance all that I have said to you." The Spirit aids us in understanding the biblical teachings and empowers us to live them out.

In conclusion, God instructs us through the rich and diverse teachings found in His Word. By appreciating the nature of these biblical teachings and relying on the Holy Spirit's guidance, we can gain a comprehensive understanding of God's will, leading us to live lives that glorify Him and serve others. The Scriptures, therefore, are not merely an ancient text; they are God's living Word, vital and applicable to our daily lives, continually guiding us towards deeper intimacy with our Creator and more profound service to His creation.

Interpreting Scripture: Rules and Principles of the Objective Historical Grammatical Method for Understanding What the Authors Meant by the Words They Used

A careful and responsible approach to biblical interpretation is crucial for a proper understanding of the Bible, the inerrant Word of God. The Objective Historical Grammatical Method (OHGM) provides a rigorous and effective framework for this task, seeking to comprehend what the original authors intended by the words they used. It is predicated on the assumption that the Bible, while divinely inspired, was also communicated in human language and within historical and cultural contexts. Thus, to accurately interpret the Scriptures, one must consider their grammatical structure, historical setting, and literary context.

Principle 1: Grammatical Analysis

The grammatical analysis involves studying the language, syntax, and structure of the biblical texts. This helps to discern the meaning of words, phrases, sentences, and paragraphs in their original languages - Hebrew for the Old Testament, and Greek for the New Testament. When Paul, in Romans 6:23 (ESV), writes, "For the wages of sin is death, but the free gift of God is eternal life in Christ Jesus our Lord," the term "wages" carries the idea of earning or deserving something, highlighting the dire consequences of sin. Understanding the grammar aids in unpacking such nuances.

Principle 2: Historical Context

Every biblical text was written within a specific historical context, which often influences its content and meaning. Knowing the circumstances, customs, politics, and geography of the time can greatly enhance our understanding. For instance, comprehending the Roman practice of crucifixion in the first century C.E. illuminates the depth of Christ's suffering and the public humiliation associated with His execution.

Principle 3: Literary Context

The literary context of a passage pertains to its genre, as well as its position within the broader narrative or argument of the book. For instance, the apocalyptic literature in the book of Revelation employs symbolic language, which is intended to be interpreted differently than the historical narrative in the book of Acts.

Principle 4: Unity of Scripture

While each biblical book has its unique context and purpose, all of them together compose the canon of Scripture. Hence, any interpretation of a specific text should align with the overarching biblical narrative and its central themes. This principle, often termed "Scripture interprets Scripture," keeps our understanding balanced and coherent.

Principle 5: Spirit-Led Understanding

While the OHGM provides a valuable methodology, it is important to remember that understanding Scripture involves more than intellectual analysis. As affirmed in 1 Corinthians 2:14 (ESV), "The natural person does not accept the things of the Spirit of God, for they are folly to him, and he is not able to understand them because they are spiritually discerned." The Holy Spirit, who inspired the biblical authors, also guides the minds of readers, steering them to grasp and apply the truths of Scripture.

EXCURSION Supplementary Note on 1 Corinthians 2:14

1 Corinthians 2:14 Updated American Standard Version (UASV)

[14] But the natural man does not accept the things of the Spirit of God, for they are foolishness to him, and he is not able to understand* them, because they are examined spiritually.

"The Greek word ginosko ("to understand") does not mean comprehend intellectually; it means know by experience. The unsaved obviously do not experience God's Word because they do not welcome it. Only the regenerate have the capacity to welcome and experience the Scriptures, by means of the Holy Spirit."— (Zuck 1991, 23)

Hundreds of millions of Christians use this verse as support that without the "Holy Spirit," we can fully understand God's Word. They would argue that without the "Spirit" the Bible is nothing more than foolish nonsense to the reader. What we need to do before, arriving at the correct meaning of what Paul meant, is grasp what he meant by his use of the word "understand," as to what is 'foolish.' In short, "the things of the Spirit of God" are the "Spirit" inspired Word of God. The natural man sees the inspired Word of God as foolish, and "he is not able to understand them."

Paul wrote, "But the natural man does not accept the things of the Spirit of God, for they are foolishness to him." What did Paul mean by this statement? Did he mean that if the Bible reader did not have the "Spirit" helping him, he would not be able to grasp the correct meaning of the text? Are we to understand Paul as saying that without the "Spirit," the Bible and its teachings are beyond our understanding?

We can gain a measure of understanding as to what Paul meant by observing how he uses the term "foolishness" elsewhere in the very same letter. At 1 Corinthians 3:19, it is used in the following way, "For the wisdom of this world is foolishness with God." This verse helps us to arrive at the use in two stages: (1) the verse states that human wisdom is foolishness with God, (2) and we know that the use of foolishness here does not mean that God cannot understand (or grasp) human wisdom. The use is that He sees human wisdom as 'foolish' and rejects it as such.

Therefore, the term "foolishness" of 1 Corinthians 3:19 is not in reference to not "understanding," but as to one's view of the text, its significance, or better yet, lack of significance, or lack of value. We certainly know that God can understand the wisdom of the world but condemns it as being 'foolish.' The same holds true of 1 Corinthians 1:20, where the verbal form of foolishness is used, "Has not God made foolish the wisdom of the world?" Thus, the term "foolishness" is used before and after 1 Corinthians 2:14 (1:20; 3:19). In all three cases, we are dealing with the significance, the value being attributed to something.

Thus, it seems obvious that we should attribute the same meaning to our text in question, 1 Corinthians 2:14. In other words, the Apostle Paul, by his use of the term "foolishness," is not saying that the unbeliever is unable to understand, to grasp the Word of God. If this were the case, why would we ever share the Word of God, the gospel message with an unbeliever? Unbelievers can understand the Word of God; however, unbelievers see it as foolish, having no value or significance. The resultant meaning of chapters 1-3 of 1 Corinthians is that the unbelieving world of mankind can understand the Word of God. However, they view it as foolish (missing value or significance). God, on the other hand, understands the wisdom of the world of mankind but views it foolish (missing value or significance). Therefore, in both cases, the information is understood or grasped; however, it is rejected because of the party considering it, believes it lacks value or significance.

We pray for the guidance of the Holy Spirit, and our spirit, or mental disposition, needs to be attuned to God and His Spirit through study and application. Now, if our mental disposition is not in tune with the Spirit, we will not come away with the right answer.

Principles for Application: Translating Scripture into Action

When we carefully read and interpret God's Word, it should not only inform our understanding but also direct our actions. This transformative power of Scripture is evident when we truly digest its meaning and begin to apply its principles in our lives. However, proper application requires a thoughtful and prayerful approach, and understanding of some guiding principles. This section seeks to explore these principles to aid us in translating Scripture into action effectively.

Understanding the Original Context

In order to apply Scripture accurately to our lives, we must first understand the original context in which it was written. Without a grasp of the historical, cultural, and grammatical contexts, we risk distorting the Scripture's true message. The Apostle Paul, writing to Timothy, admonished, "Do your best to present yourself to God as one approved, a worker who has no need to be ashamed, rightly handling the word of truth" (2 Timothy 2:15 ESV). In other words, diligent study and correct understanding of the Scriptures are prerequisites for appropriate application.

Timeless Principles vs. Time-bound Instructions

The Bible contains numerous specific instructions that were relevant to the original recipients but may not directly apply to us today. For example, the Israelites were commanded not to sow their fields with two kinds of seed (Leviticus 19:19 ASV). While this commandment may not apply directly to us, the underlying principle, which is the call to purity and separation from the practices of the pagan nations surrounding them, is timeless.

On the other hand, the moral laws, such as those found in the Ten Commandments (Exodus 20:1-17 ASV), remain universally applicable. These are timeless principles that transcend cultural and historical boundaries. It is our task, then, to distinguish between instructions specific to a particular time and those that are universally applicable.

Applying Scripture to Personal Life

Application of Scripture is not a mere intellectual exercise. It requires humility, prayer, and dependence on God. As we submit ourselves to the guidance of the Holy Spirit, we gain the ability to discern the correct application of Scripture to our lives. However, it's essential to remember that this discernment is not an excuse to twist Scripture to fit our preconceived ideas or desires. Instead, it is a means of allowing Scripture to shape and transform our thoughts and actions according to God's will.

Holistic Reading and Application

Interpreting and applying the Bible should not be a process of cherry-picking verses to suit our needs or desires. Scripture should be read holistically, with an understanding of its grand narrative of creation, fall, redemption, and restoration. This allows us to apply the Bible in a way that aligns with its overarching themes and purpose.

To illustrate, consider Paul's words in Philippians 4:13, "I can do all things through him who strengthens me" (ESV). Often, this verse is taken out of context to imply that we can achieve anything we set our minds to. However, reading the verse in its full context (Philippians 4:10-13), it becomes clear that Paul is talking about contentment in any circumstance, rather than achieving personal ambitions. Proper application, in this case, is about finding contentment in Christ, not about using Christ to attain our goals.

Application in Community

While personal application of Scripture is vital, we must not neglect its communal aspect. The Bible was written to communities of believers and includes instructions for how we should interact with one another, how we should worship, serve, and bear witness to the world. This communal dimension reminds us that the application of Scripture is not just about "me and my personal relationship with God" but also about "us as a community of believers living out God's commands together."

In conclusion, the process of translating Scripture into action is a vital aspect of Christian living. It requires diligent study, careful interpretation, humble submission to God, and active engagement with the community of faith. As we allow the inspired, inerrant Word of God to guide us, we can navigate our way in the world, honoring God in thought, word, and deed. For, as James succinctly put it, "But be doers of the word, and not hearers only, deceiving yourselves" (James 1:22 ESV).

The Power of Scripture: Personal and Community Transformation

The Bible has the power to transform lives. It has been the source of hope and strength for countless individuals throughout history, offering guidance, wisdom, and peace in a tumultuous world. It is not simply a collection of ancient texts but the living, active Word of God that continues to speak into our lives today. It is God's primary means of communicating with us, revealing His character, His will, and His plan for the redemption of the world. Through Scripture, God instructs us, equips us, and empowers us for a life of faith and service.

Personal Transformation Through Scripture

Personal transformation through the power of Scripture is at the heart of the Christian faith. When we encounter the Word of God with a receptive heart, it becomes a powerful tool for personal change and spiritual growth.

The Apostle Paul wrote to the Romans, "Do not be conformed to this world, but be transformed by the renewal of your mind, that by testing you may discern what is the will of God, what is good and acceptable and perfect" (Romans 12:2 ESV). This transformation happens as we engage with Scripture, allowing its truths to reshape our thinking, realign our values, and redirect our lives in accordance with God's will.

The Bible itself attests to its transformative power. The psalmist declares, "The law of the Lord is perfect, reviving the soul; the testimony of the Lord is sure, making wise the simple" (Psalm 19:7 ASV). Hebrews 4:12 further amplifies this by stating, "For the word of God is living and active, sharper than any two-edged sword, piercing to the division of soul and of spirit, of joints and of marrow, and discerning the thoughts and intentions of the heart" (ESV).

Through the Scriptures, we encounter the living God who searches our hearts and minds, convicts us of our sins, and leads us to repentance and faith in Jesus Christ. The Bible serves as a mirror that reveals our true selves and as a lamp that illuminates our path (James 1:23-25, Psalm 119:105). It is the primary means through which God sanctifies us, sets us apart for His service, and molds us into the image of Christ.

Community Transformation Through Scripture

While the transformative power of Scripture is deeply personal, it is not limited to individual lives. The Bible is also a potent agent for community transformation. It shapes not only our personal identities but also our collective identity as the people of God. It defines our mission, guides our communal practices, and fosters unity and mutual love among us.

Consider the early Christian community in Jerusalem. After receiving the Holy Spirit at Pentecost, they devoted themselves to the apostles' teaching, fellowship, breaking of bread, and prayers (Acts 2:42 ESV). They were a community formed and shaped by the Word of God, and their lives bore witness to its transformative power.

Through the Scriptures, God calls us to love one another, bear each other's burdens, and serve one another in love (Galatians 5:13-14; 6:2 ESV). As we submit to these instructions, our communities become reflections of God's kingdom, offering glimpses of His love, justice, and peace to a watching world.

The Bible also equips us for the work of ministry. As Paul wrote to Timothy, "All Scripture is breathed out by God and profitable for teaching, for reproof, for correction, and for training in righteousness, that the man of God may be complete, equipped for every good work" (2 Timothy 3:16-17 ESV). The Scriptures provide the theological foundation, ethical guidelines, and spiritual resources necessary for the effective functioning of the Christian community.

Conclusion: Living in the Power of Scripture

Living under the guidance of Scripture is a transformative journey. As we immerse ourselves in God's Word, we encounter the living God who loves us, saves us, and calls us to participate in His redemptive work. We are personally transformed as we are conformed to the image of Christ, and our communities are reshaped as we live out the teachings of Scripture together.

In the words of the Psalmist, "Your word is a lamp to my feet and a light to my path" (Psalm 119:105 ASV). As we continue to allow God's Word to illuminate our path, we can trust in its transformative power to guide our personal and community lives. Ultimately, Scripture is not simply a guide but the living and active Word of God, powerful and effective for transforming lives and communities in the light of God's redemptive plan.

Thus, to fully experience the transformative power of Scripture, we must approach it with reverence, study it with diligence, interpret it with care, apply it with wisdom, and live it out with faith and obedience. In doing so, we allow the inspired, inerrant Word of God to accomplish its work in us and through us, shaping us into the people God has called us to be and enabling us to participate effectively in His redemptive mission.

In conclusion, the power of Scripture lies not in its historicity, literary beauty, or moral teachings, valuable as they are, but in its divine origin, its revelation of God, and its capacity to transform lives and communities in accordance with God's will. Let us, therefore, commit ourselves to engage deeply with God's Word, allowing it to mold us, guide us, and empower us for a life of faith, hope, and love.

Misinterpretations and Misuse: Avoiding Common Pitfalls

Interacting with the Bible is not a task to be undertaken lightly. As the inspired, inerrant Word of God, the Bible holds the potential to transform our lives and guide us toward truth. However, misinterpretation or misuse of Scripture can lead to confusion, distort our understanding of God's character and will, and even facilitate harmful behaviors and ideologies. It is therefore essential that we approach the Bible with a reverent, humble, and responsible attitude, striving always to rightly handle the Word of Truth (2 Timothy 2:15 ESV).

Misinterpretation: Obstacles to Understanding

Misinterpretation typically arises from overlooking the principles of sound biblical exegesis. It's essential to respect the Bible's historical and literary context, consider the author's intent, and seek the plain meaning of the text. Misinterpretation can occur when readers impose their presuppositions, personal experiences, or cultural perspectives onto the text rather than allowing the text to speak for itself.

Consider, for instance, the misuse of Jeremiah 29:11, "For I know the plans I have for you, declares the LORD, plans for welfare and not for evil, to give you a future and a hope" (ESV). Many people interpret this verse as a universal promise of prosperity, overlooking its specific historical context. Originally, it was a message of comfort to the Israelites in Babylonian exile, assuring them of their eventual return to their homeland. Although the verse expresses God's benevolent nature, it does not guarantee individual believers a life free from adversity.

Also, understanding the genre of a biblical book is vital for correct interpretation. Reading a poetic book like Psalms requires a different approach than interpreting an epistle like Romans or a prophetic book like Isaiah. Ignoring the genre can lead to misinterpretations and misconceptions about the message of a particular passage.

Misuse: Scripture as a Weapon

Misuse of the Bible often happens when Scripture is used to justify certain behaviors, beliefs, or agendas that contradict its overarching message of love, justice, and redemption. Scripture should not be used to harm, manipulate, control, or oppress others.

A classic example is the misuse of Paul's instruction in Ephesians 5:22, "Wives, submit to your own husbands, as to the Lord" (ESV). Taken out of context, this verse has been misused to justify the domination of women. However, the broader context reveals a call to mutual submission out of reverence for Christ (Ephesians 5:21 ESV), and the model for husbands is Christ's self-sacrificing love for the church (Ephesians 5:25 ESV). Scripture should never be used to support oppression or injustice.

Avoiding Misinterpretation and Misuse

To avoid these common pitfalls, we need to cultivate a careful and thoughtful approach to the Scriptures, guided by principles of sound interpretation and a commitment to responsible use of God's Word. Here are some strategies:

- **Prioritize Context**: Always consider the immediate and broader context of a passage. Seek to understand its original historical, cultural, and literary context.

- **Respect the Genre**: Understand the genre of each biblical book and interpret accordingly. Be aware of the different literary styles in the Bible.

- **Be Aware of Presuppositions**: Recognize any presuppositions or biases you may bring to your reading of the Bible and strive to let the text speak for itself.

- **Cross-Reference**: Use Scripture to interpret Scripture. The entirety of Scripture is inspired by God and consistent in its message. If a passage seems unclear, look for other passages that speak to the same topic.

- **Seek Guidance**: Don't hesitate to seek help from reliable commentaries, Bible dictionaries, and other scholarly resources. As Proverbs 15:22 (ESV) reminds us, "Without counsel plans fail, but with many advisers they succeed."

- **Pray**: Always approach the Word with a prayerful heart, asking God to guide your understanding and application.

To honor the sanctity of Scripture and experience its transforming power, it's critical that we seek to avoid these pitfalls. By engaging with the Word of God with integrity, humility, and a deep desire to learn, we can better grasp God's revealed truth and allow it to mold our beliefs, behaviors, and attitudes, thus ensuring that we use His Word rightly as a guide for our personal lives and our communities.

Conclusion: Safeguarding the Power of Scripture

The Bible's transformative power is safeguarded by interpreting and applying it responsibly. By avoiding misinterpretation and misuse, we uphold the integrity of God's Word, furthering our understanding and application of it. Above all, we must remember that the Bible is not just a book but a divine revelation, a powerful means by which God communicates His love, wisdom, and redemptive plan for humanity. With this perspective, let us commit to engaging with Scripture in a way that honors its divine origin and purpose, facilitates personal and community transformation, and glorifies the God who has spoken to us through His Word.

Scripture as the Guide: Navigating Life's Challenges

The Bible, as the inspired, inerrant Word of God, is more than just a collection of historical narratives, poems, prophecies, and letters. It's a guidebook, a compass for navigating life's many challenges and uncertainties. This dynamic, living Word, written thousands of years ago, still speaks into our lives today with wisdom, encouragement, correction, and hope.

A Beacon in Dark Times

The world we inhabit is fraught with difficulties, ranging from personal struggles to global crises. It's not uncommon to feel lost, confused, or overwhelmed. However, the Bible offers a beacon of light in these dark times. David, in the book of Psalms, beautifully expresses this sentiment, "Your word is a lamp to my feet and a light to my path" (Psalms 119:105 ESV).

Indeed, the Scriptures illuminate our path, helping us navigate through life's storms. It does so by revealing the nature of our challenges from God's perspective and offering principles for dealing with them. For instance, in dealing with conflict, the Bible advises us to act justly, love mercy, and walk humbly with God (Micah 6:8 ASV). In dealing with anxiety, it teaches us to cast our anxieties on God because He cares for us (1 Peter 5:7 ESV).

A Source of Comfort and Hope

The Bible also serves as a source of comfort and hope in times of distress. The apostle Paul wrote, "For whatever was written in former days was written for our instruction, that through endurance and through the encouragement of the Scriptures we might have hope" (Romans 15:4 ESV). Many people throughout history have found solace in Scriptures during times of suffering, drawing strength from the knowledge of God's enduring love and faithfulness.

For example, in the midst of persecution and affliction, the early Christians found comfort in the Psalms' expressions of trust in God. They drew hope from Old Testament stories of God's deliverance and provision. They were encouraged by the teachings of Jesus and the apostles, reminding them of their heavenly reward and the transient nature of their earthly trials (2 Corinthians 4:17-18 ESV).

A Guide for Moral and Ethical Decisions

The Bible also provides guidance for moral and ethical decisions. Its teachings form a moral compass, helping us discern right from wrong in various situations. This guidance is not presented as a comprehensive list of do's and don'ts but as principles reflecting God's character and His desire for human flourishing.

In the Sermon on the Mount, Jesus provided a radical ethic of love, mercy, and humility that challenged the legalistic and self-righteous practices of His day (Matthew 5-7 ESV). Similarly, Paul's letters are filled with ethical instructions rooted in the reality of the believer's new identity in Christ (Ephesians 4:17-32 ESV).

Guarding Against Misuse

While Scripture is an indispensable guide, we must be cautious against misuse. Twisting Scripture to justify wrongdoing or to impose personal views is a grave error. Right interpretation, guided by the Holy Spirit and sound hermeneutical principles, is crucial. As already noted, it's essential to consider the historical, cultural, and literary contexts of a biblical text. Furthermore, we must approach the Bible with humility, acknowledging our biases and presuppositions and being open to correction by God's Word.

Conclusion: The Bible as Our Compass

The Bible, rightly interpreted and applied, is a reliable guide for navigating life's challenges. It's a beacon in dark times, a source of comfort and hope, and a guide for moral and ethical decisions. As we engage with the Scriptures, we must do so with reverence, humility, and a readiness to obey. In this way, we can experience the Bible's transformative power, enabling us to face life's uncertainties with confidence and hope, firmly grounded in the enduring truth of God's Word.

A Lifelong Journey with the Living Word

The Christian life is often characterized as a journey, a long and often winding path of spiritual growth and maturation. At the center of this journey stands the Bible, the inspired, inerrant Word of God. The Scripture serves not only as a source of information about God and His plan for humanity but also as a faithful guide that shapes our thoughts, convictions, actions, and overall character. Engaging with the Bible is not a one-time event but a lifelong pursuit, a journey within a journey, with the Living Word.

God's Word: An Endless Well of Wisdom

The depth and richness of Scripture are such that it can never be exhausted. As the book of Isaiah asserts, "For as the heavens are higher than the earth, so are my ways higher than your ways and my thoughts than your thoughts" (Isaiah 55:9 ESV). Despite the temporal and cultural gap between us and the original audience, the Bible continues to provide wisdom and guidance relevant to all generations.

Every passage, every verse, every word of Scripture is a fragment of the mind of God, representing an infinite wellspring of wisdom, truth, and spiritual insight. The Psalmist poetically captures this when he writes, "I rejoice at your word like one who finds great spoil" (Psalm 119:162 ESV). The treasures of wisdom and knowledge hidden in Christ and revealed through the Scriptures (Colossians 2:3 ESV) are indeed spoil for the believer, a bounty to be discovered and savored.

The Journey of Scripture Engagement

Engaging with Scripture is a lifelong journey that should ideally begin at a young age and continue until our final days. From the early stories of creation, Noah, and the Exodus that we learn in Sunday School, to the deeper explorations of doctrine, morality, and the person of Jesus Christ in adulthood, the Bible continually instructs, challenges, and inspires.

Throughout this journey, our understanding of Scripture deepens and expands. We learn to read Scripture in its historical and cultural context, to recognize its various genres, and to apply sound hermeneutical principles. As we mature, we move beyond the milk of the Word to solid food (Hebrews 5:12-14 ESV), grappling with complex theological issues and ethical dilemmas.

Moreover, the journey is not merely an intellectual endeavor. The Word of God is living and active (Hebrews 4:12 ESV). It penetrates the deepest recesses of our hearts and minds, exposing our innermost thoughts and desires. Through the Word, the Holy Spirit convicts us of sin, assures us of God's love, and transforms us into the image of Christ. The journey of Scripture engagement is thus deeply personal and transformative.

A Journey Marked by Grace

It's important to note that this journey is marked by grace. We are not left to traverse the path alone. The Holy Spirit, who inspired the authors of the Bible, assists us in understanding and applying Scripture. Jesus promised His disciples, "But the Helper, the Holy Spirit, whom the Father will send in my name, he will teach you all things and bring to your remembrance all that I have said to you" (John 14:26 ESV). While we are responsible for diligently studying the Word and seeking to understand it rightly, we rely on the Spirit's illumination to truly grasp its meaning and significance.

Moreover, we journey with the Word in the context of the community of faith. We learn from the wisdom of others, both contemporary and those who have gone before us. We engage in dialogues, discussions, and debates that sharpen our understanding and application of the Word. The Christian journey with the Living Word is thus a communal journey, marked by shared learning, mutual encouragement, and collective growth.

Conclusion: A Lifelong Commitment

In conclusion, the Christian's journey with the Living Word is a lifelong commitment that calls for diligence, humility, reliance on the Holy Spirit, and active participation in the community of faith. It's a journey that demands our time, effort, and attention. But it's also a journey filled with joy, discovery, and transformation.

On this journey, we are not merely readers of the Word. We are its students, its disciples. As we immerse ourselves in the Scripture, we come to know God more intimately, understand His will more clearly, and love Him more deeply. And as we are shaped by the Word, we become more effective witnesses of Christ, better equipped to engage our world with the truth, grace, and hope of the Gospel. Thus, the journey with the Living Word is a vital part of our greater journey as followers of Christ—a journey towards maturity, towards Christlikeness, towards our eternal home.

CHAPTER 4 Practical Faith: Integrating God's Wisdom in Everyday Decisions

Introduction: Understanding Practical Faith

Faith is often perceived as a nebulous concept, a grand spiritual idea confined to theological discussions or Sunday sermons. However, faith, when correctly understood and lived out, goes far beyond a mere intellectual assent or a private spiritual experience. It enters into the concrete, day-to-day reality of our lives, guiding our decisions, shaping our responses, and transforming our character. This is what we refer to as "practical faith."

Defining Practical Faith

At its core, practical faith is about integrating God's wisdom in our everyday decisions. It's about bringing the truths of Scripture into our workplaces, our homes, our schools, and our communities. It's about reflecting Christ's love, grace, and righteousness in our interactions with others. It's about discerning God's will and making choices that honor Him. Practical faith is faith in action, faith that produces good works, faith that "works through love" (Galatians 5:6 ESV).

To understand practical faith, it's essential to grasp the biblical view of faith. In the Bible, faith is more than intellectual assent to certain truths; it involves trust, commitment, and obedience. The author of Hebrews defines faith as "the assurance of things hoped for, the conviction of things not seen" (Hebrews 11:1 ESV). This assurance and conviction aren't abstract or passive; they lead to action, as seen in the examples of the heroes of faith in Hebrews 11. Their faith led them to obey God, even when it was hard, even when it didn't make sense, even when they couldn't see the outcome.

Practical Faith and God's Wisdom

Practical faith is deeply intertwined with God's wisdom. God's wisdom is His divine perspective on life, a perspective that transcends human understanding and experience. It's His perfect knowledge of what is true, right, and good. God's wisdom is revealed to us primarily through His Word, the Bible. "For the Lord gives wisdom; from his mouth come knowledge and understanding" (Proverbs 2:6 ESV).

As we study and meditate on the Scriptures, we gain insight into God's wisdom. We learn about His character, His purposes, His commands, His promises. We discover His blueprint for a fulfilling and godly life. The more we saturate our minds and hearts with God's Word, the more His wisdom shapes our thoughts, attitudes, and actions. In other words, our faith becomes more practical.

Practical faith isn't about having all the answers or making perfect decisions. It's about seeking God's wisdom, trusting in His providence, and striving to honor Him in all we do. It's about acknowledging, like Solomon, that "the fear of the Lord is the beginning of wisdom, and the knowledge of the Holy One is insight" (Proverbs 9:10 ESV).

In conclusion, practical faith isn't a separate aspect of our faith; it's the tangible expression of our faith in every area of our lives. It's the bridge that connects our beliefs to our behaviors, our doctrine to our duty, our faith to our works. It's an integral part of our journey with God, a journey marked not only by trust and commitment but also by wisdom and obedience. As we embark on this journey of practical faith, we find ourselves growing in maturity, reflecting more accurately the image of Christ, and experiencing more fully the abundant life that He promises (John 10:10 ESV).

The Wisdom of God: Its Source and Significance

As we navigate the intricacies of life, one of the greatest resources we have at our disposal is the wisdom of God. This divine wisdom serves as our compass, providing guidance when we feel lost, clarity when we are confused, and certainty amidst our doubts. But what exactly is God's wisdom? Where does it come from? And what significance does it have for our practical faith?

Understanding God's Wisdom

To understand God's wisdom, we need to first understand what wisdom is not. Wisdom is not mere knowledge. One can accumulate a wealth of information and yet lack wisdom. This is because wisdom is not simply knowing facts, but understanding how to apply that knowledge in practical, beneficial, and moral ways.

God's wisdom is His divine, perfect understanding that guides His actions and decisions. As the omniscient Creator, God sees the end from the beginning and knows the best course of action in every situation. His wisdom is intrinsically tied to His character; it's pure, peaceable, gentle, full of mercy, and produces good fruits (James 3:17 ESV). In essence, God's wisdom is His perfect knowledge applied in His perfect ways for His perfect purposes.

The Source of God's Wisdom

The primary source of God's wisdom is His Word, the Bible. The psalmist declares, "The law of the Lord is perfect, reviving the soul; the testimony of the Lord is sure, making wise the simple" (Psalm 19:7 ASV). In His Word, God provides principles for righteous living, models of godly character, warnings against folly, and promises to those who seek and follow His wisdom. The wisdom of God is also revealed in the person of Jesus Christ, who is described as "the power of God and the wisdom of God" (1 Corinthians 1:24 ESV).

The Significance of God's Wisdom

The significance of God's wisdom in our practical faith cannot be overstated. As we seek to integrate God's wisdom into our everyday decisions, we're not just improving our lives; we're aligning ourselves with His perfect will. We are fulfilling our calling to be His image-bearers, reflecting His character and wisdom to the world around us.

We see the significance of God's wisdom in how it shapes our decision-making. When faced with choices, we're not left to rely on our limited understanding or the shifting opinions of society. Instead, we can seek guidance from God's Word, praying for the Spirit's illumination and discerning God's wisdom.

Moreover, God's wisdom gives us perspective. In the midst of trials, it reassures us that God is working all things together for our good (Romans 8:28 ESV). It helps us see beyond our immediate circumstances to the eternal purposes that God is accomplishing.

Ultimately, the significance of God's wisdom lies in its transformative power. As we embrace God's wisdom, we find ourselves becoming more like Christ, growing in maturity, developing godly character, and living in a way that glorifies God. Practical faith thus becomes a journey of continual growth in God's wisdom, a journey that is challenging, rewarding, and ultimately transformative.

In conclusion, God's wisdom is a precious gift, a divine resource that shapes our practical faith and guides our daily lives. Its source is God's Word, and its significance lies in its transformative power. As we immerse ourselves in God's Word, seeking His wisdom and applying it to our lives, we find ourselves walking in the path of practical faith, growing in Christlikeness, and glorifying God in all we do. This is the journey of a believer, a journey marked by wisdom, obedience, and an unyielding trust in the wisdom of God.

Practical Faith in Daily Living: An Overview

Faith is not confined to the four walls of a church or the sacred moments of religious rituals; it permeates every aspect of our lives. As believers, our faith is not just a set of doctrines we affirm but a dynamic, practical reality that shapes how we live every day. This chapter offers an overview of practical faith in daily living, elucidating what it means and how it looks in real life.

Defining Practical Faith

Practical faith is the application of biblical principles in everyday life. It's not just believing in God but believing God – taking Him at His word and aligning our thoughts, words, and actions with His teachings. Practical faith is faith in action, manifested in our choices, relationships, work, and even how we handle trials and temptations.

Dimensions of Practical Faith

Practical faith unfolds in several dimensions of our lives:

1. **Moral Choices**: Every day, we face choices that test our commitment to God's moral standards. Practical faith informs these choices, enabling us to shun evil and choose what is good and pleasing to God (1 Thessalonians 5:22, ESV).

2. **Personal Relationships**: Our faith shapes how we relate with others, commanding us to love, forgive, and serve one another, and to seek peace and reconciliation (Romans 12:18, ESV).

3. **Work and Stewardship**: Practical faith shapes our work ethic and our attitude towards money and possessions. We work diligently, not just to earn a living, but to serve God and others (Colossians 3:23, ESV). We also steward our resources responsibly, recognizing that they are God's trust to us (Matthew 25:21, ESV).

4. **Handling Trials**: When faced with trials, practical faith provides a framework for understanding and responding to them. It reassures us of God's sovereignty, love, and purpose, and enables us to endure with hope and patience (James 1:2-4, ESV).

5. **Spiritual Disciplines**: Practical faith motivates our engagement with spiritual disciplines, such as prayer, Bible study, worship, and service. These disciplines nurture our relationship with God and equip us for godly living.

Nurturing Practical Faith

Nurturing practical faith is an ongoing process. It begins with immersing ourselves in God's Word, which is the lamp to our feet and light to our path (Psalm 119:105, ASV). The Holy Spirit illuminates our understanding and empowers us to live out God's truth.

Furthermore, practical faith is nurtured through community. The church serves as a nurturing ground where we learn, grow, encourage, and correct each other (Hebrews 10:24-25, ESV). The shared experiences of the community of faith often provide practical insights on living out our faith.

Practical faith is an integral aspect of our Christian journey. It is faith that touches the ground, faith that enters the marketplaces, offices, schools, homes, and every sphere of life. It's a faith that not only believes but behaves, a faith that sees every moment as an opportunity to glorify God and serve others. Such faith is not always easy or convenient, but it is rewarding and transformative, offering us a foretaste of the Kingdom of God here on earth.

Scripture and Decision Making: God's Guidance in Our Choices

In life, we are constantly faced with decisions, both trivial and life-changing. These decisions often influence the course of our lives. For believers, decision-making is not just a matter of personal preferences or societal standards but a profound spiritual exercise. This section will explore the critical role of scripture in decision-making, underscoring how God's Word guides our choices.

God's Word: The Ultimate Standard

Scripture, as God's revealed and inspired Word, provides the ultimate standard for decision-making. It lays out God's moral law, provides wisdom for living, and reveals God's purposes and promises. As the Psalmist declares, "Your word is a lamp to my feet and a light to my path" (Psalm 119:105, ASV). This lamp does not merely illuminate the path but guides the believer's steps.

Direct Guidance through Scriptural Commands and Principles

The Bible offers direct guidance through explicit commands and principles. These commands outline God's moral law and our duties to God and other people. The Ten Commandments, for instance, provide a fundamental moral framework that should inform all our decisions (Exodus 20:1-17, ASV).

Biblical principles, while not necessarily spelled out as commands, offer wisdom for a broad range of situations. For example, the principle of love and respect for all people, derived from the belief that all humans are made in God's image, should guide our relationships and choices regarding others (Genesis 1:27, ASV).

Indirect Guidance through Biblical Narratives and Wisdom Literature

The Bible also offers indirect guidance through its narratives and wisdom literature. Biblical stories illustrate the consequences of obedience and disobedience, wisdom and folly, faith and unbelief. They show us the outcomes of decisions made in faith and fear, humility and pride, love and hate.

The wisdom literature (Psalms, Proverbs, Ecclesiastes, Song of Solomon, and Job) is a rich source of practical insights for decision-making. It addresses a broad array of life's issues – from personal character to interpersonal relationships, from dealing with trials to the use of words and the stewardship of resources (Proverbs 15:1, ESV).

Interpreting and Applying Scripture

The correct interpretation and application of Scripture are crucial to its role in decision-making. We should strive to understand the original meaning of the text (what it meant to the original audience) and its timeless principle (what it means for all times) before we derive personal application (what it means for me now).

Moreover, scripture should be interpreted in light of scripture, taking into account the whole counsel of God's Word. A single verse or passage should not be taken out of context to justify a decision that contradicts the broader teachings of the Bible.

The Role of the Holy Spirit

The Holy Spirit plays a vital role in guiding us through God's Word. He illuminates our understanding of Scripture, convicts us of God's truths, and enables us to obey God's Word (John 16:13, ESV). Thus, prayerful reliance on the Holy Spirit is essential in using Scripture for decision-making.

Scripture holds a central place in Christian decision-making. It's not just a reference book we consult when faced with choices, but a living guide that shapes our values, attitudes, and actions. As believers, we need to immerse ourselves in God's Word, let it dwell in us richly, and allow it to inform our decisions, big and small. As we do this, we can be confident of walking in God's will, experiencing His peace, and bringing glory to His name.

Overcoming Paralysis by Analysis: Trust in God's Wisdom

In our quest for certainty and control, we can often find ourselves caught in the endless loop of analysis. This "paralysis by analysis" hinders our ability to make timely decisions, act with conviction, and live by faith. This section will focus on overcoming this paralysis by placing our trust in God's wisdom.

Paralysis by Analysis: The Modern Dilemma

In our information-saturated age, we have unprecedented access to knowledge, data, and viewpoints. While this can be advantageous, it can also lead to decision-making paralysis. As we seek to make the best, most informed decision, we often end up overwhelmed and immobilized, unable to move forward. This paralysis by analysis is not merely an intellectual problem but a spiritual issue, reflecting a misplaced trust in our human wisdom and understanding.

Scripture's Diagnosis: The Limitations of Human Wisdom

The Bible provides a sobering diagnosis of human wisdom. According to Proverbs, "There is a way that seems right to a man, but its end is the way to death" (Proverbs 14:12, ASV). Here we are reminded that our perspectives and analysis, however reasoned and informed, can lead us astray.

Moreover, in 1 Corinthians, Paul declares that the wisdom of the world is foolishness to God (1 Corinthians 3:19, ESV). This passage underscores the limitations of human wisdom and the folly of relying on it for ultimate decisions and matters of eternal significance.

Scripture's Prescription: Trust in God's Wisdom

In contrast to the limitations of human wisdom, God's wisdom is perfect, infallible, and infinitely reliable. Proverbs counsels us, "Trust in the LORD with all your heart, and do not lean on your own understanding. In all your ways acknowledge him, and he will make straight your paths" (Proverbs 3:5-6, ESV).

Trusting in God's wisdom doesn't mean we abandon rational thought or prudent analysis. Rather, it means we submit our understanding to God, seek His wisdom above all, and rely on His guidance in making decisions. This requires a humble recognition of our limitations and a confident faith in God's wisdom and goodness.

Applying God's Wisdom: Decision-Making in Faith

Applying God's wisdom in decision-making involves immersing ourselves in Scripture, which is God's revealed wisdom. As we study Scripture, we gain insights and principles that inform our decisions.

Furthermore, it involves prayerful discernment, seeking God's guidance and trusting that He will direct our paths. We also need to be sensitive to the Holy Spirit's prompting, remembering that He is the Spirit of wisdom and understanding (Isaiah 11:2, ASV).

Lastly, it involves stepping out in faith, not always having everything figured out but trusting in God's wisdom and guidance. As we do this, we will find freedom from paralysis by analysis, confidence in our decisions, and peace in our hearts.

Paralysis by analysis reflects a common struggle in our complex, information-overloaded world. However, as believers, we have the remedy in God's infallible wisdom. Overcoming paralysis by analysis isn't about having all the answers but about trusting in the One who does. As we trust in God's wisdom, we can navigate life's decisions with faith and confidence, knowing that He will guide us and work out His perfect plan in our lives.

Case Studies: Biblical Figures and Practical Faith

The Bible is teeming with stories of men and women who demonstrated practical faith in their everyday decisions. Through these individuals, we can see the application of God's wisdom in real life situations and learn valuable principles for our own journey. This section will focus on three biblical figures: Abraham, Esther, and Paul.

Abraham: Faith in God's Promise

The story of Abraham, known as the father of faith, offers profound insights into practical faith. Called by God from his homeland, Abraham embarked on a journey to an unknown destination, solely based on God's promise of blessing and land (Genesis 12:1-4, ASV).

Abraham's decision was not without challenges, as he grappled with the delay in God's promise, particularly concerning the birth of a son. Yet, even amid uncertainty, Abraham chose to trust God, demonstrating a faith that believed beyond what was humanly possible. As Romans 4:20-21 (ESV) states, "No unbelief made him waver concerning the promise of God, but he grew strong in his faith as he gave glory to God, fully convinced that God was able to do what he had promised."

Esther: Courageous Action for God's People

Esther, a young Jewish woman who became queen of Persia, demonstrates practical faith in her courageous decision to intercede for her people. Facing the potential annihilation of the Jews in Persia due to a royal decree, Esther chose to approach the king uninvited, a move that could cost her life (Esther 4:11, ASV).

Esther's decision was driven not by blind impulse, but by a deep faith in God's providential care for His people. Recognizing the critical nature of the situation, she requested fasting and prayer from her fellow Jews, sought God's direction, and then acted courageously (Esther 4:16, ASV).

Paul: Unwavering Dedication in Ministry

The apostle Paul offers a striking model of practical faith in his unwavering dedication to God's mission, despite immense challenges. Called by Jesus to be an apostle to the Gentiles, Paul faced numerous hardships, including persecution, imprisonment, and physical ailments.

Yet, he remained steadfast, making decisions that furthered the gospel message, grounded in his confidence in God's power and purpose.

In Philippians 1:12-14 (ESV), Paul shares, "I want you to know, brothers, that what has happened to me has really served to advance the gospel, so that it has become known throughout the whole imperial guard and to all the rest that my imprisonment is for Christ." Here, Paul's faith guided his interpretation of circumstances, leading him to see even his imprisonment as an opportunity for the gospel.

Lessons from the Case Studies

The faith journeys of Abraham, Esther, and Paul reveal valuable principles for our own practice of faith. Firstly, like Abraham, we must trust God's promises, even when the fulfilment seems delayed or impossible. Secondly, like Esther, we need courage to act, grounded in a faith that believes in God's providential care. Finally, like Paul, we should remain dedicated to God's purposes, seeing every situation as an opportunity for His work.

Practical faith, as exemplified by biblical figures like Abraham, Esther, and Paul, involves trusting God's promises, acting courageously on behalf of God's purposes, and remaining steadfast in our dedication to God. By studying their lives, we learn not only how to integrate God's wisdom in our decisions but also how to live a life of faith that glorifies God and furthers His kingdom. These lessons are invaluable as we navigate the complexities of our world, seeking to live out our faith in practical, meaningful ways.

Practical Faith and Modern Challenges: Applying God's Wisdom

In a world that's ever-changing and fraught with complex challenges, living out our faith practically may seem daunting. Yet, as believers, we are called to integrate God's wisdom into our everyday decisions, even in the face of modern difficulties. This chapter explores some of the present-day challenges that believers face and offers biblical wisdom for navigating these issues.

Technology and Ethics

The advent of technology presents a myriad of ethical questions for Christians. From the use of social media to artificial intelligence and biotechnology, the line between benefit and detriment can be blurry. So, how do we apply God's wisdom in this arena?

Scripture may not directly address these technological advancements, but it offers principles that guide our decisions. For instance, Philippians 4:8 (ESV) instructs us to think about things that are true, honorable, just, pure, lovely, commendable, excellent, and praiseworthy. This principle can guide our media consumption, reminding us to engage with content that aligns with these virtues.

Furthermore, the biblical command to love our neighbor as ourselves (Mark 12:31, ESV) can guide our interactions on social media, prompting us to engage with respect, kindness, and a consideration for the impact of our digital footprint.

Social and Political Engagement

As Christians, we are not immune to the social and political realities of our world. We grapple with questions about our role in social justice, political involvement, and navigating the often polarized landscapes of public discourse.

Here, the wisdom from Proverbs 31:8-9 (ASV) is apt, as it calls us to "Open thy mouth for the dumb, in the cause of all such as are left desolate. Open thy mouth, judge righteously, and minister justice to the poor and needy." This scripture provides a guiding principle for our social and political engagement: we are to be advocates of justice, especially for those who are marginalized.

Environmental Stewardship

One modern challenge that Christians face is the question of environmental stewardship. Amid growing concerns about climate change, pollution, and biodiversity loss, how should believers respond?

Genesis 1:28 (ASV) gives the mandate to humanity to "be fruitful, and multiply, and replenish the earth, and subdue it." This command, often called the "Creation Mandate," implies a responsibility for environmental stewardship. Hence, as believers, we are called to make decisions that uphold this mandate, including sustainable practices and advocacy for environmental justice.

Practical faith in the face of modern challenges involves actively applying biblical principles to contemporary issues. Whether it's ethical dilemmas posed by technology, our engagement in social and political matters, or environmental stewardship, the wisdom of God's Word provides guidance. As we seek to navigate these challenges, let's remember the words of James 1:5 (ESV), "If any of you lacks wisdom, let him ask God, who gives generously to all without reproach, and it will be given him."

The Role of Prayer in Decision Making

The process of decision-making in a Christian's life is often intertwined with prayer. This intimate communication with God provides us with a platform to express our concerns, seek His guidance, and ultimately, align our choices with His will. This section will explore the significance of prayer in decision-making, emphasizing the importance of acting in faith upon the guidance received rather than passively waiting for divine intervention.

Prayer as a Dialogue with God

Prayer is a two-way communication with our Creator. When we pray, we are not merely presenting our requests to God but engaging in a dialogue where we also listen for His direction. In 1 Samuel 3:9 (ASV), the young Samuel responds to God's call with, "Speak; for thy servant heareth." This illustrates the receptive attitude we ought to have in prayer. We present our decision-making dilemmas to God, then quiet our hearts and minds to listen for His guidance.

Seeking God's Guidance through Prayer

When faced with decisions, both minor and significant, it is essential to seek God's guidance through prayer. Proverbs 3:5-6 (ASV) advises us, "Trust in Jehovah with all thy heart, and lean not upon thine own understanding. In all thy ways acknowledge him, and he will direct thy paths." By presenting our choices and dilemmas to God in prayer, we acknowledge His sovereignty and wisdom. We also express our dependence on Him, opening ourselves to the direction He provides.

Acting in Faith and Obedience

Prayer in decision-making is not a passive exercise where we wait for God to make our choices or for miraculous intervention to occur. Rather, it involves active listening and subsequent obedience to God's direction. In James 2:17 (ESV), it is written, "So also faith by itself, if it does not have works, is dead." This emphasizes that our prayers must be accompanied by action. Once we receive guidance through prayer, we should act in obedience, even if the direction seems challenging or against conventional wisdom.

For instance, Noah did not merely pray when warned about the impending flood; he acted by building the ark (Genesis 6, ASV). Similarly, the Israelites, under Joshua's leadership, did not only pray for the fall of Jericho's walls but also acted by marching around the city as God instructed (Joshua 6, ASV). These examples underscore the importance of marrying prayer with faithful action.

Persevering in Prayer

Lastly, it is vital to note that guidance in decision-making may not come immediately, requiring us to persevere in prayer. In Luke 18:1-8 (ESV), Jesus shares a parable encouraging His followers "to the effect that they ought always to pray and not lose heart." In our context, this implies that we should remain persistent in seeking God's guidance, confident in His faithfulness to provide direction in His perfect timing.

In conclusion, prayer plays a pivotal role in decision-making for believers. It is a dynamic dialogue where we present our dilemmas to God and receive His guidance. Importantly, it requires us to act in faith and obedience to God's direction, illustrating a practical faith that does not sit around waiting for divine intervention, but steps out confidently knowing that we are following God's will. So, as we face decisions, may we always be guided by Philippians 4:6-7 (ESV), "Do not be anxious about anything, but in everything by prayer and supplication with thanksgiving let your requests be made known to God. And the peace of God, which surpasses all understanding, will guard your hearts and your minds in Christ Jesus."

The Dangers of Divination and Over-Spiritualizing Decisions

In our Christian journey, one of the significant pitfalls we need to guard against is the tendency towards divination and over-spiritualizing decisions. While it is crucial to seek God's will in our decisions, we must be mindful not to veer into practices and ideologies that are inconsistent with the teachings of the Bible. This chapter will delve into the dangers of divination and over-spiritualizing decisions, drawing from biblical teachings to guide us in making decisions aligned with God's wisdom.

Understanding Divination

Divination refers to the practice of seeking knowledge or guidance from a supernatural source, usually by interpreting signs or symbols. However, such practices are unequivocally condemned in the Bible. Deuteronomy 18:10 (ASV) instructs, "There shall not be found with thee anyone...that useth divination." This is because divination seeks to bypass God's wisdom and timing, relying instead on illegitimate spiritual sources. It subtly shifts our reliance away from God, breeding spiritual deception and vulnerability.

The Trap of Over-Spiritualizing Decisions

In addition to divination, there's a danger in over-spiritualizing decisions—waiting for extraordinary signs or supernatural revelations to make everyday decisions. This mindset can lead to a passive form of Christianity, where one becomes immobilized by indecision, waiting for miraculous guidance for every step taken.

For example, expecting a divine revelation to decide whether to accept a job offer, which car to purchase, or what to eat for breakfast can trivialize the serious work of discerning God's will in significant matters. This over-spiritualizing can divert our attention from biblical principles that should guide our decisions, such as wisdom, stewardship, love for neighbor, and pursuit of God's glory.

Biblical Decision Making

The Bible offers us a more balanced approach to decision-making that relies on divine wisdom rather than human divination or over-spiritualizing decisions. Scripture encourages us to seek God's wisdom through prayer and meditation on His Word (James 1:5, ESV). Moreover, we are to apply the principles of Scripture in our decision-making process and be guided by the Holy Spirit's leading in alignment with God's Word.

In Proverbs 3:5-6 (ASV), we read, "Trust in Jehovah with all thy heart, And lean not upon thine own understanding. In all thy ways acknowledge him, And he will direct thy paths." Here, the "acknowledging" does not mean waiting for miraculous signs, but actively involving God in our decision-making, seeking His guidance and wisdom.

The Role of Common Sense and Wisdom

God has gifted us with intellect, common sense, and the ability to gain wisdom. We can't neglect these gifts by over-spiritualizing our decisions or seeking guidance from divination. Rather, we must apply them within the framework of biblical truth.

For instance, when faced with financial decisions, we should apply the biblical principles of stewardship and contentment (1 Timothy 6:6-10, ESV). For ethical decisions, we rely on the Bible's moral teachings (Matthew 22:37-40, ESV). We can also seek wise counsel from other believers (Proverbs 15:22, ASV).

Developing Discernment: A Key Skill in Practical Faith

Understanding Discernment

Discernment, the ability to make responsible judgments, is a fundamental attribute of a mature Christian faith. It signifies the intellectual and spiritual capacity to distinguish between right and wrong, truth and falsehood, wisdom and folly. It's a skill, not an innate ability, that grows and matures with a person's faith walk, bible study, and prayer life.

Discernment in the Bible

The concept of discernment is a recurring theme in the Bible. The book of Proverbs, one of the wisdom books of the Old Testament, offers many verses emphasizing the importance of discernment. Proverbs 2:3, 5 (ASV) says, "Yea, if thou cry after discernment, and lift up thy voice for understanding...Then shalt thou understand the fear of Jehovah, and find the knowledge of God." These verses underscore the role of discernment as an essential tool in understanding God and His ways.

Discernment involves the interaction between the human mind and divine wisdom. It's more than a process of rational decision-making; it's a spiritual practice influenced by the Word of God and guided by the Holy Spirit. We are told in 1 Corinthians 2:14 (ESV), "The natural person does not accept the things of the Spirit of God, for they are folly to him, and he is not able to understand them because they are spiritually discerned."

The Importance of Discernment

When the ability to discern is honed, it enables individuals to make sound judgments and decisions rooted in biblical wisdom. It becomes a safeguard against false teachings and a compass in a world filled with deceptive appearances and complex moral issues. Hebrews 5:14 (ESV) says, "But solid food is for the mature, for those who have their powers of discernment trained by constant practice to distinguish good from evil."

Developing Discernment

Developing discernment is a gradual, intentional process. Firstly, it requires an intimate relationship with God and a dedication to studying His Word. Scripture, as 2 Timothy 3:16 (ESV) states, is "profitable for teaching, for reproof, for correction, and for training in righteousness," providing the primary resource for understanding God's will and developing discernment.

Secondly, a regular prayer life is crucial. James 1:5 (ESV) instructs, "If any of you lacks wisdom, let him ask God, who gives generously to all without reproach, and it will be given him." Prayer is a means through which we seek God's wisdom and guidance, invoking divine insight in our decision-making process.

Thirdly, fellowship with other believers provides a platform for growth in discernment. Through sharing experiences, discussing biblical interpretations, and mutual correction, the communal aspect of Christianity can enhance individual discernment skills.

Lastly, the consistent practice of applying God's Word in everyday decisions contributes significantly to the development of discernment. Just as a muscle strengthens with use, so does the capacity to discern through regular application of biblical wisdom in life's choices.

Applying Discernment in Decision Making

Discernment is not just about choosing between right and wrong; it's also about selecting the best among good options. Often, life presents us with multiple good choices, and it can be challenging to determine God's preferred direction. In such instances, discernment, informed by biblical wisdom, prayer, and the inner peace that the Holy Spirit provides, becomes instrumental.

However, applying discernment should not be mistaken for a formula or a foolproof method to divine God's will. There's no biblical support for the idea that we will always be led infallibly in our decision-making. The human condition means that we may sometimes make mistakes, even as we strive to discern God's will. What's important is maintaining a humble and teachable spirit, ready to learn from these errors and adjust our course as needed.

The development of discernment is not an overnight acquisition; instead, it's a lifelong journey of studying God's Word, constant prayer, fellowship, and consistent application of biblical principles in our daily lives. By doing so, we move closer to the biblical ideal of discernment, becoming better equipped to navigate the challenges of our world while adhering to the tenets of our faith.

Embracing Practical Faith as a Way of Life

Understanding Practical Faith

Practical faith refers to the daily application of biblical principles and wisdom in our decisions, actions, and lifestyle. It goes beyond a mere intellectual assent to the truths of Scripture and extends to how those truths shape our daily conduct. Practical faith is faith in action, demonstrable in the choices we make and the habits we cultivate.

The Biblical Basis for Practical Faith

The Bible makes it abundantly clear that faith should not be an abstract concept confined to our beliefs but should impact our daily lives. James 2:17 (ESV) asserts, "So also faith by itself, if it does not have works, is dead." In other words, a faith that does not influence our actions is ineffective and fruitless.

Furthermore, Jesus, in the Sermon on the Mount, explained the practical implications of faith in the Beatitudes and succeeding teachings. He didn't merely focus on beliefs but elaborated on attitudes and behaviors reflective of those beliefs (Matthew 5–7 ESV).

Embracing Practical Faith

To embrace practical faith, we must understand the importance of integrating God's wisdom in our everyday decisions. Our faith should influence our thoughts, words, actions, and attitudes. This integration is not a one-time event but a continuous process that shapes and refines us as we walk in obedience to God's Word.

Applying God's Wisdom Daily

Embracing practical faith involves applying God's wisdom in our daily lives. It means making choices aligned with biblical principles, whether it's in our relationships, financial management, work ethic, or how we treat others. Proverbs 2:6 (ASV) reminds us, "For Jehovah giveth wisdom; Out of his mouth cometh knowledge and understanding."

The Influence of Prayer and Scripture

Prayer and Scripture are crucial components in living out a practical faith. Prayer connects us to God, allowing us to seek His guidance and strength. On the other hand, Scripture provides us with divine wisdom and principles for living a godly life. 2 Timothy 3:16-17 (ESV) assures us that "All Scripture is breathed out by God and profitable for teaching, for reproof, for correction, and for training in righteousness, that the man of God may be complete, equipped for every good work."

The Role of the Holy Spirit

The Holy Spirit plays an essential role in enabling us to live out a practical faith. As we submit to the Spirit's leading, we can bear the fruit of the Spirit, which includes love, joy, peace, patience, kindness, goodness, faithfulness, gentleness, and self-control (Galatians 5:22-23 ESV). These attributes should be evident in our daily lives as we strive to reflect Christ in our conduct.

Community and Practical Faith

Community is another essential factor in embracing practical faith as a way of life. The New Testament frequently emphasizes the role of the Christian community in encouraging, teaching, correcting, and supporting one another. The communal aspect of Christianity aids in the application of faith in everyday life, as we learn from each other's experiences and grow together in Christ.

Practical Faith as a Journey

Embracing practical faith as a way of life is a journey. It's not a destination that we reach but a path we walk, continually growing in our understanding and application of God's Word. As Philippians 3:12 (ESV) notes, "Not that I have already obtained this or am already perfect, but I press on to make it my own, because Christ Jesus has made me his own."

Living out a practical faith means that our beliefs are not just theoretical but actively influence our daily lives. It means seeking to align our actions with God's wisdom, guided by prayer, Scripture, and the Holy Spirit. It's a communal journey of growth, where we strive to reflect Christ more and more in our daily decisions and interactions. Embracing practical faith as a way of life may not always be easy, but it is a rewarding and fulfilling pursuit that leads to a deeper relationship with God and a life that glorifies Him.

CHAPTER 5 The Power of Prayer: God's Way of Communication

Introduction: The Essential Role of Prayer

Prayer, in its most basic form, is communication with God. However, to confine it merely as a form of discourse would be an oversimplification of its profound nature. Prayer is not only about speaking but also listening—engaging with the Divine in a relationship that goes beyond earthly comprehension. The function of prayer in the believer's life is essential, and its influence reaches the depths of the human soul and extends to the spheres of our personal and communal existence.

Throughout the Bible, the importance of prayer is emphasized time and again. It is not presented as an optional spiritual discipline, but rather a fundamental aspect of a thriving relationship with God. Prayer is how we express our love, our fears, our confessions, and our dependence on God. It is how we align ourselves with His will and how we participate in His work.

The Apostle Paul exhorts in 1 Thessalonians 5:17 (ESV), "Pray without ceasing." This command underscores the centrality of prayer in the believer's life—it is not to be confined to specific occasions but integrated into the rhythms of our everyday lives.

Prayer as a Divine Invitation

Understanding prayer begins with recognizing it as an invitation from God. It is God who first calls us into this communion. In Jeremiah 33:3 (ASV), the Lord declares, "Call unto me, and I will answer thee, and will show thee great things, and difficult, which thou knowest not." God is both willing and desirous to engage in conversation with us, to hear us, and respond to us.

98

Prayer as a Form of Worship

Prayer is an act of worship, a means by which we affirm our faith in God, acknowledge His sovereignty, and submit to His authority. It's a practice that helps us to tune our hearts to God's heart, aligning our wills with His. When Jesus taught His disciples to pray in Matthew 6:9-13 (ESV), He began with worship, "Our Father in heaven, hallowed be your name."

Prayer as a Means of Grace

Prayer is also a channel of God's grace. Through it, we access the throne of grace where we find help in times of need (Hebrews 4:16, ESV). It's through prayer that we confess our sins and receive forgiveness (1 John 1:9, ESV). It's in prayer that we cast our anxieties on God, knowing He cares for us (1 Peter 5:7, ESV).

Prayer as Participation in God's Work

Prayer is a means by which we participate in God's work. While God is entirely sovereign and capable of accomplishing His purposes without our cooperation, He has graciously invited us to join Him in His work through prayer. When we pray for His kingdom to come and His will to be done, we are not only expressing a desire but also aligning ourselves with His purposes and availing ourselves to be used by Him.

Understanding the essential role of prayer is pivotal for our spiritual growth and relationship with God. It's an invitation to commune with God, an act of worship, a means of receiving God's grace, and a form of participation in God's work. The power of prayer lies not in the eloquence of our words or the fervency of our petitions, but in the One to whom we pray—the sovereign, gracious, and loving God who hears and answers. As we comprehend the significance of prayer, may we be driven to engage in this divine communication more passionately and consistently, experiencing the transformative power of prayer in our lives.

Defining Prayer: A Biblical Overview

Prayer is central to the Christian experience. However, before we delve deeper into its power, we must first define it from a biblical perspective. The Bible, our inerrant guide, provides varied instances of prayer from the Old Testament to the New Testament, revealing its multifaceted nature. This biblical overview of prayer seeks to paint a picture of what prayer is, as demonstrated in the Scriptures.

Prayer as Communion with God

Firstly, prayer is a form of communion with God. Genesis 3:8-10 (ASV) illustrates the initial model of communion between God and man. Despite their disobedience, God sought Adam and Eve in the cool of the day, highlighting the relationship God desires to have with humanity. This act underscores prayer as more than just a ritual or duty; it is a relational dialogue between the Creator and His creation.

Prayer as Supplication

The Bible also presents prayer as a means of supplication or petition. In 1 Samuel 1:10-11 (ASV), Hannah's prayer is one of intense petition as she pours out her soul before the Lord, requesting a child. Similarly, in the New Testament, Paul encourages believers in Philippians 4:6 (ESV) to "not be anxious about anything, but in everything by prayer and supplication with thanksgiving let your requests be made known to God."

Prayer as Intercession

Intercession is another critical aspect of prayer. We observe this when Moses intercedes for the Israelites in Exodus 32:11-14 (ASV), pleading with God to turn from His wrath. Jesus Himself intercedes for us, as we see in John 17:15 (ESV), where He prays, "I do not ask that you take them out of the world, but that you keep them from the evil one."

Prayer as Thanksgiving and Praise

Prayer serves as a platform for thanksgiving and praise. Many Psalms express heartfelt gratitude and adoration toward God, such as Psalm 100:4 (ASV), which reads, "Enter into his gates with thanksgiving, And into his courts with praise: Give thanks unto him, and bless his name." Paul echoes this sentiment in 1 Thessalonians 5:18 (ESV), advising us to "give thanks in all circumstances; for this is the will of God in Christ Jesus for you."

Prayer as Confession

The act of confession is also an integral part of prayer. David models this in Psalm 51 (ASV) after his sin with Bathsheba, providing a heartfelt example of repentance and request for forgiveness. John reaffirms this in 1 John 1:9 (ESV), assuring believers that "If we confess our sins, he is faithful and just to forgive us our sins and to cleanse us from all unrighteousness."

A Comprehensive Understanding of Prayer

In summary, prayer is a multifaceted act of communion with God that incorporates supplication, intercession, thanksgiving, praise, and confession. It is not limited to one form or function but is as diverse as the lives and experiences of those who pray. In the Biblical narrative, prayer is a heartfelt, sincere, and pivotal practice in a believer's relationship with God.

Defining prayer biblically equips us to engage with God more effectively and authentically. As we understand and implement these different aspects of prayer, we tap into its transformative power. Consequently, we are not only brought closer to God but are also better aligned with His will and purposes for our lives.

Understanding God's Communication: Hearing Through Scripture and Prayer

Understanding God's communication is a vital aspect of the Christian faith. It informs our relationship with Him and impacts our spiritual growth and transformation. Primarily, God communicates through His written word—Scripture—and through prayer. Thus, integrating these two elements into our lives deepens our relationship with Him and guides us in His will.

God Communicates Through Scripture

The Scriptures, the inspired Word of God, serve as God's primary means of communication. The Bible reveals God's character, His plans, and His instructions for humanity. In 2 Timothy 3:16-17 (ESV), Paul declares, "All Scripture is breathed out by God and profitable for teaching, for reproof, for correction, and for training in righteousness, that the man of God may be complete, equipped for every good work." This passage suggests that the Bible is not a mere historical document, but God's active and living communication tool.

Regular reading, studying, and meditating on Scripture are vital in hearing God. When we immerse ourselves in His Word, we begin to understand His character and His will for our lives more clearly. The Bible is also prophetic, offering foretelling of future events and forthtelling—God's direction, correction, and encouragement for the present. Hence, knowing Scripture is essential in distinguishing God's voice from the noise of the world.

God Communicates Through Prayer

While the Bible allows us to listen to God, prayer gives us the avenue to converse with Him. Prayer is more than asking God for our needs; it is a platform for dialogue where we express our thoughts, emotions, and desires, and in return, we listen and perceive His responses.

Prayer does not change God; instead, it changes us. As we spend time in prayer, our hearts align more with God's heart, and our desires start reflecting His desires. We learn to yield to His will as Jesus did in the Garden of Gethsemane, saying, "not as I will, but as you will" (Matthew 26:39 ESV).

How Does God Respond to Our Prayers?

God responds to our prayers in various ways. At times, His response is immediate and evident. Other times, He may choose to remain silent, teaching us to trust Him amidst uncertainties. There are also instances when God answers differently from what we expect or request, as His wisdom surpasses ours, and His plans are always for our ultimate good (Jeremiah 29:11 ESV).

However, God does not typically audibly answer our prayers, and hence we must be attentive and discerning. Often, His responses come through the illumination of Scripture, the inner conviction from the Holy Spirit, circumstances, or godly counsel from fellow believers. Therefore, cultivating a sensitive spirit towards God's quiet and gentle whispers is crucial.

The Interplay of Scripture and Prayer in God's Communication

The symbiotic relationship between Scripture and prayer is noteworthy. Our understanding of Scripture should shape our prayers, and our prayers can open our hearts to grasp God's Word more deeply. When we pray according to God's Word, we align our requests with His will. Similarly, as we pour out our hearts in prayer, we create room for the Holy Spirit to illuminate Scriptures and grant us fresh insights.

As Christians, we need both Scripture and prayer to fully engage with God's communication. Neither can be neglected without affecting our capacity to hear from God. Therefore, to truly understand God's communication, we must be people of the Word and prayer. Such a lifestyle creates an open line of communication with

God, deepening our relationship with Him, guiding us in His will, and leading us towards spiritual growth and transformation.

The Power of Prayer: Impact on Personal and Community Life

Prayer can be defined as the spiritual communication between man and God, a two-way relationship in which man should not only talk to God but also listen to Him. Prayer to God is like a child's conversation with his father. It is natural for a child to ask his father for the things he needs.

The power of prayer is not the result of the person praying. Rather, the power resides in the God who is being prayed to. 1 John 5:14-15 tells us, "And this is the confidence that we have toward him, that if we ask anything according to his will he hears us. And if we know that he hears us in whatever we ask, we know that we have the requests that we have asked of him." No matter the person praying, the passion behind the prayer, or the purpose of the prayer - God answers prayers that are in agreement with His will. His answers are not always yes, but are always in our best interest. When our desires line up with His will, we will come to understand that in time.

The power of prayer has been well documented over centuries, and miracles have occurred that science cannot explain. Indeed, the power of prayer is a testimony to the existence of a personal God who is both omnipotent and benevolent.

The Power of Prayer: Impact on Personal Life

The most noticeable impact of prayer is on one's personal life. It can lead to greater faith, spiritual growth, and self-discovery. When you talk to God, you're acknowledging His existence and demonstrating faith in Him. Jeremiah 29:12-13 states, "Then you will call upon me and come and pray to me, and I will hear you. You will seek me and find me, when you seek me with all your heart."

Personal prayer, then, is not merely about asking God for something. It's also about recognizing His power and His benevolence. It's about accepting His wisdom and His will for you. In prayer, you open yourself up to God, allowing His Spirit to guide your thoughts and emotions. Romans 8:26 says, "Likewise the Spirit helps us in our weakness. For we do not know what to pray for as we ought, but the Spirit himself intercedes for us with groanings too deep for words."

Prayer also leads to spiritual growth. As you pray, you commune with God, and the Holy Spirit can guide you into truth and help your faith to grow. In 2 Timothy 3:16-17, Paul says, "All Scripture is breathed out by God and profitable for teaching, for reproof, for correction, and for training in righteousness, that the man of God may be complete, equipped for every good work."

Additionally, prayer is an opportunity for self-discovery. Through prayer, you can gain insight into your character, your values, and your purpose. Psalm 139:23-24 says, "Search me, O God, and know my heart! Try me and know my thoughts! And see if there be any grievous way in me, and lead me in the way everlasting!"

The Power of Prayer: Impact on Community Life

In addition to personal benefits, prayer also has a profound impact on community life. It fosters unity, brings about change, and creates an atmosphere of love and respect.

Firstly, prayer can unite people from different walks of life. Acts 2:42 says, "And they devoted themselves to the apostles' teaching and the fellowship, to the breaking of bread and the prayers." As the believers prayed together, they shared in each other's burdens, celebrated victories, and bore witness to God's power and grace.

Prayer also brings about change in the community. It can shift attitudes, incite action, and usher in transformation. James 5:16 says, "Therefore, confess your sins to one another and pray for one another, that you may be healed. The prayer of a righteous person has great power as it is working."

Lastly, prayer cultivates an atmosphere of love and respect among people. As they come together in prayer, they learn to appreciate each other's strengths, understand each other's weaknesses, and support each other in times of need. In Ephesians 6:18, Paul urges, "Praying at all times in the Spirit, with all prayer and supplication. To that end, keep alert with all perseverance, making supplication for all the saints."

In conclusion, prayer is a powerful tool in both personal and community life. It allows us to tap into God's power and wisdom, encourages spiritual growth and self-discovery, and fosters unity and change in the community. But most importantly, prayer is a way to maintain an intimate relationship with God. Our prayers should not just be requests or intercessions but a continual surrender of our lives in reverence and love to our Creator and Savior.

Prayer as Dialogue: Expressing Our Hearts and Hearing God

The very essence of prayer lies in expressing our hearts to God, not just our words or our requests, but the core of our beings. There is a profound truth in the statement that prayer is not just about speaking but also about revealing our hearts to God. It's about opening up our deepest desires, fears, concerns, hopes, and dreams, laying them bare before the One who knows us best.

As David wrote in Psalm 62:8, "Trust in him at all times, O people; pour out your heart before him; God is a refuge for us." This suggests the idea of prayer as a pouring out, a complete, heartfelt expression of our inner self. It's an invitation to let go of our inhibitions and express our thoughts and feelings in their most raw and honest form.

Similarly, the book of Lamentations shows Jeremiah expressing deep and raw emotions to God amidst immense suffering. In Lamentations 2:19, he encourages, "Arise, cry out in the night, at the beginning of the night watches! Pour out your heart like water before the presence of the Lord! Lift your hands to him for the lives of your children."

Prayer as an expression of our hearts is not just a monologue but a dialogue with God. And the other part of that dialogue is to pause, to listen, to allow God to speak to our hearts as well.

Hearing God

While expressing our hearts to God forms one part of the dialogue, an equally, if not more crucial part, is hearing from God. But how can we hear God's voice?

In John 10:27, Jesus says, "My sheep hear my voice, and I know them, and they follow me." As believers in Christ, we have the privilege of hearing His voice, being guided by His words, and being known by Him.

Listening to God in prayer involves being still, focusing our minds on Him, and reading His Word. Psalm 46:10 says, "Be still, and know that I am God. I will be exalted among the nations, I will be exalted in the earth!"

A crucial way God speaks to us is through His Word, the Bible. In 2 Timothy 3:16-17, Paul says, "All Scripture is breathed out by God and profitable for teaching, for reproof, for correction, and for training in righteousness, that the man of God may be complete, equipped for every good work." Thus, by reading and meditating on the Scriptures, we tune our hearts to hear God's voice and understand His will.

To truly hear God, we must approach Him with an open heart, ready to receive whatever He has to say. This means putting aside our agendas, quieting our minds, and focusing entirely on Him. As James 1:19 advises, "Know this, my beloved brothers: let every person be quick to hear, slow to speak, slow to anger."

Prayer as Dialogue

When we think of prayer as dialogue, we recognize it is a two-way communication. This perspective transforms our prayer life, as we stop viewing it merely as a list of requests or a one-way monologue. Instead, we engage in a divine conversation with our Creator, expressing our hearts and actively listening to His response.

In 1 Samuel 3, the young Samuel provides a model of how we should approach this dialogue with God. When Samuel hears God calling him in the night, he responds, "Speak, for your servant is listening." This response is one of humility, readiness, and eagerness to hear what God has to say.

In conclusion, prayer is a dialogue in which we express our hearts to God and listen to His voice. It involves complete honesty, openness, and attentiveness. Through this divine communication, we deepen our relationship with God, gain wisdom and guidance, and align ourselves more closely with His will. It's not just about asking but also about seeking and knocking. As Matthew 7:7-8 says, "Ask, and it will be given to you; seek, and you will find; knock, and it will be opened to you. For everyone who asks receives, and the one who seeks finds, and to the one who knocks it will be opened."

Posture of Prayer: Humility, Honesty, and Persistence

The Scriptures are replete with teachings on the value of approaching prayer with humility. Humility in prayer is acknowledging our dependence on God, recognizing our inability to control or change circumstances without His help. It is an attitude that honors God as our Creator and Sustainer, and it sets the tone for a meaningful and sincere dialogue with Him.

One of the most powerful illustrations of humility in prayer is found in Luke 18:9-14, in the parable of the Pharisee and the Tax Collector. The Pharisee stands self-righteously in the temple, boasting of his supposed righteousness, while the tax collector, standing far off, would not even lift his eyes to heaven, but beat his breast, saying, "God, be merciful to me, a sinner!" Jesus concludes the story stating that it was the tax collector, not the Pharisee, who went home justified, "for everyone who exalts himself will be humbled, but the one who humbles himself will be exalted."

This humility in prayer also involves submission to God's will. In the Garden of Gethsemane, as He faced His impending death on the cross, Jesus prayed, "My Father, if it is possible, let this cup pass from me; nevertheless, not as I will, but as you will" (Matthew 26:39). In His moment of deepest anguish, Jesus modeled the ultimate submission and humility before God's will.

Posture of Prayer: Honesty

Honesty in prayer reflects our authenticity and transparency before God. It's about revealing our true selves, expressing our deepest thoughts and emotions, and laying bare our needs and desires. Being honest in prayer means not hiding any part of ourselves from God.

The Psalms provide numerous examples of such raw honesty in prayer. The Psalmists cried out to God in their distress, questioned Him in their confusion, and even expressed feelings of anger and abandonment. Psalm 13 begins with David asking, "How long, O Lord? Will you forget me forever? How long will you hide your face from me?"

Honesty in prayer also means confessing our sins and acknowledging our need for God's forgiveness. In 1 John 1:9, we read, "If we confess our sins, he is faithful and just to forgive us our sins and to cleanse us from all unrighteousness." Honesty paves the way for confession, and confession leads to forgiveness and restoration.

Posture of Prayer: Persistence

The final posture of prayer we examine is persistence. Persistence in prayer is an expression of our faith in God's goodness and power. It demonstrates our commitment to seek God's will, trust His timing, and wait patiently for His response.

Jesus emphasized the importance of persistent prayer in Luke 18:1-8, through the parable of the persistent widow. The widow consistently pleads with the unjust judge for justice, and because of her persistence, the judge eventually grants her request. Jesus uses this parable to encourage us to "always pray and not lose heart."

Another biblical example of persistent prayer is the apostle Paul's request for the removal of his "thorn in the flesh" (2 Corinthians 12:7-10). Despite God's refusal to remove the thorn, Paul's faith remains unshaken. His persistent prayers lead him to a deeper understanding of God's grace, as he hears the Lord's response, "My grace is sufficient for you, for my power is made perfect in weakness."

In conclusion, the posture of prayer—humility, honesty, and persistence—is an integral part of our communication with God. This approach acknowledges our dependence on God, opens the door for genuine dialogue, and patiently seeks His will. As we develop these attitudes in prayer, we can expect to grow in our understanding and experience of God's love, grace, and wisdom.

Common Misconceptions about Prayer: Addressing Misunderstandings

Misconception 1: Prayer Is a Way to Manipulate God

One common misconception about prayer is that it is a means of manipulating God. This is a fundamentally flawed understanding of the purpose and power of prayer. Prayer is not a magic formula or a way to coerce God into acting according to our whims. It is a means of aligning our will with God's will. In Matthew 6:10, Jesus instructed His followers to pray, "Your will be done, on earth as it is in heaven." This is a petition for God's will to be accomplished, not our own.

Misconception 2: God Will Answer All Prayers the Way We Want

Another misconception is the belief that if we pray fervently and faithfully, God will always answer our prayers in the way we want. This belief can lead to disappointment and disillusionment when the outcome is not what we expected. But as we see in Scripture, God's ways are not our ways, and His thoughts are not our thoughts (Isaiah 55:8). Sometimes, God answers our prayers in unexpected ways, or His answer may be "no" or "wait." The Apostle Paul prayed three times for his "thorn in the flesh" to be removed, but God's answer was, "My grace is sufficient for you" (2 Corinthians 12:9).

Misconception 3: Prayer Is Only for Times of Crisis

The idea that prayer is solely a crisis-management tool is another misunderstanding. Many people turn to prayer only in times of crisis, treating it as a last resort when all other options have failed. However, the Bible encourages us to "pray without ceasing" (1 Thessalonians 5:17), implying a continuous, ongoing conversation with God that includes praise, thanksgiving, confession, and requests.

Misconception 4: The More People Praying, The More Likely God Is to Answer

The belief that God is more likely to answer our prayers if more people are praying, sometimes referred to as the "prayer chain" concept, is a misunderstanding of the nature of prayer. While the Bible encourages collective prayer and there is power in praying together (Matthew 18:20), it is not the number of people praying that influences God's response. God values sincere, heartfelt prayer, whether it comes from one person or a multitude.

Misconception 5: You Must Pray in a Certain Posture or Location for Your Prayers to Be Heard

Some believe that prayers must be offered in a particular posture or location to be effective. But the Bible shows that people prayed in various positions - standing, kneeling, sitting, and even lying down - and in various places - in the temple, on mountains, by the sea, in the wilderness, and in homes. God is interested in our hearts, not our physical posture or location. "The LORD is near to all who call on him, to all who call on him in truth" (Psalm 145:18).

Edward D. Andrews

Misconception 6: God Doesn't Hear the Prayers of Sinners

Another misconception is that God doesn't hear the prayers of sinners. While it is true that sin can hinder our relationship with God (Isaiah 59:2), it is also true that God is gracious and merciful, ready to hear when we confess our sins and seek His forgiveness (1 John 1:9). The tax collector in Luke 18:13 was justified before God when he humbly prayed, "God, be merciful to me, a sinner!"

Misconception 7: God Listens Only to the Prayers of Righteous People

This misconception arises from a literal interpretation of verses like Proverbs 15:29, which says, "Jehovah is far from the wicked, but he hears the prayer of the righteous," and Proverbs 28:9, which states, "If one turns away his ear from hearing the law, even his prayer is an abomination." While it is true that God values righteousness and obedience, these verses should not be understood to mean that God completely disregards the prayers of those who have sinned.

God is omniscient, meaning He has complete knowledge of everything, including every prayer that is prayed. Therefore, the phrase "God does not listen to the prayers of the wicked" should not be interpreted to mean that God is unaware of such prayers. Instead, it means that God does not honor or respond affirmatively to prayers that are not offered in righteousness, sincerity, and obedience to His commands.

It is important to note that none of us is perfectly righteous in our own right. As Romans 3:10 states, "None is righteous, no, not one." Our righteousness comes from faith in Jesus Christ, who died for our sins and rose again to give us eternal life (Romans 3:22). Therefore, even when we fall short, we can approach God in prayer, confess our sins, and receive forgiveness and cleansing because of Christ's sacrifice (1 John 1:9).

In essence, God is more interested in the condition of our hearts than in our external behavior. He values humility, sincerity, and a contrite spirit over empty words and hypocritical actions (Psalm 51:17). Even those who have sinned can approach Him in prayer, confess their wrongdoings, and be assured of His forgiveness and acceptance. In the Parable of the Pharisee and the Tax Collector (Luke 18:9-14), Jesus teaches that the humble, penitent prayer of the tax collector was more acceptable to God than the self-righteous prayer of the Pharisee.

So, yes, while God desires us to strive for righteousness and obedience, it is also true that He hears the prayers of those who humbly confess their sins and seek His mercy and forgiveness. It is not our righteousness, but the righteousness of Christ, that makes our prayers acceptable to God. This perspective not only deepens our understanding of prayer but also reinforces the grace, mercy, and forgiveness of God, who "desires all people to be saved and to come to the knowledge of the truth" (1 Timothy 2:4).

Understanding these misconceptions about prayer can lead us to a more biblically informed perspective. Prayer is a privilege and a spiritual discipline that draws us closer to our Heavenly Father. It is a means of communication with God who invites us into a loving relationship with Him, listens to our prayers, and responds according to His perfect wisdom and love. Prayer is not about getting what we want; it's about getting to know God better and aligning our lives with His will.

Practical Guide to Prayer: Techniques and Tips for Effective Communication

Prayer is an integral part of the Christian faith, providing a channel for communication with God. Despite its importance, many believers struggle with how to pray effectively. Using principles gleaned from Scripture, this guide provides practical techniques and tips for enhancing your prayer life.

Understanding the Purpose of Prayer

Prayer is not just about asking God for things. It is about cultivating a relationship with our Creator. Therefore, our prayers should not just be requests; they should also involve worship, thanksgiving, confession, and listening to God.

Worship

Begin your prayers by acknowledging God's nature and character. This places the focus on God and aligns our hearts with His. The Lord's Prayer starts this way: "Our Father in heaven, hallowed be your name" (Matthew 6:9, ESV). Worship involves praising God for who He is.

Thanksgiving

God instructs us to enter His presence with thanksgiving (Psalm 100:4, ASV). Before you bring your requests to God, thank Him for His blessings and grace. This cultivates a heart of gratitude and helps us to remember God's faithfulness.

Confession

Confession is agreeing with God about our sins and turning away from them. As 1 John 1:9 (ESV) assures us, "If we confess our sins, he is faithful and just to forgive us our sins and to cleanse us from all unrighteousness." Begin your prayers by confessing your sins to God.

Petition

After worship, thanksgiving, and confession, present your requests to God. Be specific about your needs and desires, but always pray with the understanding that God's will is perfect. As we read in Matthew 6:10 (ESV), "Your kingdom come, your will be done, on earth as it is in heaven."

Listening

Prayer is a dialogue, not a monologue. Therefore, it's crucial to quiet your heart and listen to what God might be saying. God speaks to us through His Word, so reading the Bible should be a regular part of our prayer time.

Maintaining the Right Attitude

The Bible highlights three key attitudes we should maintain in prayer: faith, persistence, and humility.

Faith

Jesus says in Mark 11:24 (ESV), "Therefore I tell you, whatever you ask in prayer, believe that you have received it, and it will be yours." Faith is crucial in prayer. Believe in God's ability to answer your prayers according to His perfect will.

Persistence

The parable of the persistent widow (Luke 18:1-8, ESV) encourages us to persist in prayer. Do not be discouraged if your prayers are not answered immediately. Keep praying.

Humility

Prayer should be characterized by a humble acknowledgment of our dependence on God. As the tax collector prayed in Luke 18:13 (ESV), "God, be merciful to me, a sinner!"

Creating a Prayer Schedule

A consistent prayer schedule can enhance your prayer life. The Psalmist declares, "Seven times a day I praise you for your righteous rules" (Psalm 119:164, ASV). Set specific times for prayer throughout your day.

Keeping a Prayer Journal

A prayer journal can help keep track of prayer requests, answers to prayer, and insights gained during prayer and Bible study. Writing down our prayers can help to focus our thoughts and can serve as a testimony of God's faithfulness over time.

Utilizing Scripture in Prayer

Praying Scripture is a powerful way to align our prayers with God's will. You can use the Psalms as a guide or pray specific promises of God found in Scripture.

Conclusion

Effective prayer is not about following a formula but cultivating a relationship with our heavenly Father. Incorporating these techniques and tips into your prayer life can help make that time more enriching and powerful. Remember, God does not require eloquence or lengthy prayers; He desires sincere hearts that seek His will above all else. So let us approach the throne of grace with confidence, knowing that our prayers reach the ears of a loving and compassionate God.

The Role of Prayer in Problem-Solving – Acting on Behalf of Our Prayers

Prayer holds a unique position within the Christian faith as a mechanism of divine intervention and personal change. Its role in problem-solving is profound, allowing believers to present their challenges to God and seek His wisdom. Beyond mere utterances, acting on behalf of our prayers is a tangible demonstration of faith that complements the spiritual discipline of prayer.

Prayer as a Tool for Problem-Solving

In the face of difficulties, the Bible instructs us to pray. James 1:5 (ESV) says, "If any of you lacks wisdom, let him ask God, who gives generously to all without reproach, and it will be given him." Prayer is the first recourse for believers in any circumstance, serving as a tool for accessing divine wisdom and guidance in solving problems.

A Divine Dialogue

Prayer is not a one-way monologue; it is a divine dialogue between God and believers. It's not about bombarding heaven with requests but about seeking God's will. When faced with the weight of the cross, Jesus prayed, "not as I will, but as you will" (Matthew 26:39, ESV). As we present our problems to God, we must listen attentively to His responses, usually found within His Word, and act according to His direction.

Faith in Action

As James 2:17 (ESV) states, "So also faith by itself, if it does not have works, is dead." Simply praying about a problem is not enough; we must put our faith into action. God often answers prayers through ordinary means, which requires us to act. For instance, if we are praying about a job opportunity, we should still prepare for interviews and submit applications. Our actions demonstrate our faith in God's providence.

God's Wisdom and Our Effort

When we pray for wisdom in problem-solving, it does not mean that we abdicate our responsibility to think and act. Proverbs 14:15 (ASV) warns, "The simple believeth every word; But the prudent man looketh well to his going." While we depend on God's wisdom, He also expects us to use the intelligence He has given us to navigate our situations. Prayer does not exclude the necessity for action and careful planning; rather, it should inspire and guide these efforts.

Praying for Courage and Strength

Often, the answers to our prayers require courage to implement. The Israelites prayed for deliverance from Egypt, but they had to step out in faith when the time came (Exodus 14, ESV). Therefore, in our prayers, we should ask for the courage and strength to follow through on the actions required to solve our problems.

Praying Continually

1 Thessalonians 5:17 (ESV) encourages believers to "pray without ceasing." In problem-solving, this means continually seeking God's wisdom and guidance as we take steps to resolve our issues. Our prayers should not end when we start taking action but should accompany every step of our problem-solving process.

The Peace of God in Problem-Solving

In the midst of problem-solving, peace can often seem elusive. However, Philippians 4:6-7 (ESV) offers a promise: "Do not be anxious about anything, but in everything by prayer and supplication with thanksgiving let your requests be made known to God. And the peace of God, which surpasses all understanding, will guard your hearts and your minds in Christ Jesus." As we pray and act on our prayers, we can experience God's peace, knowing that we are aligning ourselves with His will and acting in faith.

Conclusion

The role of prayer in problem-solving goes beyond asking God for solutions. It includes seeking His will, acting in faith, using divine wisdom in conjunction with our efforts, and experiencing His peace as we navigate our challenges. Prayer is a profound tool for problem-solving, but it requires our participation and action. We need to remember that prayer is not about changing God's mind but about aligning our hearts with His will and stepping out in faith to solve our problems as we are guided by His Spirit and Word.

Case Studies: Examining Prayer in the Lives of Biblical Figures

The Bible is rich with narratives of individuals who sought God's guidance and intervention through prayer. Their experiences offer insights into the role of prayer in the life of a believer, its power, and its principles.

Abraham: Intercession for Sodom and Gomorrah

Abraham's intercession for Sodom and Gomorrah in Genesis 18:16-33 (ASV) is a prime example of the role of prayer as intercession. Abraham pleads with God to spare the cities if there are righteous people within them. His prayer exhibits a selfless concern for others, a characteristic that should define our prayers. It also shows that God is open to our requests and is willing to engage with us in dialogue, a principle that holds true in the New Testament as well (James 5:16, ESV).

Hannah: Prayer for a Child

In 1 Samuel 1 (ASV), Hannah's prayer for a child showcases the power of sincere, heartfelt prayer. Despite her deep anguish and sorrow, Hannah turns to God, pouring out her soul before Him. Her experience demonstrates that God hears the cries of His people and responds to their prayers, especially when they commit to serving Him faithfully.

David: A Man of Prayer

King David, known as "a man after God's own heart," offers an extensive record of prayers throughout the Psalms. His prayers range from cries of despair to songs of rejoicing, revealing an intimate relationship with God. In Psalm 51 (ASV), David's prayer for forgiveness following his sin with Bathsheba shows the power of confession and the necessity of a contrite heart in prayer.

Daniel: Prayer under Persecution

Daniel's prayer life is exemplary, particularly in the face of persecution (Daniel 6, ASV). His commitment to prayer, even when threatened with death, underscores the importance of consistency in prayer. His experience demonstrates that God hears and honors the prayers of those who faithfully serve Him.

Jesus Christ: Our Perfect Example

Our Lord Jesus Christ, the epitome of perfect prayer, offers a model in the Gospels. Jesus' prayer in the Garden of Gethsemane (Matthew 26:36-46, ESV) reveals the depth of His relationship with the Father. It shows us that prayer is not only about making requests but also about aligning our will with God's.

Paul: Prayers for the Church

The Apostle Paul's prayers for the early Church, as seen in Ephesians 1:15-23 (ESV), are rich in substance and depth. Paul doesn't focus on physical or material needs but prays for spiritual wisdom, revelation, and growth. His prayers teach us that intercessory prayer should aim at the spiritual wellbeing of others.

Conclusion

These biblical case studies provide insights into prayer's crucial role in the lives of believers. They reveal that prayer is a medium of intimate communication with God, driven by faith, sincerity, and a deep understanding of God's will. These narratives remind us that our prayers should be characterized by persistence, humility, and a commitment to God's glory, irrespective of our circumstances. They assure us that God listens to and answers the prayers of His people, urging us to make prayer a pivotal part of our Christian journey. These examples, as different as they may be, have a common thread – a testament of faith, woven through prayer, linking the human heart with the divine.

Cultivating a Life of Prayer

The Importance of Prayer in a Believer's Life

Cultivating a life of prayer is a central component of the Christian journey. It is through prayer that we communicate with God, seek His guidance, express our adoration, confess our sins, and plead for our needs. As Apostle Paul writes, "pray without ceasing" (1 Thessalonians 5:17, ESV), underscoring the need for constant, unwavering prayer in the life of a believer.

Establishing a Daily Routine of Prayer

To cultivate a life of prayer, one must establish a daily routine. As observed in the life of Daniel, he prayed three times a day, maintaining his practice even in the face of severe opposition (Daniel 6:10, ASV). One can set specific times for prayer, such as morning, afternoon, and night. These do not replace spontaneous prayers but serve as the framework upon which a consistent prayer life can be built.

Praying with a Right Heart

An effective prayer life is not just about the frequency of prayers, but also the condition of the heart. The Psalmist David prayed, "Create in me a clean heart, O God, and renew a right spirit within me" (Psalm 51:10, ASV). A humble, repentant heart is crucial for a sincere and meaningful prayer life. In prayer, we should continually seek God's forgiveness and cleansing to maintain a heart that is right with God.

Understanding the Role of the Holy Spirit in Prayer

Recognizing the role of the Holy Spirit in prayer is pivotal. The Apostle Paul explains, "the Spirit helps us in our weakness. For we do not know what to pray for as we ought, but the Spirit himself intercedes for us with groanings too deep for words" (Romans 8:26, ESV). Inviting the Holy Spirit to guide our prayers enables us to align our requests according to God's will.

Using Scripture as a Guide for Prayer

Scripture can serve as an effective guide in prayer. By praying the Scriptures, we align ourselves with God's will as expressed in His Word. For instance, the Lord's Prayer provided by Jesus in Matthew

6:9-13 (ESV) offers a template that covers various elements of prayer, such as adoration, confession, thanksgiving, and supplication. Meditating on and praying through Psalms and other biblical prayers can enrich our prayer life.

Practicing Intercessory Prayer

Intercessory prayer, or praying on behalf of others, is an integral aspect of a vibrant prayer life. Paul often included intercessions in his prayers for the early churches (Ephesians 1:16, ESV). Regularly praying for others—be they fellow believers, family members, government authorities, or those who do not yet know Christ—expands our prayer life beyond our own needs and reflects God's heart for all people.

Perseverance in Prayer

Persisting in prayer, especially during challenging times or when answers seem delayed, is vital. The parable of the persistent widow in Luke 18:1-8 (ESV) illustrates the need for perseverance in prayer. When faced with trials, it is essential to remain steadfast in prayer, trusting in God's perfect timing and sovereign will.

Conclusion

Cultivating a life of prayer requires commitment, discipline, and reliance on the Holy Spirit. It involves daily communication with God, possessing a heart aligned with His will, employing Scripture as a guide, practicing intercession, and displaying perseverance. A consistent, dynamic prayer life leads to a deeper, more intimate relationship with God and forms the backbone of a flourishing Christian walk. This is the beauty and the challenge of a life of prayer, and it's a journey well worth embarking upon.

CHAPTER 6 Nurturing Your Spiritual Growth: The Importance of Personal Responsibility

Introduction: The Intersection of Spiritual Growth and Personal Responsibility

The Christian journey is marked by continual spiritual growth, and personal responsibility plays a pivotal role in this process. Although the Holy Spirit empowers and guides us, we are personally accountable for nurturing our spiritual life. This intersection of spiritual growth and personal responsibility forms the basis for a maturing faith, as exemplified by the Apostle Paul's analogy of the spiritual growth process in 1 Corinthians 3:6-7 (ESV).

Personal Responsibility in Spiritual Growth

Personal responsibility in spiritual growth involves an active engagement with spiritual disciplines, such as studying the Word, prayer, fasting, and fellowship. These practices, according to 2 Timothy 2:15 (ASV), demand diligent effort on our part to "study to show thyself approved unto God, a workman that needeth not to be ashamed, rightly dividing the word of truth."

Intentional Engagement with Scripture

Our responsibility begins with an intentional engagement with Scripture. The Psalmist declares, "Your word is a lamp to my feet and a light to my path" (Psalm 119:105, ASV). Regular study and meditation on the Bible enable us to grow in our understanding of God and His will for us.

123

Devotion to Prayer

Next, devotion to prayer, as urged by Paul in 1 Thessalonians 5:17 (ESV) to "pray without ceasing," is another personal responsibility that fosters spiritual growth. Through prayer, we communicate with God, expressing our joys, sorrows, fears, and hopes, thus deepening our relationship with Him.

The Role of Fasting

Fasting, often paired with prayer in Scripture, is another spiritual discipline that fosters growth. Fasting, as Jesus taught in Matthew 6:16-18 (ESV), is a personal commitment that, when done sincerely for God's glory, can bring about spiritual breakthroughs and deeper understanding of God's Word.

Christian Fellowship and Its Significance

Christian fellowship also holds a significant role in spiritual growth. "And let us consider how to stir up one another to love and good works, not neglecting to meet together, as is the habit of some, but encouraging one another, and all the more as you see the Day drawing near" (Hebrews 10:24-25, ESV). Regular interaction with other believers fosters encouragement, accountability, and mutual edification, which are critical for spiritual growth.

Spiritual Growth as a Lifelong Process

It is essential to understand that spiritual growth is a lifelong process. Philippians 1:6 (ESV) reminds us that "he who began a good work in you will bring it to completion at the day of Jesus Christ." We need to continually strive for growth, understanding that spiritual maturity is a progressive journey that lasts a lifetime.

The Role of Trials in Spiritual Growth

Trials and difficulties, too, play a role in spiritual growth. James 1:2-4 (ESV) encourages believers to consider trials as joy, as they produce steadfastness leading to maturity. Through these hardships, we learn to rely on God's strength, leading to spiritual fortitude and deepened faith.

Conclusion: Personal Responsibility – The Key to Spiritual Growth

In conclusion, personal responsibility is a key component in nurturing spiritual growth. Engaging in spiritual disciplines, persevering in faith amidst trials, and recognizing spiritual growth as a lifelong process are all facets of this personal responsibility. As we faithfully discharge our spiritual duties, we can rely on the Holy Spirit's guidance to facilitate growth, leading us to become more Christ-like in our thoughts, words, and actions.

Nurturing spiritual growth is not a passive event but an active, lifelong journey. The Holy Spirit does not bypass our will but works in conjunction with our active participation. Hence, personal responsibility is not just a choice but a necessity in our quest for spiritual maturity and deeper intimacy with God. In the end, our efforts are not in vain, for "your labor in the Lord is not in vain" (1 Corinthians 15:58, ESV).

The Biblical Basis for Personal Responsibility

Introduction: Understanding Personal Responsibility

Personal responsibility is a theme that echoes throughout the Bible, both in the Old and New Testaments. It refers to the acknowledgment and acceptance of the individual's role in their actions and the consequences thereof. The essence of personal responsibility lies in owning our actions, decisions, and their outcomes, understanding that our choices can lead to blessings or consequences.

Personal Responsibility in the Old Testament

In the Old Testament, personal responsibility is a recurring theme. This concept is succinctly encapsulated in the book of Deuteronomy, where Moses addresses the Israelites, urging them to choose life by loving and obeying God (Deuteronomy 30:19-20, ASV). This scripture places the onus on the individual to make the conscious choice to follow God's commandments.

Ezekiel 18:20 (ASV) further underscores personal responsibility by stating that "the son shall not bear the iniquity of the father, neither shall the father bear the iniquity of the son." Each individual is held accountable for their actions, reinforcing the principle of personal responsibility.

Personal Responsibility in the New Testament

In the New Testament, Jesus' teachings often emphasized personal responsibility. For instance, in the Parable of the Talents (Matthew 25:14-30, ESV), each servant was given resources according to their abilities and was expected to steward them well. The parable underscores that each of us will be held accountable for how we utilize the resources and gifts God has entrusted to us.

The Apostle Paul also emphasized personal responsibility in his epistles. In Galatians 6:4-5 (ESV), he states, "But let each one test his own work, and then his reason to boast will be in himself alone and not in his neighbor. For each will have to bear his own load." This passage affirms the need for personal accountability in spiritual matters.

Personal Responsibility and Free Will

The biblical narrative from Genesis to Revelation recognizes the human capacity for decision-making, referred to as free will. This free will presents each individual with a choice, and it is here that personal responsibility becomes evident. The choice to obey or disobey God, to do good or evil, all hinge on personal responsibility. Joshua's declaration to the Israelites in Joshua 24:15 (ASV), "choose you this day whom ye will serve," exemplifies this interplay between free will and personal responsibility.

Personal Responsibility and Christian Living

The principle of personal responsibility is integral to Christian living. Paul's words in 2 Corinthians 5:10 (ESV) remind us that "we must all appear before the judgment seat of Christ, so that each one may receive what is due for what he has done in the body, whether good or evil." This future judgment underscores the need for personal responsibility in the present, influencing our actions, words, and attitudes.

Conclusion: Embracing Personal Responsibility

In conclusion, the Bible offers a strong foundation for the concept of personal responsibility. It is a call to accountability in our actions, decisions, and their consequences. It is an invitation to live in a way that honors God, embraces integrity, and respects others. This responsibility, while at times daunting, is integral to our spiritual growth and maturity. Embracing personal responsibility leads to a life that mirrors the teachings of Christ, impacting not just our personal lives, but also the world around us.

To paraphrase the words of the Apostle Paul in 1 Corinthians 9:24 (ESV), "So run [your race] that you may obtain [the prize]." The race is individual, and each one of us is responsible for how we run it. This is the essence of personal responsibility. It is an inextricable part of our spiritual journey, compelling us to live mindful, purposeful lives dedicated to the glory of God.

Understanding Spiritual Growth: An Ongoing Journey

Introduction: The Process of Spiritual Growth

Spiritual growth is a vital component of the Christian journey. It encompasses the transformative process of becoming more like Christ through the power of the Holy Spirit. This maturation process is not instantaneous but is a lifelong journey that requires commitment, perseverance, and the grace of God.

The Biblical Perspective on Spiritual Growth

The Bible provides a robust framework for understanding spiritual growth. In 2 Peter 3:18 (ESV), believers are exhorted to "grow in the grace and knowledge of our Lord and Savior Jesus Christ." This verse encapsulates the dual aspects of spiritual growth—growing in God's unmerited favor (grace) and increasing in our understanding of Jesus Christ.

The Apostle Paul likened spiritual growth to the natural process of physical development. In 1 Corinthians 3:1-2 (ASV), Paul describes the believers in Corinth as spiritual infants who could only digest "milk" (basic spiritual truths) and were not ready for "solid food" (deeper spiritual teachings). This analogy illustrates that spiritual growth is a progressive journey, moving from spiritual infancy to maturity.

The Role of the Holy Spirit in Spiritual Growth

The Holy Spirit plays a crucial role in spiritual growth. According to Galatians 5:22-23 (ESV), the Holy Spirit produces the "fruit of the Spirit" in the lives of believers, which includes love, joy, peace, patience, kindness, goodness, faithfulness, gentleness, and self-control. These virtues represent the character of Christ, and their presence in a believer's life signifies spiritual growth.

Moreover, Romans 8:26-27 (ESV) outlines how the Holy Spirit intercedes for us, guiding our prayers and aligning our desires with God's will. This inner work of the Spirit is integral to our spiritual development.

Personal Responsibility in Spiritual Growth

As we've seen earlier, personal responsibility is pivotal in the process of spiritual growth. While it is the Holy Spirit that enables and empowers growth, believers must actively engage in spiritual practices that facilitate this process. This includes the study of Scripture (Psalm 119:11, ASV), prayer (1 Thessalonians 5:16-18, ESV), fellowship with other believers (Hebrews 10:24-25, ESV), and service (Matthew 20:26-28, ESV).

The Journey Towards Spiritual Maturity

The ultimate goal of spiritual growth is maturity, signified by Christlikeness. Ephesians 4:13-15 (ESV) describes this goal as attaining "the measure of the stature of the fullness of Christ," growing in every way into Him who is the head, Christ. This journey towards spiritual maturity is marked by increasing love for God and others, a deepening understanding of God's word, and a life marked by the fruit of the Spirit.

The Challenges and Rewards of Spiritual Growth

The journey of spiritual growth is not without its challenges. It involves wrestling with sin (Romans 7:15-25, ESV), enduring trials (James 1:2-4, ESV), and contending against spiritual forces (Ephesians 6:12, ESV). Yet, these struggles are not in vain. They serve to refine our faith, cultivate perseverance, and shape us into the image of Christ.

The rewards of spiritual growth are profound. They include experiencing deep intimacy with God (Psalm 63:1-5, ASV), finding joy in God's presence (Psalm 16:11, ASV), and anticipating the future glory in heaven (Romans 8:18, ESV).

Conclusion: An Ongoing Journey

In conclusion, spiritual growth is an ongoing journey of becoming more like Christ through the work of the Holy Spirit and our active participation. It's a process filled with challenges and rewards, calling for steadfast commitment, personal responsibility, and reliance on God's grace. No matter where we are on this journey, let us press on towards the goal for the prize of the upward call of God in Christ Jesus (Philippians 3:14, ESV). After all, spiritual growth is not about reaching a destination but about becoming more Christlike in the journey.

Role of Personal Responsibility in Spiritual Development

Introduction: The Connection Between Personal Responsibility and Spiritual Development

Spiritual development, the process of growing in our relationship with God and becoming more Christlike, is at the heart of the Christian life. Although God's grace and the work of the Holy Spirit are fundamental to this process, personal responsibility plays a vital role as well. The spiritual journey requires active engagement and dedication on our part.

Understanding Personal Responsibility in the Bible

Personal responsibility, as reflected in the Bible, involves accountability for one's actions, decisions, and attitudes. This concept is deeply woven into the fabric of biblical teachings. In Galatians 6:5 (ESV), the Apostle Paul states, "For each will have to bear his own load." This verse underscores the personal responsibility every Christian has in their spiritual growth.

Spiritual Disciplines and Personal Responsibility

The practice of spiritual disciplines is a powerful demonstration of personal responsibility. These disciplines include Bible study, prayer, fasting, worship, and service, among others. By intentionally engaging in these practices, believers take personal responsibility for their spiritual growth.

In 2 Timothy 2:15 (ASV), Paul urges Timothy to "give diligence to present thyself approved unto God, a workman that needeth not to be ashamed, handling aright the word of truth." This exhortation emphasizes the believer's responsibility to actively study and rightly understand God's Word.

Similarly, in 1 Thessalonians 5:17 (ESV), believers are instructed to "pray without ceasing," reflecting the believer's responsibility to maintain ongoing communication with God.

The Responsibility to Resist Sin and Pursue Righteousness

Personal responsibility in spiritual development also involves the conscious effort to resist sin and pursue righteousness. Romans 6:12-13 (ESV) admonishes believers not to let sin reign in their bodies but to present themselves to God as instruments of righteousness. The choice to yield to sin or righteousness lies within the believer's sphere of personal responsibility.

Cultivating Godly Relationships and Community

Believers also have a responsibility to foster godly relationships and actively participate in a faith community. Hebrews 10:24-25 (ESV) encourages believers to "consider how to stir up one another to love and good works, not neglecting to meet together." These verses point to the believer's responsibility to contribute to the spiritual growth of others and the overall health of the Christian community.

Persevering in Trials

Part of our personal responsibility involves steadfastness in trials, understanding that they can contribute to our spiritual growth. James 1:2-4 (ESV) reminds us that trials produce steadfastness, leading to maturity and completeness in our faith. Navigating trials with a godly attitude is an aspect of our spiritual responsibility.

Conclusion: A Balanced Perspective on Personal Responsibility and Grace

In conclusion, personal responsibility is paramount in spiritual development. However, it's important to maintain a balanced perspective. Our efforts alone, apart from God's grace and the empowering work of the Holy Spirit, will not result in true spiritual growth. Philippians 2:12-13 (ESV) captures this balance well, "work out your own salvation with fear and trembling, for it is God who works in you, both to will and to work for his good pleasure." Our responsibility and God's enabling work go hand in hand in the journey of spiritual growth.

Thus, while we take personal responsibility in our spiritual development, we do so relying on God's grace, trusting in His promises, and depending on the Holy Spirit's work within us. This balanced approach enables us to grow and mature in our faith, becoming more like Christ, which is the ultimate goal of spiritual development.

Practical Steps for Nurturing Spiritual Growth

Introduction: The Pursuit of Spiritual Growth

The pursuit of spiritual growth is a fundamental aspect of the Christian journey. This lifelong process of transformation brings us closer to God, molds us into the likeness of Christ, and empowers us to live lives pleasing to the Lord. While spiritual growth is ultimately a work of the Holy Spirit, our involvement and cooperation play a critical role in the process.

Regular Bible Study and Meditation

The Bible is the inspired Word of God, providing guidance, wisdom, and revelation about God's character and His plans for humanity. Studying and meditating on the Scriptures are indispensable practices for spiritual growth. Joshua 1:8 (ASV) provides a compelling promise regarding consistent engagement with the Scriptures, "This book of the law shall not depart out of thy mouth, but thou shalt meditate thereon day and night."

Consistent Prayer Life

Prayer is our direct line of communication with God. The Apostle Paul, in 1 Thessalonians 5:17 (ESV), urges us to "pray without ceasing." Regular prayer is not just about presenting our needs to God, but it also involves listening to His voice, expressing our gratitude, confessing our sins, and interceding for others.

Cultivating Godly Relationships

Our relationships can significantly influence our spiritual growth. Surrounding ourselves with fellow believers who encourage, challenge, and support us in our faith is invaluable. Proverbs 27:17 (ASV) illustrates this point: "Iron sharpeneth iron; So a man sharpeneth the countenance of his friend."

Involvement in a Local Church

Active involvement in a local church offers opportunities for worship, fellowship, service, and learning from God's Word collectively. In Hebrews 10:25 (ESV), believers are encouraged not to neglect gathering together. Being part of a community of faith is essential for spiritual nurturing.

Fasting

Fasting, the voluntary abstention from food for spiritual purposes, can deepen our dependence on God, heighten our spiritual discernment, and invigorate our prayer lives. In Matthew 6:16-18, Jesus assumes that His followers will fast and provides instructions for doing so in a manner pleasing to God. Fasting is no longer biblically obligatory. It is a personal choice.

Obedience and Submission to God's Will

Jesus says in John 14:15 (ESV), "If you love me, you will keep my commandments." Obedience to God's commands is a significant aspect of spiritual growth. It involves a willingness to submit to God's will as revealed in His Word, even when it's difficult or against our natural inclinations.

Service and Ministry

Serving others is not only an expression of love, but it also contributes to our spiritual growth. In Galatians 5:13 (ESV), Paul reminds believers to use their freedom to serve one another through love. By ministering to others, we mirror Christ's servant-heart, contributing to our spiritual development.

Perseverance in Trials

Trials can serve as catalysts for spiritual growth when navigated with faith and a godly perspective. James 1:2-4 (ESV) reminds us to consider it joy when facing trials, knowing that the testing of our faith produces steadfastness leading to maturity.

Conclusion: Embracing the Journey of Spiritual Growth

In summary, nurturing spiritual growth is a multifaceted process involving a range of practices and attitudes. It's a dynamic journey that requires our ongoing commitment and effort. Yet, as we remain faithful in these practical steps, we can trust that God, through His Spirit, will complete the good work He has begun in us (Philippians 1:6). Remember, spiritual growth isn't about achieving perfection, but rather, it's about continual transformation into the likeness of Christ.

Overcoming Spiritual Stagnation: Recognizing and Breaking Barriers

Introduction: The Reality of Spiritual Stagnation

The Christian journey isn't always a steady uphill climb. There are times when believers may encounter spiritual stagnation, a state where growth seems to halt, and spiritual vitality dwindles. Recognizing this reality and understanding how to break through these barriers are crucial to renewing and deepening our relationship with God.

Identifying Spiritual Stagnation

Spiritual stagnation is often characterized by a lack of spiritual progress or decline in spiritual fervor. It may manifest as diminished interest in prayer, Bible study, and fellowship with other believers. Moreover, there may be an increase in sinful patterns, a lack of fruitfulness, and feelings of distance from God. Recognizing these symptoms is the first step in addressing the problem.

Understanding the Causes

There are several potential causes of spiritual stagnation. Persistent, unconfessed sin can create a barrier between the believer and God, leading to spiritual dryness. Additionally, neglecting spiritual disciplines like prayer and Bible study can result in a lack of spiritual nourishment. Other possible causes include prolonged exposure to false teaching, unforgiveness, unresolved hurt, or prioritizing worldly pursuits over spiritual growth.

Addressing Unconfessed Sin

"Behold, Jehovah's hand is not shortened, that it cannot save, or his ear dull, that it cannot hear; but your iniquities have made a separation between you and your God, and your sins have hidden his face from you so that he does not hear" (Isaiah 59:1-2, ESV). Sin creates a chasm between us and God. Confession and repentance are the bridge that closes that gap. Regular self-examination and confession are essential to maintaining spiritual vitality.

Reviving Spiritual Disciplines

The spiritual disciplines are channels of grace that God uses to nourish and mature us. If neglected, our spiritual growth can become stunted. Re-establishing consistent prayer, Bible study, fellowship, and worship are key to breaking out of spiritual stagnation.

Seeking Godly Counsel

When struggling with spiritual stagnation, seeking counsel from mature believers or church leaders can provide valuable insight and encouragement. Proverbs 11:14 (ASV) states, "Where no wise guidance is, the people falleth; But in the multitude of counselors there is safety."

Detaching from Worldly Distractions

Worldly distractions can divert our focus from our spiritual growth. As believers, we're called to be in the world but not of it (John 17:16, ESV). We must evaluate our lives and, if necessary, reduce engagements that are hindering our spiritual progress.

Embracing Trials as Opportunities for Growth

God often uses trials to spur spiritual growth. James 1:2-4 (ESV) says, "Consider it pure joy, my brothers and sisters, whenever you face trials of many kinds because you know that the testing of your faith produces perseverance. Let perseverance finish its work so that you may be mature and complete, not lacking anything."

Conclusion: Overcoming Spiritual Stagnation

In conclusion, overcoming spiritual stagnation requires a proactive, intentional approach. It begins with recognizing the signs, understanding the possible causes, and taking decisive steps to revive our spiritual growth. As we commit to breaking down these barriers, we rely not on our strength, but on God's enabling power. For it's God "who works in you, both to will and to work for his good pleasure" (Philippians 2:13, ESV). With His help, we can overcome spiritual stagnation and continue progressing in our spiritual journey.

Case Studies: Examples of Personal Responsibility in Biblical Figures

Introduction: Personal Responsibility in the Bible

The Bible presents numerous instances of individuals who exemplified personal responsibility in their relationship with God and their spiritual growth. We can gain valuable insights from studying these examples as we endeavor to cultivate personal responsibility in our own spiritual journey.

Daniel: Personal Responsibility in Maintaining Spiritual Disciplines

The story of Daniel in the Old Testament provides an excellent model of personal responsibility. Despite being in a foreign land, he maintained his spiritual disciplines, including prayer. Daniel 6:10 (ASV) states, "And when Daniel knew that the writing was signed, he went into his house (now his windows were open in his chamber toward Jerusalem); and he kneeled upon his knees three times a day, and prayed, and gave thanks before his God, as he did aforetime." Even under the threat of death, Daniel took personal responsibility for his relationship with God.

Job: Personal Responsibility Amidst Suffering

Job's narrative portrays personal responsibility in the face of suffering. Even when he lost everything, Job chose to worship God, demonstrating a profound sense of responsibility for his spiritual attitude, regardless of his circumstances (Job 1:20-21, ESV).

Peter: Personal Responsibility in Repentance and Restoration

The apostle Peter presents a case study in personal responsibility for one's actions and spiritual restoration. After denying Christ three times (John 18:15-27, ESV), Peter took responsibility for his actions. His heartfelt repentance is evident in his weeping (Matthew 26:75, ESV), and later, he reaffirmed his love for Christ three times (John 21:15-17, ESV), mirroring his previous denials.

Paul: Personal Responsibility in Spiritual Growth and Ministry

Paul is another excellent example. After his encounter with Christ (Acts 9:1-19, ESV), Paul took responsibility for his spiritual growth, spending time in Arabia before beginning his ministry (Galatians 1:17-18, ESV). He also felt a personal responsibility to spread the gospel, declaring, "Woe to me if I do not preach the gospel!" (1 Corinthians 9:16, ESV).

Joshua: Personal Responsibility in Leading and Decision-Making

Joshua, chosen to lead the Israelites into the Promised Land, displayed personal responsibility in his leadership and decision-making. He committed himself and his household to serve God, declaring, "As for me and my house, we will serve the LORD" (Joshua 24:15, ASV). His resolve set a precedent for the people he led.

Conclusion: Lessons from Biblical Figures

These biblical figures provide rich examples of personal responsibility in various aspects of spiritual life, from maintaining spiritual disciplines, dealing with suffering, repentance, spiritual growth, and ministry to making critical life decisions. They serve as models and offer lessons for believers today as we seek to take personal responsibility in our spiritual journey.

Personal responsibility plays an integral role in our relationship with God. The Christian life calls for more than passive faith; it requires active engagement in our spiritual growth and service. Studying the lives of these biblical figures who demonstrated personal responsibility can inspire and guide us in our spiritual walk.

Personal responsibility is a crucial aspect of our spiritual growth. It underlines our part in cooperating with God's work in us – a dynamic relationship that spurs us towards spiritual maturity. After all, as Paul reminds us in Philippians 2:12-13 (ESV), "Therefore, my beloved, as you have always obeyed, so now, not only as in my presence but much more in my absence, work out your own salvation with fear and trembling, for it is God who works in you, both to will and to work for his good pleasure." God works in us, but we also have a part to play – that's personal responsibility.

The Danger of Spiritual Passivity: Addressing Misconceptions

Introduction: Understanding Spiritual Passivity

In spiritual circles, a dangerous misconception often arises: that one's spiritual journey simply happens, requiring no personal effort or responsibility. This belief can lead to spiritual passivity, a state of inaction or indifference in one's spiritual growth. This state is not only unbiblical but can lead to spiritual stagnation or decline.

Edward D. Andrews

Misconception 1: Spiritual Growth is Automatic

One prevalent misconception is the belief that spiritual growth is automatic once a person becomes a Christian. While the Holy Spirit indwells believers at conversion and works in them (Romans 8:9-11, ESV), this does not mean that spiritual growth happens without any active participation from the believer. Paul encourages believers to "work out your own salvation with fear and trembling" (Philippians 2:12, ESV). This verse indicates a cooperative effort: God provides the power for spiritual growth, but believers must actively engage in spiritual disciplines and pursue godliness.

Misconception 2: Spiritual Passivity is Humility

Another misconception is equating spiritual passivity with humility. While humility is indeed a Christian virtue, it does not involve passivity. Humility is an active posture of recognizing God's authority and our need for Him, not an excuse for spiritual inaction. Jesus, our perfect example of humility (Philippians 2:5-8, ESV), was anything but passive in His ministry and obedience to the Father.

Misconception 3: God Will Do Everything

This misconception stems from misunderstanding God's sovereignty. While God is indeed sovereign over all things, this does not imply that we have no role in our spiritual growth or service to Him. The apostle Paul emphasizes the believer's active role in spiritual growth, saying, "I beat my body and make it my slave so that after I have preached to others, I myself will not be disqualified for the prize" (1 Corinthians 9:27, ESV).

The Danger of Spiritual Passivity

Spiritual passivity poses several dangers. Firstly, it can lead to spiritual stagnation. Without active engagement in spiritual disciplines—such as prayer, Bible study, and fellowship—spiritual growth is hindered. As Hebrews 5:11-14 (ESV) warns, those who fail to progress in understanding and applying God's Word become "dull of hearing."

Secondly, spiritual passivity can result in vulnerability to false teaching. Ephesians 4:14 (ESV) warns that spiritual immaturity can lead to being "tossed to and fro by the waves and carried about by every wind of doctrine."

Lastly, spiritual passivity can lead to unfruitfulness in the Christian life. Jesus warns in John 15:1-6 (ESV) that branches in Him that do not bear fruit will be cut off. Fruitfulness comes from abiding in Christ, an active, ongoing relationship, not passivity.

Overcoming Spiritual Passivity

Overcoming spiritual passivity requires recognizing and addressing these misconceptions with biblical truth. We must understand that spiritual growth involves our active participation, that true humility leads to obedience and service, not passivity, and that while God is sovereign, He calls us to an active role in our spiritual development and service to Him.

Additionally, engaging in spiritual disciplines is crucial in overcoming spiritual passivity. Regular Bible study, prayer, fellowship with other believers, and other practices are necessary for spiritual growth (Acts 2:42, ESV).

Finally, we must seek the Holy Spirit's guidance and empowerment. While we have a role in our spiritual growth, we are dependent on the Spirit to produce spiritual fruit in us (Galatians 5:22-23, ESV). Therefore, seeking His guidance and empowerment should be a consistent practice in our lives.

In conclusion, spiritual passivity is a dangerous state that arises from misconceptions about the nature of spiritual growth and our role in it. Recognizing and addressing these misconceptions, actively engaging in spiritual disciplines, and seeking the Holy Spirit's guidance and empowerment are crucial steps in overcoming spiritual passivity and nurturing robust spiritual growth.

The Relationship Between Faith, Works, and Spiritual Growth

Introduction: A Harmonious Trio

In the New Testament, faith, works, and spiritual growth form an interconnected trio. Understanding their relationship is crucial to a biblical understanding of Christian discipleship. In this exploration, we'll unravel this intricate relationship, addressing how faith and works relate to each other and their collective role in fostering spiritual growth.

Faith: The Root of Spiritual Life

Our spiritual journey begins with faith. Ephesians 2:8-9 (ESV) tells us, "For by grace you have been saved through faith. And this is not your own doing; it is the gift of God, not a result of works, so that no one may boast." Faith in Jesus Christ's redemptive work on the cross is the doorway to eternal life and the starting point of our spiritual growth. It is a personal acceptance and trust in the finished work of Jesus Christ, acknowledging that our righteousness stems from Him, not ourselves.

Works: The Fruit of Genuine Faith

While faith is the root of our spiritual life, works are the fruit of genuine faith. As James 2:17 (ESV) states, "So also faith by itself, if it does not have works, is dead." The Apostle James isn't contradicting Paul's teachings on salvation by grace through faith alone. Instead, James emphasizes that a faith that does not produce works is not true faith at all. Works are not the means of our salvation but the evidence of our saving faith.

The Relationship Between Faith and Works

There exists a symbiotic relationship between faith and works in the believer's life. We must be clear that works do not contribute to our salvation. It is only by faith in Jesus Christ that we are saved. However, this faith, when genuinely held, inevitably leads to actions that glorify God. These "works" are manifestations of the transformative power of the Gospel in our lives.

In essence, faith is the root, and works are the fruit. Our deeds, whether acts of love, patterns of obedience, or expressions of holiness, stem from the transformation that faith instigates in our hearts.

Spiritual Growth: The Progressive Maturation of Faith and Works

If faith is the starting point and works are the evidence of our spiritual journey, then spiritual growth is the progressive maturation of both. It's the ongoing process in which we become more like Christ in our thoughts, desires, and actions, often referred to as sanctification.

Our faith deepens as we grow in our understanding of God's character and His Word, resulting in a more profound trust in Him. In turn, our works, spurred by this matured faith, become more aligned with God's will. We become more loving, more holy, and more obedient as we grow spiritually.

The Role of the Holy Spirit

The Holy Spirit plays an indispensable role in this process. As Jesus tells His disciples in John 14:26 (ESV), "But the Helper, the Holy Spirit, whom the Father will send in my name, he will teach you all things and bring to your remembrance all that I have said to you." The Holy Spirit illuminates our understanding of God's Word, deepening our faith. He also convicts us of sin and empowers us to live righteously, leading to the good works that testify to our faith.

Conclusion: An Interdependent Relationship

In conclusion, faith, works, and spiritual growth share a dynamic, interdependent relationship in the believer's life. Faith is the root, works are the fruit, and spiritual growth is the ongoing process of the deepening of faith and the increasing fruitfulness of works in our lives. This triad, powered by the Holy Spirit, forms the framework of our spiritual journey, reminding us that faith without works is dead and that both are necessary for genuine spiritual growth.

Lifelong Learning: Embracing an Ongoing Commitment to Growth

Introduction: The Concept of Lifelong Learning

Lifelong learning is the ongoing, self-motivated pursuit of knowledge for personal or professional reasons. This process enhances not only social inclusion, active citizenship, and personal development, but it is also a critical aspect of spiritual maturity and growth. The Bible is clear about the importance of continually growing and learning in our faith and understanding of God's Word.

Learning in Scripture: A Command, Not an Option

In the Bible, the pursuit of knowledge and wisdom is not presented as an option but as a command. Proverbs 1:5 (ASV) says, "A wise man will hear, and will increase in learning; and a man of understanding shall attain unto sound counsels." This verse encapsulates the biblical view of lifelong learning: it is a process that involves active listening, understanding, and applying what we learn.

The Apostle Paul: A Model of Lifelong Learning

The Apostle Paul provides a model for lifelong learning. Despite his extensive religious training and experience, Paul never stopped learning and growing in his understanding of God's truth. He continually studied the Scriptures, sought God in prayer, and taught others the truths he had discovered (Philippians 3:12-14, ESV).

Continuous Learning and Spiritual Growth

Continuous learning is integral to spiritual growth. A stagnated learning process can lead to spiritual stagnation, while an active pursuit of knowledge in the things of God fuels spiritual maturity. According to 2 Peter 3:18 (ESV), we are to "grow in the grace and knowledge of our Lord and Savior Jesus Christ." Growing in knowledge is not separate from growing in grace; the two go hand in hand.

Commitment to Learning: A Catalyst for Transformation

Our commitment to learning has transformative effects on our lives. It equips us to discern God's will and make wise decisions, as Romans 12:2 (ESV) indicates: "Do not be conformed to this world, but be transformed by the renewal of your mind, that by testing you may discern what is the will of God, what is good and acceptable and perfect." The renewing of our minds is an ongoing, lifelong process that involves constant learning and application of God's Word.

Practical Steps to Lifelong Learning

To embrace lifelong learning, we must be intentional about studying and meditating on God's Word (Psalm 1:2, ESV). It involves establishing regular habits of Bible study and prayer, seeking sound biblical teaching, and participating in fellowship with other believers for mutual encouragement and edification (Hebrews 10:24-25, ESV).

Additionally, we should stay open to correction and rebuke, recognizing that we never outgrow the need for discipline and instruction (Proverbs 12:1, ESV). The willingness to learn from our mistakes and make necessary changes is a vital aspect of lifelong learning.

Lifelong Learning: A Journey, Not a Destination

In conclusion, lifelong learning is not a destination but a journey. It's a journey that requires humility, acknowledging that we don't have all the answers and that we can always grow in our understanding of God and His Word. It requires persistence, pressing on in the face of difficulties and discouragement. And it requires a love for God and His truth, a desire to know Him more deeply and live in a manner worthy of His calling.

By embracing lifelong learning, we are not just accumulating knowledge; we are growing in our relationship with God, becoming more like His Son Jesus Christ, and preparing ourselves for a lifetime of service in His Kingdom.

Embracing Personal Responsibility in Your Spiritual Journey

Introduction: The Intersection of Personal Responsibility and Spirituality

Personal responsibility plays a significant role in the life of a believer. It's a vital aspect of our spiritual journey, impacting our growth, our relationships with others, and our relationship with God. In the Bible, we see clear mandates for personal responsibility as an integral part of spiritual maturity.

Defining Personal Responsibility in a Spiritual Context

In a spiritual context, personal responsibility involves owning our actions, making decisions that align with God's Word, and accepting the consequences of our choices. Proverbs 14:12 (ASV) says, "There is a way which seemeth right unto a man; but the end thereof are the ways of death." This verse is a stark reminder that we have the freedom to choose our path, but we must also accept the results of our decisions.

Personal Responsibility in Scripture: Adam, Eve, and Beyond

From the Genesis account of Adam and Eve, we see that God holds us accountable for our actions (Genesis 3:12-19, ASV). Adam and Eve were given clear instructions, but they chose to disobey and experienced the consequences. Throughout Scripture, this theme of personal responsibility continues with numerous examples, affirming that each person is responsible for his or her actions.

Personal Responsibility and Spiritual Growth

The act of taking personal responsibility is instrumental in spiritual growth. In the context of our spiritual journey, personal responsibility includes areas such as the consistent study of God's Word, cultivating a prayer life, and making choices in line with biblical principles. Philippians 2:12 (ESV) implores us to "work out your own salvation with fear and trembling." This verse emphasizes the role of personal responsibility in our spiritual growth.

The Dangers of Neglecting Personal Responsibility

When we neglect personal responsibility, we inhibit our spiritual growth and potentially damage our witness to others. Proverbs 28:13 (ESV) warns, "Whoever conceals his transgressions will not prosper, but he who confesses and forsakes them will obtain mercy." Concealing our failures and avoiding responsibility leads to spiritual stagnation, while acknowledging our faults and repenting leads to mercy and growth.

Embracing Personal Responsibility: Practical Steps

Embracing personal responsibility involves a commitment to self-examination and honesty before God. It requires consistent engagement with God's Word, allowing it to "discern the thoughts and intentions of the heart" (Hebrews 4:12, ESV). It also entails a readiness to confess and repent of our sins, as 1 John 1:9 (ESV) promises that if we confess our sins, He is faithful to forgive us.

Another practical step is to foster accountability relationships with fellow believers who can lovingly challenge us and encourage us in our spiritual journey (Galatians 6:1-2, ESV). Such relationships are invaluable for fostering personal responsibility.

Conclusion: A Life-Long Commitment

In conclusion, embracing personal responsibility is a lifelong commitment in our spiritual journey. It's not a one-time event, but an ongoing process that contributes to our spiritual maturity. As we take responsibility for our actions and decisions, we align ourselves with God's Word, which in turn, facilitates spiritual growth. By taking responsibility for our spiritual growth, we position ourselves for deeper relationships with God and others and set a strong example for those around us. It's a vital component of our spiritual journey and a powerful tool for growth and transformation in Christ.

CHAPTER 7 A Call to Action: God's Expectation for Our Participation

Introduction: Understanding God's Call to Action

God's call to action is a theme that runs throughout the entirety of the Bible. From the earliest accounts in Genesis to the concluding remarks in Revelation, it's clear that God involves His people in His redemptive plan for humanity and expects them to actively participate in His work. This chapter will delve into the importance of this active participation in the light of Scripture, illustrating how God's expectations are key to our spiritual growth and service.

Defining God's Call to Action

God's call to action is the divine summons to live in obedience to His commands, actively participate in His plans, and embrace our roles in His story. As Paul writes in Ephesians 2:10 (ESV), "For we are his workmanship, created in Christ Jesus for good works, which God prepared beforehand, that we should walk in them."

Case Studies from the Bible

Throughout Scripture, there are countless examples of men and women who heeded God's call to action. For instance, Noah built the ark (Genesis 6:22, ASV), Abraham left his homeland (Genesis 12:1-4, ASV), and Moses led the Israelites out of Egypt (Exodus 3:10, ASV). In the New Testament, the disciples left their nets to follow Jesus (Matthew 4:19-20, ESV), and Paul dedicated his life to spreading the gospel (Acts 9:15-16, ESV). These individuals actively participated in God's plans, setting examples for all believers to follow.

149

The Role of Faith and Obedience

Answering God's call to action requires faith and obedience. Faith, as defined in Hebrews 11:1 (ESV), is "the assurance of things hoped for, the conviction of things not seen." It is through faith that we trust God and move forward in obedience, even when the path ahead is unclear. Without faith, it is impossible to please God (Hebrews 11:6, ESV).

Obedience, on the other hand, is our response to faith. It's an active expression of our trust in God and a fundamental aspect of our relationship with Him. As Jesus states in John 14:15 (ESV), "If you love me, you will keep my commandments."

Practical Steps to Respond to God's Call

Responding to God's call to action requires daily commitment to seek His will through prayer and Scripture study. It requires a willingness to step out of our comfort zones, to be flexible in the face of change, and to make sacrifices when needed. Romans 12:1-2 (ESV) aptly summarises this process, "I appeal to you therefore, brothers, by the mercies of God, to present your bodies as a living sacrifice, holy and acceptable to God, which is your spiritual worship. Do not be conformed to this world, but be transformed by the renewal of your mind, that by testing you may discern what is the will of God, what is good and acceptable and perfect."

Conclusion: Embracing Active Participation in God's Plans

In conclusion, God's call to action is an essential aspect of our spiritual journey. It's an invitation to participate in His divine plan and to engage actively in His work. Through faith and obedience, we can respond to this call, bearing witness to the transforming power of the gospel and playing our part in the grand narrative of God's redemptive work. As we yield to God's call to action, we grow spiritually, become more like Christ, and impact the world around us in meaningful ways.

Biblical Foundation: God's Expectation for Human Participation

From Genesis to Revelation, the Bible provides a solid foundation for understanding God's expectations for human participation in His divine plans. This participation is not just a passive acceptance but involves active engagement, thoughtful decision-making, and a willingness to walk in the path God lays out.

The Beginning: Genesis and Human Participation

The Bible's first book, Genesis, sets the stage for understanding God's expectation of our involvement. When God creates humanity in His image (Genesis 1:27, ASV), He commissions them to rule over and care for the earth (Genesis 1:28, ASV). This mandate involves active engagement in God's creation, demonstrating His expectation for human participation right from the start.

The Exodus: Moses' Example of Active Participation

Moses is another profound example of God's expectation for human participation. When God calls Moses to lead the Israelites out of Egypt, Moses initially resists (Exodus 3-4, ASV). However, after God reassures him, Moses takes up the challenge and plays an integral role in God's plan to liberate His people. This story underscores that while God's calling may be daunting, He provides the strength and guidance we need to fulfill our roles.

The Prophets: Speaking For God

The prophets of the Old Testament also exhibit God's expectation for human participation. God appointed prophets as His spokespersons, commissioning them to convey His messages to His people. Whether it was Isaiah's visions of coming judgment and hope (Isaiah 6:1-8, ASV), or Jonah's reluctant mission to Nineveh (Jonah 1-4, ASV), each prophet had to actively engage in their God-given task.

Jesus' Ministry: Inviting Others to Participate

In the New Testament, Jesus continues this theme of inviting human participation. He called twelve disciples to join Him, participate in His ministry, and learn from His teachings (Matthew 4:18-22, ESV). Jesus' invitation to the disciples was not just to observe, but to engage in His mission actively. They were sent out to preach, heal, and cast out demons (Matthew 10:1-8, ESV).

Paul's Teachings: The Body of Christ

Paul, in his letters, consistently teaches about the role of each believer in the body of Christ. In 1 Corinthians 12:12-27 (ESV), Paul uses the analogy of a body to illustrate that every believer has a unique function in the church. This further emphasizes God's expectation for all believers to participate actively in the work of His kingdom.

Revelation: The Call to Overcome

In the book of Revelation, John delivers messages from Jesus to the seven churches (Revelation 2-3, ESV). In each message, Jesus exhorts the church to overcome challenges, promising rewards for those who do. These exhortations underscore God's expectation for believers to actively engage in the spiritual battles they face.

Conclusion: Active Participation in God's Story

The biblical foundation for God's expectation of human participation is clear. Whether it's through the mandate given to Adam and Eve, the call of Moses, the missions of the prophets, Jesus' invitation to His disciples, Paul's teachings, or the messages to the seven churches, Scripture repeatedly highlights God's desire for His people to play an active role in His divine plan. This active participation is not just an expectation but an invitation – an invitation to engage with our Creator, to grow in our faith, and to contribute to His redemptive work in the world. By embracing this call, we become co-laborers with God, experiencing the joy and purpose found in walking in His will.

God's Plan and Human Agency: A Partnership

The relationship between God's sovereign plan and human agency is a critical theme throughout the Bible. It is a divine partnership, which demonstrates that while God is the ultimate orchestrator of all things, He invites humanity to actively participate in His redemptive plans.

God's Sovereignty and Human Agency: A Biblical Perspective

Scripture asserts the sovereignty of God; He is the author and finisher of all things (Hebrews 12:2, ESV). Simultaneously, it is clear that God has given humans free will and the capacity to make choices. Deuteronomy 30:19 (ASV) presents this tension: "I call heaven and earth to witness against you this day, that I have set before thee life and death, the blessing and the curse: therefore choose life, that thou mayest live, thou and thy seed." The recognition of this tension helps us understand the coexistence of God's divine plan and human agency.

Creation and the Fall: Human Agency in Action

From the onset, in the account of creation, human agency is evident. God gives Adam and Eve the authority to tend to and rule over the earth (Genesis 1:28, ASV). However, their decision to disobey God leads to the Fall (Genesis 3:1-24, ASV). Despite the devastating consequences, God sets in motion His redemptive plan, showing His sovereignty even in the face of human error.

Abraham: Faith and Action

God's relationship with Abraham serves as a vivid demonstration of the interaction between God's plan and human participation. God

153

initiates the relationship by promising Abraham descendants and land (Genesis 12:1-3, ASV). Abraham responds in faith and action by leaving his homeland (Genesis 12:4, ASV). Throughout his life, Abraham's choices, both good and bad, shape his journey, yet God's promises come to pass, reinforcing God's sovereign control.

Moses: Responding to God's Call

Moses' life is another example of this dynamic interplay. Despite his initial hesitations, Moses answers God's call to lead the Israelites out of Egypt (Exodus 3-4, ASV). Though it is God's power that liberates the Israelites, Moses' decisions and actions play a pivotal role in God's deliverance plan.

Jesus: Divine Plan and Human Participation

In the New Testament, Jesus, though divine, exemplifies perfect human agency aligned with God's will. His prayer in the Garden of Gethsemane, "not my will, but yours, be done" (Luke 22:42, ESV), displays His active decision to submit to God's redemptive plan. Following Jesus' ascension, His disciples, empowered by the Holy Spirit, carry on His mission, actively participating in the spread of the Gospel (Acts 1:8, ESV).

Paul: A Chosen Instrument

Paul's conversion and subsequent ministry further illustrate this partnership. Paul, originally a persecutor of Christians, becomes a "chosen instrument" to carry God's name to the Gentiles (Acts 9:15, ESV). Paul's active obedience, coupled with God's transformative power, results in the rapid spread of the Gospel and the establishment of numerous churches.

Conclusion: A Divine Collaboration

In conclusion, the Bible presents a profound mystery and a divine collaboration between God's sovereign plan and human agency. While

God is the designer and executor of the master plan, He invites and allows human participation. God incorporates our decisions, actions, and even mistakes, into His redemptive narrative, never compromising His sovereignty or perfect will. It's a divine partnership that calls us to action, to live out our faith with responsibility, and to participate actively in God's work in the world. It's a call that ensures our lives have eternal significance as we co-labor with God in His grand narrative of redemption.

Remember, our actions matter to God. As we actively respond to His call, we can be confident that He is working all things together for good (Romans 8:28, ESV), intertwining our choices with His perfect will, and using us to accomplish His divine purposes. Thus, it is essential to understand and embrace our roles in this divine partnership, knowing that we are part of something infinitely greater than ourselves.

Case Studies: Examples of God's Call to Action in the Bible

God's call to action is a consistent theme throughout Scripture. His call challenges individuals to move beyond their comfort zones and step out in faith, often leading to transformative experiences. Here, we explore several notable instances in the Bible where God's call to action is clearly demonstrated.

Noah: A Call to Obedience

Noah's life exemplifies God's call to obedient action. Amid a sinful generation, Noah finds favor in God's sight (Genesis 6:8, ASV). God commands Noah to build an ark, a monumental task, to ensure his family's survival during the imminent global flood (Genesis 6:13-22, ASV). Despite the mockery and disbelief he undoubtedly faced, Noah faithfully obeys God's instructions, illustrating obedience in response to God's call to action.

2Abraham: A Call to Sacrifice

In Abraham's life, God's call to action involves leaving his homeland and journeying into an unknown land (Genesis 12:1-4, ASV). Later, God's call reaches a critical point when He commands Abraham to offer his son Isaac as a sacrifice (Genesis 22:1-2, ASV). Abraham's willingness to obey, despite the unimaginable pain it must have caused, displays an exemplary response to God's challenging call to action.

Moses: A Call to Deliverance

Moses is called by God to deliver the Israelites from Egyptian bondage (Exodus 3:10, ASV). Although initially reluctant, Moses eventually steps into this role, confronting Pharaoh and leading the Israelites towards the Promised Land. His journey underscores the transformational power of responding to God's call to action.

David: A Call to Kingship

David, a shepherd boy, is chosen by God to be Israel's king (1 Samuel 16:1-13, ASV). His faith in God, demonstrated when he bravely confronts Goliath (1 Samuel 17, ASV), reveals his willingness to act in response to God's call. David's life, though marked by failures, ultimately illustrates a heart responsive to God's command.

Esther: A Call to Courage

Esther, a Jewish queen in a Persian kingdom, is called by God to risk her life to save her people (Esther 4:14, ASV). She responds courageously to God's call to action, demonstrating the impact one person can have when they step out in faith.

The Disciples: A Call to Follow

In the New Testament, Jesus calls His disciples to leave their ordinary lives and follow Him (Matthew 4:18-22, ESV). Their willingness to abandon everything to follow Jesus sets a powerful example of responding to God's call to action.

Paul: A Call to Preach

Paul, initially an enemy of Christians, is dramatically called by God to spread the Gospel (Acts 9:15, ESV). His transformative response results in extensive missionary journeys that significantly expand the early Christian church.

Conclusion: Responding to God's Call to Action

These examples provide a comprehensive overview of how God calls individuals to participate in His divine plan actively. They remind us that God continues to call His people to action today. Whether it's a call to obedience, sacrifice, deliverance, kingship, courage, or preaching the Gospel, God invites us to join Him in His redemptive work.

Recognizing and responding to God's call to action is an essential part of the Christian journey. As we faithfully respond to His call, God uses our actions to fulfill His purposes, and in the process, transforms our lives. Let us take courage from these biblical examples and embrace our role in God's divine narrative, always ready to respond to His call to action.

Personal Responsibility: The Keystone of Our Faithful Actions

Central to the Christian journey is the concept of personal responsibility. It encompasses our response to God's grace, obedience to His commands, and the pursuit of moral conduct. Our personal responsibility is a cornerstone of our relationship with God, significantly influencing our spiritual growth and witness to the world.

Recognizing the Role of Personal Responsibility in Our Relationship with God

Our relationship with God is deeply intertwined with the concept of personal responsibility. This relationship begins with our response to God's gracious offer of salvation. Although salvation is a divine gift, made possible through the sacrifice of Jesus Christ (Ephesians 2:8-9, ESV), it requires a human response—faith, repentance, and obedience (Acts 20:21, ESV). This call to personal responsibility is not a work that earns salvation, but a response to God's saving grace.

Further, we are individually accountable for cultivating our relationship with God. Just as relationships in the natural world require effort and commitment, our relationship with God necessitates personal involvement—through prayer, study of God's Word, and obedience (Psalm 119:15, ASV; James 1:22, ESV). God has provided the means for relationship—His Word and the Holy Spirit—but the responsibility to seek and maintain this relationship lies with us.

Personal Responsibility in Moral Conduct

God's Word provides clear guidelines for moral conduct. It's our personal responsibility to adhere to these commands and apply them in our daily lives (James 1:22, ESV). From the Ten Commandments in the Old Testament (Exodus 20:1-17, ASV) to Jesus' teachings in the New Testament (Matthew 5-7, ESV), scripture continually emphasizes personal responsibility in moral living.

Christians are not merely called to avoid sin, but to proactively pursue righteousness (Romans 6:13, ESV). This pursuit includes acts of kindness, justice, and mercy, in line with Jesus' teachings (Micah 6:8, ASV; Matthew 22:37-40, ESV). The initiative lies with the individual, and it's our responsibility to live a life that reflects God's character and commands.

Personal Responsibility in Spiritual Growth

Spiritual growth, too, is undergirded by personal responsibility. While it's God who provides the growth (1 Corinthians 3:7, ESV), we're called to participate in the process. This involvement includes disciplines such as prayer, Bible study, worship, and fellowship with other believers (Acts 2:42, ESV).

Moreover, we are called to "work out" our salvation with "fear and trembling" (Philippians 2:12, ESV). This does not imply earning salvation, but it does underscore the role of personal responsibility in sanctification—the process of becoming more like Christ.

Personal Responsibility in Our Witness to the World

As believers, we bear the responsibility of being Christ's ambassadors to the world (2 Corinthians 5:20, ESV). We're called to share the Gospel, making disciples of all nations (Matthew 28:19-20, ESV). This mission requires initiative, intentionality, and consistent witness in our words and deeds.

Conclusion: Embracing Personal Responsibility in Our Faith Journey

Personal responsibility is a keystone of faithful action. It underpins our relationship with God, moral conduct, spiritual growth, and witness to the world. By recognizing and embracing this responsibility, we become active participants in God's redemptive work, fostering a dynamic relationship with God, pursuing moral integrity, nurturing spiritual growth, and effectively witnessing to the world.

As we grow in our understanding of personal responsibility, let us be reminded of Paul's words: "So then, each of us will give an account of himself to God" (Romans 14:12, ESV). Let this awareness inspire us to live faithfully, making the most of the opportunities God gives us for relationship, growth, and witness.

The Role of Faith in Action: Beyond Belief

The Christian faith is a living faith, marked not only by mental assent to theological truths but by actions that align with those beliefs. From its genesis in the Biblical narrative to its manifestation in the life of a believer, faith is inseparable from action. As James aptly summarizes: "So also faith by itself, if it does not have works, is dead" (James 2:17, ESV). This view, far from degrading faith to a mere formula of deeds, reveals the dynamic interplay of faith and works, emphasizing the active nature of genuine faith.

Faith as Action in the Old Testament

The Old Testament presents numerous instances where faith and action are deeply interconnected. For instance, the faith of Abraham, the father of the faithful, was not a mere intellectual affirmation. His faith was proven by his willingness to leave his homeland (Genesis 12:1-4, ASV), to believe in God's promise of a son (Genesis 15:6, ASV), and to offer that son in obedience to God's command (Genesis 22:1-18, ASV). His faith was not a static belief but was actualized in obedience and action.

Moses, too, demonstrated his faith through action. By choosing to identify with the Hebrew slaves rather than enjoy the privilege of Egyptian royalty (Hebrews 11:24-26, ESV), and by leading the Israelites out of Egypt (Exodus 14:15-16, ASV), Moses displayed a faith that moved beyond mere belief to tangible action.

Faith as Action in the New Testament

The New Testament continues this theme of faith in action. The Gospels portray Jesus repeatedly teaching and demonstrating that genuine faith is inseparable from works. Whether it was healing the paralytic based on the faith exhibited by his friends (Mark 2:1-12, ESV), or commending the woman who anointed His feet as a result of her faith (Luke 7:37-50, ESV), Jesus validated faith that was expressed through actions.

The Apostle Paul, though emphasizing justification by faith apart from works of the law (Romans 3:28, ESV), did not discount the necessity of works. In fact, he underscored that believers are "created in Christ Jesus for good works" (Ephesians 2:10, ESV). He urged the Galatians to express their faith through love (Galatians 5:6, ESV) and instructed Titus that those who believe in God should be careful to devote themselves to good works (Titus 3:8, ESV).

Faith and Action in the Christian Life

In the life of a believer, faith and action must work hand in hand. Faith is the catalyst for transformation, fueling the pursuit of righteousness and godly living. As believers, we're called to express our faith through love (Galatians 5:6, ESV), maintain good works (Titus 3:8, ESV), and show our faith by our works (James 2:18, ESV).

Such works are not a means of earning salvation but are the evidence of our faith and the fruit of God's transformative work within us. It's essential to note that works aren't a way to curry God's favor or earn salvation. Rather, works are the natural outpouring of faith. It is faith, rooted in God's grace, that produces works pleasing to God.

Conclusion: Faith in Action - A Dynamic Expression of Belief

The biblical narrative makes it abundantly clear that faith extends beyond intellectual assent. It propels actions that reflect God's character, obey His commands, and promote His kingdom. This is not a one-time act, but a lifelong journey of faithful obedience.

Faith, when deeply rooted in the heart of the believer, inevitably bursts forth in acts of love, obedience, and service. It is active and vibrant, shaping our character, guiding our decisions, and influencing our interactions with others. Far from being a static entity, faith is a dynamic force that propels us into meaningful action, testifying to the transformative power of the Gospel.

Therefore, let us follow in the footsteps of those biblical figures who demonstrated their faith through their actions. As Hebrews 11:1 (ESV) notes, "Now faith is the assurance of things hoped for, the conviction of things not seen." It is by this faith that we hope for a better country, a heavenly one, and God is not ashamed to be called our God, for He has prepared a city for us (Hebrews 11:16, ESV). Let us then live by this faith, demonstrating it in our actions as we await the fulfilment of His promises.

Identifying Our Personal Call to Action: Spiritual Gifts and Talents

As believers in Christ, we have been uniquely equipped by God with spiritual gifts and natural talents to participate in His Kingdom's work. Recognizing and employing these gifts and talents aligns us with our personal call to action and allows us to actively serve in ways that glorify God and benefit others.

Understanding Spiritual Gifts

Spiritual gifts, according to Scripture, are divinely given abilities distributed by the Holy Spirit for the edification of the church. As stated in 1 Corinthians 12:7 (ESV), "To each is given the manifestation of the Spirit for the common good." These gifts range from prophecy, service, teaching, exhortation, generosity, leadership, to mercy (Romans 12:6-8, ESV), among others. Each Christian is endowed with at least one spiritual gift, emphasizing the role each believer has in contributing to the body of Christ.

Discovering Your Spiritual Gifts

The process of discovering our spiritual gifts often involves prayer, self-assessment, and feedback from others. First, pray for guidance and discernment, asking God to reveal how He has equipped you for service. Second, self-assessment can involve reflecting on what activities you feel drawn to and energized by within the context of ministry. Lastly, feedback from others can provide valuable insight into areas where others have observed God's gifting in your life.

Understanding Natural Talents

Natural talents, on the other hand, are innate abilities or skills that an individual possesses. These can range from artistic abilities, communication skills, problem-solving capabilities, leadership qualities, and more. While these talents might not be explicitly termed 'spiritual gifts' in the Bible, they are undoubtedly part of God's creative work in individuals and can be used to honor Him and serve others.

Aligning Spiritual Gifts and Talents with Personal Action

Our spiritual gifts and talents should guide our personal call to action. For example, if you have the gift of teaching, you could serve by leading a Bible study or mentoring younger believers. If you have a natural talent for organization, you could help in planning church events or managing projects.

It's essential to remember that our spiritual gifts and talents should be used in a way that aligns with God's overarching commands to love Him and our neighbors. Regardless of the specific gifts or talents we have, they should drive us toward these fundamental aspects of Christian living.

Conclusion: A Personal Call to Dynamic Christian Service

Recognizing and utilizing our spiritual gifts and natural talents aligns us with our personal call to action. The apostle Peter encapsulates this beautifully when he writes, "As each has received a gift, use it to serve one another, as good stewards of God's varied grace" (1 Peter 4:10, ESV).

As we each respond to our personal call to action, it's important to remember that our value in God's eyes is not based on the number or nature of the gifts we possess. Instead, it's based on our identity as His children, saved and loved by Him. Our service, then, is not a means to earn His favor but a grateful response to His grace.

In conclusion, identifying our spiritual gifts and natural talents is a crucial step in embracing our call to action. God has uniquely equipped each of us to serve and glorify Him. As we discover and utilize our gifts and talents, we align ourselves with His purposes, actively participating in His kingdom's work. This active participation is not a burdensome obligation, but a joyful expression of our faith, love, and gratitude to our gracious God.

Action as Worship: Serving God through Active Participation

Worship, often narrowly defined within the context of singing and praying in a church setting, holds a much broader biblical definition. It encompasses not only expressions of praise but also the entirety of a believer's life, particularly the actions one takes in service to God. The Bible presents a compelling picture of active participation in God's work as a vital form of worship.

The Biblical Perspective on Action as Worship

The idea of action as worship originates from the understanding that worship, in its truest form, involves offering our whole selves to God. As the apostle Paul wrote in Romans 12:1 (ESV), "I appeal to you therefore, brothers, by the mercies of God, to present your bodies as a living sacrifice, holy and acceptable to God, which is your spiritual worship."

This verse calls us to a life of active obedience and service, offering our daily lives as an act of worship to God. Our actions, whether grand or small, when done in obedience to God and out of love for Him, become a powerful act of worship.

Serving God: A Manifestation of Worship

Service to God is a crucial aspect of our worship. The prophet Micah sums up God's expectation of His people in Micah 6:8 (ASV), "What doth Jehovah require of thee, but to do justly, and to love kindness, and to walk humbly with thy God?" Here, action is intertwined with faith, suggesting that worship is not just about ceremonies or rituals but also about how we live our lives daily.

The Parable of the Good Samaritan: An Example of Action as Worship

The parable of the Good Samaritan (Luke 10:25-37, ESV) provides a poignant example of action as worship. The Samaritan, moved by compassion, actively helps the wounded man by bandaging his wounds, providing him shelter, and ensuring his care. His actions, driven by love for his neighbor, exemplify the essence of worship.

The Active Role of Believers in the New Testament

The New Testament continually emphasizes believers' active role in serving others as part of their worship. James 1:27 (ESV) states, "Religion that is pure and undefiled before God, the Father, is this: to visit orphans and widows in their affliction, and to keep oneself unstained from the world."

Furthermore, in Matthew 25:31-46 (ESV), Jesus places significant emphasis on the importance of serving others, indicating that acts of kindness to the "least of these" are, in fact, acts of service to Him.

Active Participation: Faith in Action

Our actions—born out of faith, guided by love, and aimed at serving God and others—serve as a testament to our worship of God. As stated in James 2:17 (ESV), "So also faith by itself, if it does not have works, is dead." Our faith is authenticated and enlivened by our actions. It is through our active participation in God's work that our faith becomes a living, vibrant aspect of our worship.

Conclusion: Embracing Action as Worship

In conclusion, worship in the Bible encompasses far more than words of praise; it includes our actions and our daily lives. When we serve God and others, we express our love, gratitude, and reverence for God, transforming our actions into acts of worship.

As we learn to see our service and active participation in God's work as an act of worship, our perspective changes. The ordinary becomes sacred, our everyday actions become holy offerings, and our lives become a continual act of worship. We recognize that each moment presents an opportunity to worship God, not just through words, but through our actions.

By embracing action as worship, we align ourselves more closely with God's heart. We begin to see people through His eyes and respond to the world around us with His compassion and love. As we live out our faith, we make our lives a testimony of worship, showing the world a glimpse of God's Kingdom here on earth.

Overcoming Fear and Procrastination: Roadblocks to Action

Fear and procrastination are significant roadblocks to action. They hinder us from fully participating in God's plan and fulfilling our call to action. Understanding the roots of these hindrances and biblical principles for overcoming them is crucial in transforming our faith into action.

Understanding Fear and Procrastination

Fear, according to the Bible, is not always harmful. The fear of God, for instance, is a beginning of wisdom (Proverbs 9:10, ASV). However, debilitating fear that prevents us from obeying God's commands or fulfilling our God-given potential is detrimental to our spiritual growth.

Procrastination, on the other hand, is the habit of delaying an action or task, usually because it is challenging or unpleasant. It is a major obstacle to productivity and action, causing us to delay or avoid tasks God has called us to do.

Fear: A Biblical Perspective

The Bible addresses fear repeatedly. From Genesis to Revelation, God's message to humanity often begins with the phrase, "Do not fear." For instance, in Isaiah 41:10 (ESV), God reassures us, "Fear not, for I am with you; be not dismayed, for I am your God; I will strengthen you, I will help you, I will uphold you with my righteous right hand."

God's encouragement to His people not to fear does not mean that we will not encounter fearful situations. Instead, it underscores the promise that God is with us in every situation and circumstance.

Procrastination: A Biblical Perspective

The Bible also provides guidance on procrastination. Proverbs 6:4 (ASV) says, "Give not sleep to thine eyes, nor slumber to thine eyelids." This verse warns against the perils of procrastination and exhorts us to take immediate action.

The parable of the ten virgins in Matthew 25:1-13 (ESV) also provides insight on procrastination. The five foolish virgins who were not prepared for the bridegroom's arrival represent those who procrastinate, emphasizing the importance of being ready and taking timely action.

Overcoming Fear

The antidote to fear is faith. Faith in God's sovereignty, His love for us, and His promises can help us overcome fear. 2 Timothy 1:7 (ESV) tells us, "For God gave us a spirit not of fear but of power and love and self-control." Fear is not from God. He equips us with power, love, and self-control to overcome fear and engage in the work He has called us to.

167

Overcoming Procrastination

The key to overcoming procrastination lies in understanding the value of time and the importance of diligent work. Ephesians 5:15-16 (ESV) says, "Look carefully then how you walk, not as unwise but as wise, making the best use of the time because the days are evil." As followers of Christ, we are called to use our time wisely and work diligently, overcoming procrastination and fulfilling our call to action.

Practical Steps to Overcoming Fear and Procrastination

Prayer and meditation on God's Word can help us conquer fear and procrastination. Philippians 4:6-7 (ESV) encourages us to present our anxieties to God in prayer, and His peace will guard our hearts and minds.

Creating a plan of action and setting achievable goals can help us overcome procrastination. Breaking down tasks into manageable steps and prioritizing them can reduce the overwhelm often associated with big tasks.

Fear and procrastination are common obstacles to action. However, with God's help, we can overcome these roadblocks and engage fully in the work He has called us to. Through faith in God's promises, diligent work, prayer, and strategic planning, we can conquer fear and procrastination and transform our faith into action.

The Ripple Effect: The Impact of Our Actions on Others

The concept of the "ripple effect" refers to the notion that a single action can have far-reaching effects, much like a stone thrown into a pond creates ripples that spread outwards. The Bible frequently illustrates this principle, reminding us that our actions, words, and decisions can significantly impact the lives of others and, consequently, the world around us.

Understanding the Ripple Effect

The ripple effect concept emphasizes our interconnectedness and the profound influence we can have on others, intentionally or unintentionally. It's an idea that underscores the power of individual actions to set forth cascades of events, reinforcing the responsibility that comes with our choices.

The Ripple Effect in the Old Testament

The Old Testament provides several examples of how individual actions can lead to significant consequences for others. One of the most striking examples is in the story of Achan, recorded in Joshua 7:1 (ASV). Achan's disobedience to God's command not to take anything from the conquered city of Jericho led to Israel's defeat in the battle of Ai and his family's death. This story underlines how our actions can affect not just our lives but those around us too.

The Ripple Effect in the New Testament

The New Testament also offers numerous illustrations of the ripple effect. The apostle Paul, for example, had a profound influence on early Christianity. His conversion and subsequent work spread the gospel throughout the Roman Empire, establishing many early churches. Paul's letters to these churches form a significant part of the New Testament and continue to impact Christianity today.

The Influence of Our Actions

Our actions and decisions often have unforeseen and far-reaching consequences. As followers of Christ, we are called to "walk in a manner worthy of the calling to which you have been called," as stated in Ephesians 4:1 (ESV). Our behavior, words, and choices should reflect Christ's love and teachings, impacting others positively.

The Impact of Our Actions on Others

Our actions can serve as a powerful testimony of our faith. By living out our faith through our actions, we can influence others towards Christ. Matthew 5:16 (ESV) says, "In the same way, let your light shine before others, so that they may see your good works and give glory to your Father who is in heaven." Our actions can lead others to acknowledge God's presence and power, causing a positive ripple effect.

The Negative Ripple Effect

However, it's also crucial to understand that our actions can lead to negative ripple effects. Sinful actions can lead to damaging consequences for ourselves and others around us. This calls for accountability and repentance.

Conclusion: Our Responsibility

Understanding the ripple effect of our actions underscores our responsibility as Christians. Each decision we make, each action we undertake, can send ripples through the lives of those around us, influencing them in ways we may never fully comprehend. We are, therefore, called to live with intention, discernment, and love, recognizing the potential impact of our actions on others and ultimately on God's Kingdom. As Galatians 6:7 (ESV) reminds us, "Do not be deceived: God is not mocked, for whatever one sows, that will he also reap."

Responding to God's Call with Commitment and Action

The Christian journey is one marked by a divine call to action, an invitation from God to participate actively in His work. This calling requires a dual response: commitment and action. Both are essential elements of the Christian faith and have been demonstrated throughout biblical history.

God's Call in the Old Testament

Throughout the Old Testament, we observe God calling individuals to specific roles or tasks. For instance, Moses' call at the burning bush in Exodus 3:4-12 (ASV) was a pivotal moment. This encounter characterized by God's divine initiative, Moses' sense of inadequacy, and God's assurance of His presence illustrates the dynamic of God's call and the commitment required to respond to it.

God's Call in the New Testament

In the New Testament, the theme of divine calling is prevalent as well. Jesus' call of His disciples exemplifies this. In Matthew 4:18-22 (ESV), Simon Peter and his brother Andrew were called to leave their nets and follow Jesus, to become "fishers of men." Their immediate response of leaving their nets signified their commitment and prompt action in obedience to Jesus' call.

Commitment: The First Step in Responding to God's Call

Commitment is the first step in responding to God's call. It involves a conscious decision to devote oneself to God's plan and purpose, as illustrated by Ruth's statement to Naomi in Ruth 1:16-17 (ASV), "for whither thou goest, I will go." This commitment goes beyond mere verbal assent—it demands a transformation of life and priorities.

Action: The Manifestation of Commitment

Once commitment is established, it must be coupled with action. James 2:17 (ESV) underscores this when it declares that "faith by itself, if it does not have works, is dead." Our actions manifest our commitment, substantiate our faith, and demonstrate our obedience to God's call.

Examples of Action Rooted in Commitment

The Bible is replete with examples of action rooted in commitment. One such instance is Nehemiah's response to God's call to rebuild the walls of Jerusalem in Nehemiah 2:5 (ASV). Despite facing opposition and discouragement, Nehemiah acted on his commitment, leading the people to rebuild the city's walls in record time.

Perseverance in Commitment and Action

Responding to God's call requires perseverance in both commitment and action. Despite facing obstacles, we are called to remain steadfast. As recorded in 1 Corinthians 15:58 (ESV), "Therefore, my beloved brothers, be steadfast, immovable, always abounding in the work of the Lord, knowing that in the Lord your labor is not in vain."

Conclusion: Living Out Our Commitment through Action

The call to respond to God with commitment and action is a fundamental aspect of Christian life. It requires us to submit to God's sovereignty, embrace His plan, and actively participate in His work. By embodying our commitment through action, we participate in God's transformative work in the world and affirm the authenticity of our faith. As Ephesians 2:10 (ESV) reminds us, "For we are his workmanship, created in Christ Jesus for good works, which God prepared beforehand, that we should walk in them."

CHAPTER 8 Seeking Wisdom: How God Teaches Us Through Life Experiences

Introduction: Life Experiences as God's Classroom

Life can often feel like an intricate tapestry of experiences. Some threads are vibrant, full of joy and success, while others are darker, interwoven with pain, failure, or uncertainty. As believers, we understand these experiences are more than random occurrences; they are often God's classroom, where we are taught wisdom and molded in character.

The Concept of Wisdom in the Bible

The Bible often speaks of wisdom not as an accumulation of knowledge but as the practical application of knowledge, particularly in relation to honoring and obeying God. In Proverbs 9:10 (ASV), it says, "The fear of Jehovah is the beginning of wisdom," signifying that true wisdom starts with a right relationship with God. Wisdom, therefore, is intrinsically linked to our spiritual growth and understanding of God.

Learning Through Life Experiences

As we journey through life, our experiences become catalysts for learning and spiritual growth. In Romans 5:3-4 (ESV), Paul notes, "we rejoice in our sufferings, knowing that suffering produces endurance, and endurance produces character, and character produces hope." These verses illustrate how God uses life's trials and tribulations to teach us resilience, shape our character, and ultimately, instill hope.

173

Wisdom Through Triumphs

Our moments of success, too, can teach us important lessons. King Solomon's prosperous and peaceful reign in 1 Kings 3:12 (ASV), for example, was not just a period of wealth and prosperity. Solomon's wisdom, granted by God, enabled him to rule justly and peacefully, teaching him—and us—the importance of humility and reliance on God, even in times of triumph.

The Role of Scripture in Gaining Wisdom

While life experiences are significant teachers, Scripture remains our primary source of wisdom. As stated in 2 Timothy 3:16-17 (ESV), "All Scripture is breathed out by God and profitable for teaching, for reproof, for correction, and for training in righteousness, that the man of God may be complete, equipped for every good work." The Bible provides divine wisdom that guides our actions, informs our decisions, and molds our character.

The Holy Spirit as Our Teacher

God does not leave us alone to navigate our life experiences. The Holy Spirit is our Helper and Teacher, illuminating our minds to understand and apply God's truth to our circumstances. John 14:26 (ESV) promises, "But the Helper, the Holy Spirit, whom the Father will send in my name, he will teach you all things and bring to your remembrance all that I have said to you."

Prayer: Seeking Wisdom from God

Prayer is a crucial aspect of seeking wisdom from God. In James 1:5 (ESV), we are encouraged, "If any of you lacks wisdom, let him ask God, who gives generously to all without reproach, and it will be given him." Prayer invites God into our learning process, expressing our dependence on Him for wisdom.

Conclusion: Wisdom—The Fruit of Experience and Divine Instruction

Life experiences, under God's sovereign control, serve as a classroom where we learn wisdom. From trials to triumphs, we glean insights that, when coupled with the timeless wisdom from Scripture and the Holy Spirit's teaching, deepen our understanding of God and our role in His grand narrative. Our journey then becomes an opportunity to grow in wisdom and live in alignment with God's purposes and plans, ensuring that our life experiences are not merely random happenings but divinely orchestrated lessons in wisdom. As the writer of Proverbs 3:13 (ASV) noted, "Happy is the man that findeth wisdom, and the man that getteth understanding."

Biblical Wisdom: What It Is and Why It Matters

The Bible, an inspired and infallible book, places significant emphasis on wisdom. It is mentioned hundreds of times throughout both the Old and New Testaments, demonstrating its fundamental role in spiritual development and moral living. The question arises, what exactly is Biblical wisdom, and why does it matter?

Understanding the Nature of Biblical Wisdom

Unlike worldly wisdom, which often emphasizes knowledge or intelligence, Biblical wisdom is deeply spiritual and relational. The Bible defines wisdom as the fear of the Lord. Proverbs 9:10 (ASV) states, "The fear of Jehovah is the beginning of wisdom; And the knowledge of the Holy One is understanding." Wisdom begins with acknowledging God's sovereign authority and nurturing a deep, reverential respect for Him.

Biblical Wisdom vs. Worldly Wisdom

Worldly wisdom often places a high premium on self-reliance, personal achievement, and the pursuit of material wealth. In contrast,

Biblical wisdom is grounded in humility, obedience, and the pursuit of righteousness. While worldly wisdom leads to fleeting satisfaction, Biblical wisdom leads to eternal life. As noted in Proverbs 3:13-14 (ASV), "Happy is the man that findeth wisdom, And the man that getteth understanding. For the gaining of it is better than the gaining of silver, And the profit thereof than fine gold."

The Source of Biblical Wisdom

Biblical wisdom is a divine gift, bestowed by God upon those who seek it. James 1:5 (ESV) assures believers that "if any of you lacks wisdom, let him ask God, who gives generously to all without reproach, and it will be given him." By turning to God in prayer, believers acknowledge their dependence on Him for guidance and understanding.

The Role of Scripture in Gaining Wisdom

Scripture is the primary conduit through which God imparts His wisdom. In 2 Timothy 3:16-17 (ESV), Paul affirmed, "All Scripture is breathed out by God and profitable for teaching, for reproof, for correction, and for training in righteousness, that the man of God may be complete, equipped for every good work." By studying and meditating on Scripture, believers can gain insight into God's wisdom, informing their understanding of the world and guiding their decisions.

Living Out Biblical Wisdom

Biblical wisdom is not simply about gaining knowledge; it is about living in alignment with God's commands. It involves making moral decisions, treating others with love and respect, and seeking justice. Living out Biblical wisdom, as expressed in James 3:17 (ESV), means to demonstrate that "the wisdom from above is first pure, then peaceable, gentle, open to reason, full of mercy and good fruits, impartial and sincere."

Why Biblical Wisdom Matters

Biblical wisdom matters because it serves as the compass guiding our conduct, shaping our character, and informing our understanding of God's will. It is the foundation for a life lived in alignment with God's commands, a life that reflects His love, mercy, and justice.

Furthermore, Biblical wisdom offers the promise of eternal life. As Proverbs 8:35 (ASV) proclaims, "For whoso findeth me findeth life, And shall obtain favor of Jehovah." The pursuit of Biblical wisdom, therefore, is not just a quest for knowledge, but a quest for life in its fullest sense—life that is abundant, purposeful, and eternal.

Conclusion: The Pursuit of Biblical Wisdom

In the vast and often tumultuous ocean of life, Biblical wisdom serves as the compass that directs us towards the safe harbor of God's will. It instructs us on how to navigate life's storms, illuminates the path to eternal life, and draws us closer to the heart of God. By acknowledging our need for God's wisdom and diligently seeking it in His Word, we equip ourselves to lead lives of profound spiritual significance, reflecting God's glory through our actions and attitudes. The pursuit of Biblical wisdom, then, is not just a journey—it's a destination. It's where we find life, love, and the very presence of God.

The Role of Experience in Shaping Wisdom

Life experiences are often the furnace in which wisdom is forged. The Bible emphasizes this in several places, elucidating how personal encounters, struggles, and victories can be instrumental in enhancing our understanding of God's wisdom. But what exactly is the role of experience in shaping wisdom?

Experience: The Catalyst for Growth

Every believer's journey with God is marked by various experiences—some joyful, some challenging, and some utterly transformative. These experiences serve as a catalyst for growth. As expressed in James 1:2-4 (ESV), "Count it all joy, my brothers, when you meet trials of various kinds, for you know that the testing of your faith produces steadfastness. And let steadfastness have its full effect, that you may be perfect and complete, lacking in nothing."

The trials and experiences we go through are not random or purposeless. They serve to test our faith, to cultivate resilience, and ultimately to shape us into more mature believers. It's through these experiences that we gain a deeper, more nuanced understanding of life and God's wisdom.

From Knowledge to Wisdom: The Crucible of Experience

While knowledge and wisdom are related, they are not synonymous. Knowledge refers to the acquisition of facts, while wisdom involves understanding the deeper significance of those facts and applying them effectively in our lives. Experience serves as the crucible where knowledge is transformed into wisdom.

In experiencing life's ups and downs, we gain a practical understanding of God's truths, bringing the scriptural teachings to life. The Psalmist wrote, "It is good for me that I was afflicted, that I might learn your statutes." (Psalm 119:71, ESV). Here we see the transformative power of experience, taking the knowledge of God's laws and turning it into wisdom through the furnace of affliction.

Learning from Mistakes: The Wisdom of Repentance

Even our mistakes and failures can be instrumental in shaping wisdom. Proverbs 28:13 (ASV) states, "He that covereth his transgressions shall not prosper: But whoso confesseth and forsaketh them shall obtain mercy." By acknowledging our failures and seeking

God's forgiveness, we learn valuable lessons about the consequences of our actions, the nature of God's grace, and the path to righteousness. Repentance thus becomes a powerful teacher, instilling wisdom borne of humble introspection and divine mercy.

Experience and Empathy: Understanding the Human Condition

Experience also fosters empathy, a critical component of wisdom. When we endure trials and tribulations, we gain a deeper understanding of the human condition, making us more capable of offering comfort and guidance to others. As Paul stated in 2 Corinthians 1:3-4 (ESV), "Blessed be the God and Father of our Lord Jesus Christ, the Father of mercies and God of all comfort, who comforts us in all our affliction, so that we may be able to comfort those who are in any affliction, with the comfort with which we ourselves are comforted by God."

Conclusion: Embracing Experience as God's Teaching Tool

In the grand tapestry of our spiritual journey, each thread of experience—be it joy or sorrow, victory or defeat—contributes to the vibrant pattern of wisdom that defines our relationship with God. By embracing life experiences as God's teaching tools, we open ourselves to the growth and maturation that these lessons offer.

Indeed, life experiences are more than mere events; they are the classroom in which we learn the profound lessons of Biblical wisdom. As we navigate the varied landscapes of life, may we continually seek to discern God's hand at work, shaping us into vessels of His divine wisdom.

Edward D. Andrews

Case Studies: Wisdom Gained from Biblical Characters' Experiences

The Bible offers us a unique window into the lives of countless individuals, each with their own experiences, struggles, victories, and lessons learned. Through these case studies, we can gain a profound understanding of how experience shapes wisdom. The experiences of biblical characters such as King Solomon, Job, Peter, and Paul provide rich insights into how wisdom is cultivated through personal journeys.

King Solomon: Wisdom Through Divine Intervention

King Solomon, known as the wisest man in the Bible, offers a unique case. His wisdom was a direct result of divine intervention. In 1 Kings 3:9 (ASV), Solomon asks God for "an understanding heart to judge thy people, that I may discern between good and evil." God granted this request, and Solomon became renowned for his wisdom.

Yet, Solomon's wisdom was also shaped by his experiences. Despite his God-given wisdom, he made serious mistakes, such as allowing his foreign wives to lead him into idolatry (1 Kings 11:4, ESV). From Solomon's experience, we learn that wisdom is not a shield against sin or poor decisions, and that constant vigilance and obedience to God's laws are crucial.

Job: Wisdom Through Suffering

Job's experiences offer another compelling case study. Despite being a righteous man, Job suffered immensely, losing his family, his wealth, and his health. His friends, believing that his suffering must be a punishment for sin, urged him to confess his wrongdoings. However, Job maintained his innocence.

In the end, God affirmed Job's righteousness and restored his fortunes. From Job's story, we learn that wisdom sometimes comes through enduring inexplicable suffering. Job's wisdom grew as he clung to his faith amidst his trials, reminding us that wisdom often involves trusting God, even when His ways are beyond our understanding (Job 42:3, ESV).

Peter: Wisdom Through Failure and Restoration

Simon Peter, one of Jesus' closest disciples, presents another insightful case. Peter was quick to profess his faith and devotion, yet he denied Jesus three times before the crucifixion. This experience of failure was a turning point for Peter.

After Jesus' resurrection, He restored Peter, who became a fearless leader in the early church. Peter's experience teaches us that wisdom can emerge from our failures, especially when they lead to repentance, forgiveness, and transformed lives. As Peter writes in 1 Peter 5:10 (ESV), "And after you have suffered a little while, the God of all grace, who has called you to his eternal glory in Christ, will himself restore, confirm, strengthen, and establish you."

Paul: Wisdom Through Transformation

The Apostle Paul's experience was one of dramatic transformation. From a persecutor of Christians, he became one of the most influential apostles. His conversion on the Damascus road (Acts 9, ESV) was just the start of a journey marked by hardships, including imprisonment, beatings, and shipwrecks.

Despite these trials, Paul continued to proclaim the gospel, gaining wisdom through his experiences. He learned to rejoice in hardships, understanding that they produce endurance, character, and hope (Romans 5:3-4, ESV). Paul's life reminds us that wisdom is often shaped in the crucible of personal transformation and steadfast commitment to God's calling.

Conclusion: Lessons from the Lives of the Wise

Through these case studies, we see that the path to wisdom often involves experiences of divine intervention, suffering, failure, and transformation. These biblical characters, each in their unique way, demonstrate that wisdom is not merely about intellectual understanding. It is about a deep, experiential knowledge of God that is shaped by our life journey and our responses to the challenges we face.

These biblical narratives remind us that wisdom is not a destination but a journey, one that involves continual learning, personal growth, and an ever-deepening relationship with God. As Proverbs 9:10 (ASV) reminds us, "The fear of Jehovah is the beginning of wisdom; And the knowledge of the Holy One is understanding." As we navigate our own experiences, may we, like these biblical characters, grow in wisdom that is rooted in reverence for God and shaped by our journey with Him.

Personal Testimonies: Lessons Learned from Modern-Day Christians

Personal testimonies are the lifeblood of the Christian experience. They are the tangible stories of God's grace and action in the world today, offering wisdom and insights drawn from real-life experiences. As such, they serve as powerful teaching tools, helping us navigate our own journeys of faith.

Conversion Experiences: The Dramatic Turning Points

One of the most impactful types of personal testimony comes from individuals who have experienced a profound transformation in their lives, not unlike the Apostle Paul's encounter on the Damascus road. These are often individuals who, despite living in direct opposition to Christian principles, encounter Christ and experience a radical transformation.

A striking example can be seen in the life of Nicky Cruz, a former gang leader in New York City. Cruz's life was marked by violence and crime until he encountered the evangelist David Wilkerson. Cruz's conversion led to a complete turnaround, from a life of violence to one dedicated to evangelism and helping others escape the path he once walked.

Lessons from such testimonies remind us of the transformative power of God's grace and the truth of 2 Corinthians 5:17 (ESV), which states, "Therefore, if anyone is in Christ, he is a new creation. The old has passed away; behold, the new has come."

Perseverance in Trials: The Power of Faith

Other powerful testimonies come from Christians who have faced immense trials and tribulations. These modern-day Jobs show us the power of faith and the importance of perseverance.

One such example is Joni Eareckson Tada, who became quadriplegic due to a diving accident at the age of 17. Despite her physical limitations and the challenges she faced, Tada's faith in God not only remained intact but grew stronger. She went on to establish a worldwide ministry, using her experience to encourage others facing hardships.

Her story echoes Romans 5:3-5 (ESV), "Not only that, but we rejoice in our sufferings, knowing that suffering produces endurance, and endurance produces character, and character produces hope."

Everyday Faithfulness: The Steadfast Walk

Testimonies of everyday faithfulness may not be as dramatic as conversions or trials, but they are equally important. These are the stories of individuals who exemplify steadfast commitment to walking with God in the mundane and routine of daily life.

Consider a committed Sunday School teacher who, over decades, impacts hundreds of lives through her faithful service. Or a Christian businessman who maintains integrity in a cutthroat industry. Their testimonies remind us that God calls us not only to moments of dramatic faith but to a lifetime of everyday faithfulness, living out Colossians 3:23 (ESV), "Whatever you do, work heartily, as for the Lord and not for men."

Conclusion: The Ongoing Story of God's Work

The personal testimonies of modern-day Christians provide a rich tapestry of lessons about faith, perseverance, and faithfulness. They show us how God continues to work in our world, transforming lives and empowering His people to overcome challenges.

These testimonies remind us that each of us has a role to play in God's story, as we too live out our faith, endure trials, and strive for faithfulness. As we learn from these modern-day testimonies, may we also become testimonies of God's grace, demonstrating His love and power to the world around us.

Embracing Trials: Finding Wisdom in Life's Challenges

In the Christian life, trials and tribulations are an inevitable part of our mortal existence. However, the Bible encourages believers to find strength, endurance, and ultimately, wisdom from these trials. In the book of James, we read, "Count it all joy, my brothers, when you meet trials of various kinds, for you know that the testing of your faith produces steadfastness" (James 1:2-3, ESV). While this perspective can be challenging to grasp, it provides invaluable insight in our navigation of life's adversities.

Understanding Trials: Not God's Doing, but Part of Human Life

Trials come in different forms—health crises, financial difficulties, or personal losses. They can be immensely challenging and can sometimes shake our faith. Importantly, it must be clear that God is not the author of these trials, as "with evil things God cannot be tried, nor does he himself try anyone" (James 1:13, ASV).

When we understand that trials are not divine punishments but part of our imperfect, human life, we can start to see them as opportunities for personal growth and spiritual development.

184

Moreover, by resisting the hardships and adversities we face, we can manifest God's strength and grace in our lives.

Finding Wisdom in Trials

While God does not inflict pain or hardship upon us, we, as believers, can use our trials to gain wisdom and spiritual maturity. Embracing trials becomes a pathway to wisdom—a deep, Godly wisdom that transcends human understanding. As the Bible tells us, "If any of you lacks wisdom, let him ask God, who gives generously to all without reproach, and it will be given him" (James 1:5, ESV).

Biblical Examples: Gaining Wisdom from Trials

The Bible provides numerous accounts of individuals who faced severe trials and used these experiences to grow in wisdom. Consider Job, who experienced immense personal losses, yet maintained his faith in God. At the end of his trials, Job had acquired a profound understanding of God's sovereignty and love, stating, "I know that you can do all things; no purpose of yours can be thwarted" (Job 42:2, ESV).

Similarly, the Apostle Paul underwent numerous trials for his faith, including imprisonment and beatings. Yet, these hardships only served to strengthen his faith and deepen his wisdom, as he stated, "I consider that our present sufferings are not worth comparing with the glory that will be revealed in us" (Romans 8:18, ESV).

Modern-day Application: Gaining Wisdom from Our Trials

Today, as believers, we are not exempt from trials. However, we have the choice to use these hardships for our spiritual growth and for God's glory. When we face challenges, we are called to lean on God, seek His wisdom, and find comfort in His promises.

During these times, prayer, immersing oneself in Scripture, and fellowship with other believers can provide comfort and guidance.

Remember, embracing trials is not about denying the pain or pretending to be unscathed, but about acknowledging the pain and yet choosing to remain steadfast in faith, using these trials to grow in wisdom and grace. This, in turn, reflects God's strength and sovereignty, bringing honor and glory to His name.

Learning from Success: Celebrations as Opportunities for Wisdom

In a Christian's journey, success is not merely measured by worldly standards of wealth, power, or prestige. Rather, success is about faithfully walking with God, doing His will, and bearing spiritual fruit. Even when we achieve milestones that society defines as success, it's important to see them as blessings from God and opportunities for further wisdom. The biblical Joseph rose to power in Egypt (Genesis 41), yet he never lost sight of God's guidance in his life. Success, for believers, is thus as much a spiritual lesson as any hardship could ever be.

Seeing Success as God's Blessing

When believers experience success, it's essential to remember that it is God's blessing, not merely our own effort. Proverbs 16:3 in ASV says, "Commit thy works unto Jehovah, and thy purposes shall be established." Any success we attain is a testament to God's faithfulness and favor. We must respond with gratitude, humility, and the understanding that these blessings are opportunities for further wisdom.

Learning Wisdom in Times of Success

Success, when viewed through the lens of wisdom, provides crucial lessons for believers. First, success teaches us about God's providence. As we trace our journey, we realize that God's hand guided us, opening doors and guiding our steps. This deepens our faith and trust in Him.

Second, success teaches humility. Recognizing our achievements as God's grace prevents pride from taking root. As stated in Proverbs 16:18 (ESV), "Pride goes before destruction, and a haughty spirit before a fall." The wisdom gained here is knowing that our achievements do not make us superior to others.

Lastly, success gives us the wisdom of stewardship. Any blessing from God, including success, isn't just for our own benefit. We are called to be good stewards of our God-given resources and opportunities (1 Peter 4:10, ESV). This means using our success to glorify God and bless others.

Biblical Examples: Wisdom from Success Stories

The Bible offers numerous success stories, each rich with wisdom. Solomon, for instance, asked God for wisdom, which led him to become one of the most successful kings in Israel's history. Yet, his life warns us about the danger of letting success lead to spiritual complacency (1 Kings 11).

Joseph's success story, from a favored son to a slave, and finally to a high-ranking Egyptian official, teaches us that success is always under God's control. Despite being in an influential position, Joseph maintained his faith in God and used his success to save his people.

Modern-day Application: Success as an Avenue to Wisdom

In our lives, every success story—be it big or small—can be an opportunity for gaining wisdom. Whenever we achieve a goal, reach a milestone, or overcome a significant challenge, it's a moment to pause, thank God, and draw lessons.

What has the journey taught us about God's faithfulness? What has the success story taught us about humility and stewardship? How can we use the success to bless others and glorify God?

In conclusion, success in the Christian journey is not merely about self-congratulation. It's an opportunity to learn wisdom—wisdom about God's providence, humility, and stewardship. It's a reminder to stay grounded in God and use our achievements for His glory. Celebrating success, therefore, becomes a celebration of God's goodness, and each triumph becomes a testament to His grace and favor.

The Importance of Reflection: Processing Life's Lessons

Reflection is an indispensable part of the Christian journey. It is in the quiet moments of introspection that we process our experiences, understand God's work in our lives, and apply the wisdom we've gleaned. This practice is far from a modern invention; it's a pattern evident in the lives of biblical characters and commended in Scripture itself. Psalm 1:2 in ASV states, "But his delight is in the law of Jehovah; And on his law doth he meditate day and night." This meditation is, in essence, reflection—processing God's word and its implications for life.

Reflection in the Biblical Context

Throughout the Bible, there are accounts of characters who exemplified the practice of reflection. David, for instance, was a man after God's own heart (Acts 13:22, ESV), and many of his psalms show him reflecting on God's goodness, his personal failings, and God's faithfulness in times of distress. His reflections helped him maintain his faith in difficult times and repent when he strayed.

The apostle Paul's letters often show a reflective mind at work. From pondering the mystery of God's grace in his life (1 Timothy 1:12-16, ESV) to exhorting believers to examine themselves (2 Corinthians 13:5, ESV), Paul's writings encourage the process of deep, personal reflection.

The Role of Reflection in Processing Life's Lessons

Reflection is a crucial tool for processing life's lessons. It allows us to take a step back and examine our experiences under the light of Scripture. We discern patterns, understand cause-effect relationships, gain insights into God's character, and identify areas of growth or repentance.

Reflection gives us the chance to learn from our past, understanding our failures and successes in their proper context. It enables us to celebrate God's grace in our victories and see His guiding hand in our challenges. Through reflection, we convert experience into wisdom and understanding, as noted in Proverbs 24:3 in ASV: "Through wisdom is a house builded; And by understanding it is established."

Reflection as a Gateway to Spiritual Growth

By cultivating a habit of reflection, we create room for spiritual growth. Reflection encourages humility as we see our own failings and God's perfection. It fosters gratitude as we recognize God's blessings. It deepens our faith as we recall God's faithfulness in past trials, strengthening us for future ones. It is through reflective examination that we can heed Paul's advice in Romans 12:2 (ESV): "Do not be conformed to this world, but be transformed by the renewal of your mind, that by testing you may discern what is the will of God, what is good and acceptable and perfect."

Applying Reflection in Modern-Day Christian Living

Applying reflection to our daily lives starts with setting aside dedicated time for it. Whether it's a few quiet minutes each morning or an hour at week's end, this intentional pause is invaluable. During this time, we can contemplate our experiences, read and reflect on Scripture, and pray for wisdom.

Reflection may involve journaling, a practice that allows us to record and revisit our insights. Writing out our thoughts can bring clarity and reveal deeper insights. It also provides a tangible record of God's faithfulness that can encourage us in difficult times.

Conclusion: Reflection as an Ongoing Pursuit of Wisdom

In conclusion, the practice of reflection stands as an integral part of the Christian journey, serving as a bridge between experience and wisdom. Through reflection, we learn to see our lives from a God-centered perspective, appreciate His work in us, and understand life's lessons more deeply. It is an ongoing pursuit, an ever-renewing process that shapes us into the image of Christ and enables us to navigate our journey with grace, wisdom, and resilience. As we follow the biblical model of reflection, we equip ourselves to process life's lessons, grow spiritually, and deepen our relationship with God.

Wisdom and Decision Making: Applying Lessons Learned

A key benefit of wisdom is its profound impact on decision making. Acquired through experience and reflection, wisdom is not merely about knowledge; it's about understanding and discerning what is truly important, enabling us to make choices that align with God's will. Proverbs 2:6 (ASV) says, "For Jehovah giveth wisdom; Out of his mouth cometh knowledge and understanding."

Biblical Examples of Wisdom in Decision Making

In Scripture, we find numerous examples of characters who displayed wisdom in their decision-making processes. King Solomon, known for his wisdom, made decisions that ensured peace and prosperity during his reign. His wisdom, granted by God, equipped him to rule judiciously and make decisions that had lasting positive impacts (1 Kings 3:5-14, ESV).

The Apostle Paul also demonstrated wisdom in decision-making, particularly in his missionary journeys. Guided by the Holy Spirit, he made strategic choices about where to travel and preach, leading to the establishment of numerous Christian communities (Acts 16:6-10, ESV).

Applying Wisdom to Life's Choices

In daily life, wisdom can guide our decisions in various areas, such as relationships, career choices, stewardship of resources, and how we spend our time. It helps us to discern the right paths and make choices that glorify God and contribute to our spiritual growth. Proverbs 3:5-6 (ASV) underscores this, urging us to, "Trust in Jehovah with all thy heart, And lean not upon thine own understanding: In all thy ways acknowledge him, And he will direct thy paths."

Cultivating Wisdom for Decision Making

Cultivating wisdom begins with fearing the Lord, as Proverbs 9:10 (ASV) states, "The fear of Jehovah is the beginning of wisdom; And the knowledge of the Holy One is understanding." This reverential fear is about recognizing God's sovereignty, righteousness, and love. It invites us to align ourselves with God's character and will, fostering wisdom.

Studying God's Word is another essential practice. As we delve into Scripture, we gain insights into God's nature and His principles for living. Regular Bible study equips us with a godly perspective, influencing our choices.

Prayer, too, is a critical component. In prayer, we seek God's guidance, express our dependence on Him, and ask for wisdom. James 1:5 (ESV) assures us, "If any of you lacks wisdom, let him ask God, who gives generously to all without reproach, and it will be given him."

Making Wise Decisions in Modern Christian Life

As modern-day Christians, we face countless decisions. Whether deciding on a career path, choosing a spouse, managing finances, or navigating ethical dilemmas, wisdom is our invaluable guide. As we encounter new experiences, the lessons we've learned, processed through reflection, become the basis for making wise choices.

In each decision, it's crucial to seek God's guidance, consult Scripture, and consider the wisdom we've accumulated from past experiences. By doing so, we align our decision-making with God's will, leading to choices that honor Him and promote spiritual growth.

Conclusion: Wisdom—The Compass for Life's Decisions

Wisdom, gleaned from experiences and reflections, acts as a compass guiding our decision-making. It aligns our choices with God's will, leading to decisions that honor Him, benefit others, and foster our spiritual growth. As we continue to cultivate wisdom through reverence for God, study of His Word, and prayer, we equip ourselves to navigate life's myriad decisions with spiritual discernment and integrity.

The Pitfall of Pride: A Barrier to Gaining Wisdom

Pride, the inflated sense of one's self-importance, often serves as a significant barrier to gaining wisdom. Proverbs 16:18 (ASV) warns, "Pride goeth before destruction, And a haughty spirit before a fall." This cautionary verse underscores how pride can lead to downfall, obstructing our path to acquiring wisdom.

Pride in the Bible: Cases and Consequences

Scripture provides numerous accounts where pride led to grave consequences, hindering the acquisition of wisdom. King Nebuchadnezzar of Babylon is a prime example. His pride led him to boast about his achievements, forgetting that it was God who had given him his kingdom. Consequently, he was humbled by God until he acknowledged that "the Most High rules the kingdom of men and gives it to whom he will" (Daniel 4:25, ESV).

The New Testament also provides a stark example with the Pharisees. Their pride, rooted in their self-righteousness and strict adherence to the law, blinded them to Christ's message and ministry. Instead of gaining wisdom from Jesus' teachings, they became adversaries, ultimately contributing to His crucifixion (Matthew 26:3-4, ESV).

Understanding the Nature of Pride

Pride is essentially an overestimation of one's self, often manifesting as arrogance or haughtiness. It blinds individuals to their limitations, flaws, and dependence on God. Pride can also lead to an underappreciation of others' contributions and a resistance to accepting advice or correction.

Such self-exalting tendencies contradict the spirit of humility necessary for gaining wisdom. Proverbs 11:2 (ASV) emphasizes this point, stating, "When pride cometh, then cometh shame; But with the lowly is wisdom."

Combating Pride: Cultivating Humility

To gain wisdom, we must counteract pride by cultivating humility. This begins with acknowledging our dependence on God and recognizing our limitations. James 4:6 (ESV) offers assurance in this regard, "But he gives more grace. Therefore it says, 'God opposes the proud but gives grace to the humble.'"

Practically, humility involves acknowledging our mistakes, being open to correction, and valuing others' contributions. It means acknowledging that we don't have all the answers and that we can learn from various sources – God's Word, the guidance of the Holy Spirit, and the experiences of others.

The Role of Reflection in Fostering Humility

Reflection plays a pivotal role in fostering humility. By reviewing our actions and attitudes, we can identify instances of pride and take steps to address them. Reflection also helps us recognize God's hand in our lives, reinforcing our dependence on Him and promoting humility.

Pride and Wisdom in Modern Christian Life

In our modern context, pride can subtly infiltrate our lives. It might appear as a reluctance to accept help, a resistance to admitting mistakes, or an insistence on our ways. Such attitudes hinder us from learning and growing – they obstruct the path to wisdom.

As Christians, we must remain vigilant against pride and continuously cultivate humility. This involves regular self-examination, acknowledgment of God's sovereignty, and a commitment to learning and growth.

Conclusion: Disarming the Barrier of Pride

In our pursuit of wisdom, pride is a formidable barrier. It fosters self-reliance and arrogance, blinding us to our need for God's guidance and the wisdom of others. However, through the cultivation of humility, guided by reflection and a recognition of God's sovereignty, we can disarm this barrier. Doing so, we open the pathway to wisdom, enhancing our relationship with God and our ability to make godly decisions. Ultimately, by rejecting pride and embracing humility, we align ourselves more closely with the character of Christ, the epitome of wisdom and humility.

Committing to Seek Wisdom in All Life's Experiences

The pursuit of wisdom should not be a sporadic endeavor, only sought in times of difficulty or decision-making. Instead, the quest for wisdom must be a continual, unwavering commitment encompassing all life's experiences. The book of Proverbs provides timeless wisdom on this subject, stating, "The beginning of wisdom is this: Get wisdom. Though it cost all you have, get understanding" (Proverbs 4:7, ESV).

Recognizing Wisdom's Value

First, we need to acknowledge wisdom's immense value. Scripture repeatedly emphasizes wisdom's inestimable worth. Job 28:18 (ASV) declares, "No mention shall be made of coral or of crystal: The price of wisdom is above rubies." Recognizing wisdom's value allows us to prioritize its pursuit in all aspects of life.

The Breadth of Wisdom

Wisdom does not exist in a vacuum; it's broad and all-encompassing. It involves discernment, understanding, knowledge, and righteous decision-making. It spans our relationships, career choices, moral decisions, crisis responses, and even our thought life. Every experience, every interaction, every decision is an opportunity for gaining and applying wisdom.

Wisdom in Success and Failure

Both success and failure present rich opportunities for acquiring wisdom. Success teaches us the principles that lead to positive outcomes and the importance of humility amid achievements. Failure, on the other hand, offers us invaluable lessons on perseverance, humility, and the necessity of corrective measures. The Bible underscores this point in Proverbs 24:16 (ESV), "For the righteous falls seven times and rises again, but the wicked stumble in times of calamity."

Wisdom in Joy and Sorrow

Joy and sorrow, the high peaks and deep valleys of our life journey, also hold potential for wisdom. Joy can teach us gratitude and the value of savoring God's blessings. Conversely, sorrow, while painful, can deepen our empathy, resilience, and reliance on God. As Psalm 119:71 (ASV) states, "It is good for me that I have been afflicted; That I may learn thy statutes."

The Role of Scripture and Prayer in Seeking Wisdom

Our primary resource for wisdom is the Bible, the inspired, inerrant Word of God. Through its teachings, we glean principles for righteous living, examples of wise and foolish actions, and the revelation of God's character. As 2 Timothy 3:16 (ESV) affirms, "All Scripture is breathed out by God and profitable for teaching, for reproof, for correction, and for training in righteousness."

Prayer is another indispensable tool. James 1:5 (ESV) instructs, "If any of you lacks wisdom, let him ask God, who gives generously to all without reproach, and it will be given him." Through prayer, we can request wisdom, seek guidance, and gain a clearer understanding of God's Word and His will.

The Community Factor in Wisdom Acquisition

Our relationships also serve as a source of wisdom. The insights, experiences, and counsel of fellow believers can enrich our understanding and help us navigate life's complexities. Proverbs 27:17 (ASV) encapsulates this concept, "Iron sharpens iron; So a man sharpens the countenance of his friend."

Conclusion: The Lifelong Commitment

To seek wisdom in all life's experiences is a lifelong commitment. This pursuit requires us to stay vigilant, ready to learn from every situation, whether it's filled with joy or sorrow, success or failure. It involves regular engagement with the Bible, fervent prayer, and intentional community interaction. As we commit to this pursuit, we can trust that God, the source of all wisdom, will generously grant us the understanding we seek. His promise remains true: "For the Lord gives wisdom; from his mouth come knowledge and understanding" (Proverbs 2:6, ESV).

CHAPTER 9 The Art of Discernment: Learning to Make God-Centered Choices

Introduction: Discernment in the Christian Life

Discernment is an indispensable aspect of the Christian life. It involves the ability to make wise, godly decisions and judgments, distinguishing between right and wrong, truth and falsehood, and the will of God versus our desires. Discernment requires a grounded understanding of God's Word, a sincere heart, and an open mind attuned to God's guiding presence. As Hebrews 5:14 (ESV) asserts, "solid food is for the mature, for those who have their powers of discernment trained by constant practice to distinguish good from evil."

The Biblical Basis for Discernment

The Bible, the inspired, inerrant Word of God, serves as our primary resource for discernment. The principles, teachings, and narratives within the scriptures provide a framework for understanding God's character, His moral standards, and His vision for human life. "Your word is a lamp to my feet and a light to my path," says Psalm 119:105 (ESV), indicating the guiding role of scripture in decision-making.

Prayer and Discernment

Prayer is an essential aspect of discernment. As we communicate with God, we not only present our requests and express our gratitude, but we also seek His wisdom and guidance. Through prayer, we can receive divine insight and clarity in our decision-making. James 1:5

(ESV) assures us that "If any of you lacks wisdom, let him ask God, who gives generously to all without reproach, and it will be given him."

Discernment and the Holy Spirit

The Holy Spirit, who dwells within believers, plays a crucial role in discernment. The Spirit illuminates our understanding of God's Word, helps us recognize God's leading, and convicts us of sin and righteousness. As Jesus promises in John 16:13 (ESV), "When the Spirit of truth comes, he will guide you into all the truth."

Discernment in Practice

Discernment extends to all areas of life: our relationships, careers, ministries, and everyday choices. The practice of discernment involves examining these areas under the light of scripture, prayerful consideration, and the guidance of the Holy Spirit.

For instance, when making a decision, we should ask: Does this align with God's Word? What is the Holy Spirit's prompting in my heart? Have I sought God's wisdom through prayer? Am I acting out of selfish desire or God-centered purpose?

Discernment and Christian Community

The Christian community is another valuable resource in discernment. Godly friends, mentors, and leaders can provide insightful advice, accountability, and support as we make decisions. Proverbs 15:22 (ASV) wisely notes, "Where no counsel is, the people fall; But in the multitude of counselors there is safety."

Conclusion: Cultivating a Lifestyle of Discernment

Discernment is not an isolated act but a lifestyle. It requires a deep commitment to knowing God's Word, a consistent prayer life, sensitivity to the Holy Spirit's leading, and an active engagement with the Christian community.

The pursuit of discernment is an ongoing journey, requiring intentionality and patience. But the rewards are immense: a life aligned with God's will, decisions that honor Him, and a deeper understanding of His character and purposes. As we continually commit to discernment, we can find assurance in God's promise in Proverbs 2:6-7 (ESV): "For the Lord gives wisdom; from his mouth come knowledge and understanding; he stores up sound wisdom for the upright; he is a shield to those who walk in integrity."

The Definition of Discernment: A Biblical Perspective

The term "discernment" often evokes a sense of keen insight, perception, or the ability to distinguish between subtleties that may escape the casual observer. From a biblical perspective, discernment takes on a deeper, more profound meaning. It isn't merely an intellectual exercise or a product of natural intuition, but an active engagement with God's Word, a receptivity to the Holy Spirit's guidance, and a committed pursuit of God's will.

Discernment in the Old Testament

In the Old Testament, discernment is closely tied to wisdom and understanding. Solomon, renowned for his wisdom, asked God for "an understanding mind to govern your people, that I may discern between good and evil" (1 Kings 3:9, ESV). Discernment, therefore, involves the ability to make morally sound decisions based on God's standards of righteousness.

Discernment in the New Testament

In the New Testament, discernment expands to incorporate spiritual realities. Paul's prayer for the Philippians reveals this aspect: "And it is my prayer that your love may abound more and more, with knowledge and all discernment" (Philippians 1:9, ESV). Here, discernment is connected with love and knowledge, enabling believers to "approve what is excellent" and live blameless lives (Philippians 1:10, ESV).

Discernment as Distinguishing Truth from Error

A key aspect of discernment is the ability to distinguish truth from error, especially regarding doctrinal matters. In the early church, discernment was crucial in identifying and rejecting false teachers. As 1 John 4:1 (ESV) admonishes, "Beloved, do not believe every spirit, but test the spirits to see whether they are from God, for many false prophets have gone out into the world."

Discernment as Understanding God's Will

Discernment also involves understanding God's will, both in specific circumstances and in the broader scope of one's life. This requires an intimate knowledge of God's Word and a sensitivity to the Holy Spirit's guidance. As Paul writes in Romans 12:2 (ESV), "Do not be conformed to this world, but be transformed by the renewal of your mind, that by testing you may discern what is the will of God, what is good and acceptable and perfect."

Discernment as Perception of Spiritual Realities

Beyond discerning moral, doctrinal, and divine aspects, discernment in the biblical sense also includes perceiving spiritual realities. It involves a heightened awareness of the spiritual forces at work around us and an understanding of how they influence our lives. The spiritual armor described in Ephesians 6:10-18 (ESV) serves as a practical tool for believers to employ their discernment against the spiritual forces of evil.

Discernment as a Spiritual Gift

The New Testament lists discernment, or "distinguishing between spirits," as one of the spiritual gifts bestowed by the Holy Spirit (1 Corinthians 12:10, ESV). Those with this gift have an enhanced ability to distinguish between the work of the Holy Spirit and the work of other spirits, making it an invaluable asset for the health and wellbeing of the church.

Conclusion: The Rich Complexity of Biblical Discernment

The biblical concept of discernment is rich and multi-faceted. It involves wisdom, understanding, moral acuity, doctrinal clarity, awareness of God's will, perception of spiritual realities, and can even be a specific spiritual gift. As followers of Christ, our pursuit of discernment should not be optional or sporadic. Rather, it should be an intentional and ongoing quest, a vital part of our relationship with God, and a crucial aspect of our service to others.

In an age rife with misinformation, deceptive ideologies, and moral ambiguity, biblical discernment is more crucial than ever. It guides us in truth, protects us from error, and equips us to live faithfully as God's people. As we deepen our understanding of God's Word, rely on the guidance of the Holy Spirit, and remain committed to pursuing God's will, we develop and sharpen our discernment. In doing so, we learn to make God-centered choices, honoring Him with our lives and serving as effective witnesses to His truth.

The Need for Discernment: Making God-Centered Choices

The need for discernment in the life of a Christian cannot be overstated. The world presents us with a deluge of information, opinions, ideologies, and philosophies, each claiming to offer truth, happiness, or fulfillment. Yet, as Christians, we are called to live in alignment with God's truth, making choices centered on His will and purposes. Discernment is the spiritual compass that helps navigate this complex landscape, enabling us to make God-centered choices.

The Role of Discernment in Making Moral Decisions

One of the most significant areas where discernment is required is in making moral decisions. As followers of Christ, we are called to live according to God's standards of righteousness. Discernment helps us to "distinguish good from evil" (Hebrews 5:14, ESV). Through discernment, we can understand God's moral law, as revealed in Scripture, and apply it to situations and decisions in our lives.

Discernment in Discerning True Doctrine from False

As Paul warned the Ephesian elders, "fierce wolves will come in among you, not sparing the flock; and from among your own selves will arise men speaking twisted things, to draw away the disciples after them" (Acts 20:29-30, ESV). Discernment equips us to distinguish sound doctrine from false teachings, safeguarding our faith and ensuring that we remain grounded in the truth of the Gospel.

Discernment in Understanding God's Will

Paul's admonition to the Romans highlights another crucial area where discernment is required: understanding God's will. "Do not be conformed to this world, but be transformed by the renewal of your mind, that by testing you may discern what is the will of God, what is good and acceptable and perfect" (Romans 12:2, ESV). Understanding God's will for our lives is a daunting task. It requires a deep immersion in God's Word, a listening ear for the Spirit's prompting, and a discerning heart that is attuned to God's ways.

The Importance of Discernment in Relationships

Discernment also plays a significant role in the realm of relationships. The wisdom literature in the Bible, particularly the book of Proverbs, frequently emphasizes the importance of careful discernment in choosing companions and friends. "Whoever walks with the wise becomes wise, but the companion of fools will suffer harm" (Proverbs 13:20, ESV). Discernment helps us evaluate the character and influence of others, steering us toward edifying relationships that encourage spiritual growth.

Discernment as a Guard against Deception

Finally, discernment serves as a guard against the many forms of deception that abound in our world. The New Testament writers often warn about the deceitfulness of sin (Hebrews 3:13, ESV), the world's corrupting influence (James 4:4, ESV), and the schemes of the devil (Ephesians 6:11, ESV). Through discernment, we can recognize these threats, resist them, and remain steadfast in our commitment to Christ.

Conclusion: The Indispensable Need for Discernment

In conclusion, discernment is an indispensable aspect of Christian living. It is not a luxury or an optional extra, but a necessity for anyone who desires to live a life that is pleasing to God, fruitful in service, and effective in witness. Whether in moral decision-making, discerning true doctrine from false, understanding God's will, fostering healthy relationships, or guarding against deception, discernment plays a pivotal role.

By cultivating discernment, we can navigate life's complexities with wisdom and grace, making God-centered choices that reflect our allegiance to Christ and our commitment to His kingdom. The need for discernment underscores the importance of remaining rooted in Scripture, sensitive to the Spirit's leading, and steadfast in prayer. For it is through these means that God cultivates discernment in His people, equipping us to live for His glory in every aspect of life.

Sources of Wisdom: Scripture, Prayer, and Community

In our pursuit of God-centered discernment, we can find direction from three pivotal sources: Scripture, prayer, and community.

These channels work synergistically, offering us guidance and insights that illuminate the path of wisdom.

Scripture: The Primary Source of Wisdom

As conservative Bible scholars, we assert that Scripture is the primary and authoritative source of wisdom. "All Scripture is breathed out by God and profitable for teaching, for reproof, for correction, and for training in righteousness" (2 Timothy 3:16, ESV). We regard the Bible as the inspired, inerrant Word of God, absolutely infallible in the original writings and in literal translations. It is the lens through which we understand God, ourselves, and the world around us.

The Bible is replete with teachings, commandments, and principles that guide us in discerning right from wrong, truth from error, and wisdom from folly. The Psalms exclaim, "Your word is a lamp to my feet and a light to my path" (Psalm 119:105, ESV). The Word of God, properly understood and rightly applied, provides the light we need to navigate the twists and turns of life's journey.

Prayer: A Dialogue with Wisdom's Source

Prayer is another crucial source of wisdom. James reminds us, "If any of you lacks wisdom, let him ask God, who gives generously to all without reproach, and it will be given him" (James 1:5, ESV). Prayer is not a one-way request for wisdom but an ongoing dialogue with the ultimate source of wisdom—God Himself. Through prayer, we acknowledge our dependence on God, align our hearts with His will, and seek His guidance for our decisions.

Importantly, however, prayer does not function like a slot machine. God does not dispense wisdom without requiring engagement and effort from us. We must act in ways that align with our prayers, immersing ourselves in God's Word, seeking to understand it, and striving to apply its truths in our lives.

Community: A Context for Applying Wisdom

The third source of wisdom is the Christian community. As believers, we are not meant to live our faith in isolation. We belong to a community of faith, the body of Christ, where we learn from one another, bear one another's burdens, and encourage one another in the faith.

Community offers a context for applying wisdom. Proverbs asserts, "Where there is no guidance, a people falls, but in an abundance of counselors there is safety" (Proverbs 11:14, ESV). In the Christian community, we have the privilege of engaging with fellow believers, who, grounded in the Word and guided by a collective desire to honor God, provide valuable insights and perspectives that help us make wise decisions.

The interplay of Scripture, prayer, and community shapes the practice of discernment. Scripture gives us the principles and precepts that define wisdom, prayer opens our hearts to receive wisdom from God, and community provides the context for applying wisdom. Engaging with these sources of wisdom nurtures a discerning heart, equipping us to make decisions that honor God and advance His Kingdom.

Conclusion: Embracing Scripture, Prayer, and Community

In conclusion, the pursuit of discernment involves a dynamic engagement with Scripture, prayer, and community. These sources of wisdom, integrated and balanced, enable us to make God-centered choices that reflect a maturing faith and a growing understanding of God's will. As we engage with Scripture, commune with God in prayer, and interact within our Christian community, we foster the art of discernment, a critical skill for navigating the complexities of life in a manner that glorifies God.

The Role of the Holy Spirit in Discernment

Understanding the role of the Holy Spirit in discernment requires recognizing the Spirit's primary work: inspiring the sacred Scriptures. As we embrace a conservative Bible scholar perspective, we acknowledge the Holy Spirit's role not in the sense of a miraculous indwelling guiding us subjectively, but as the divine author of Scripture, who provides us with God-breathed words to guide us when we correctly understand and apply them.

The Holy Spirit: The Divine Inspirer of Scripture

The Bible asserts that the Holy Spirit moved human authors to write the Scriptures. "No prophecy of Scripture comes from someone's own interpretation. For no prophecy was ever produced by the will of man, but men spoke from God as they were carried along by the Holy Spirit" (2 Peter 1:20-21, ESV). This passage underscores that the Holy Spirit's function is to deliver God's truth through the Scriptures.

As the divine Inspirer of Scripture, the Holy Spirit plays a pivotal role in our discernment. The Spirit-inspired Scriptures are our authoritative guide for belief and conduct. As such, it is through understanding and correctly applying the Bible that we engage the Holy Spirit's guidance.

The Holy Spirit and Scripture: Interconnected in Discernment

In discernment, the Holy Spirit and Scripture are inseparably interconnected. When we speak of the Spirit's leading, we refer to the insights, principles, and wisdom found in the Scripture, which the Spirit has inspired. Therefore, it is not about seeking subjective feelings or impressions but about earnestly studying and applying the Spirit-breathed Word.

The Apostle Paul's letter to Timothy affirms, "All Scripture is breathed out by God and profitable for teaching, for reproof, for correction, and for training in righteousness, that the man of God may be complete, equipped for every good work" (2 Timothy 3:16-17, ESV). Thus, Scripture—inspired by the Holy Spirit—is central to our discernment process, equipping us to make God-centered choices.

The Holy Spirit, Scripture, and Action: The Triad of Discernment

The role of the Holy Spirit in discernment does not eliminate our responsibility for action. The Spirit's guidance comes through understanding and applying Scripture, and this requires diligent study, prayer, meditation, and thoughtful application.

James calls for this action-oriented response in our pursuit of wisdom, which is essentially the exercise of discernment: "But be doers of the word, and not hearers only, deceiving yourselves" (James 1:22, ESV). Being "doers of the word" implies taking action based on the understanding and application of Scripture, not on mystical impressions or subjective feelings.

Conclusion: Embracing the Spirit's Role in Discernment through Scripture

In conclusion, the Holy Spirit's role in discernment is intrinsically linked to the Scriptures. The Spirit, as the divine inspirer of Scripture, provides guidance and wisdom through the Word. Consequently, discernment does not come from seeking subjective leadings from the Spirit but from diligently studying and rightly applying the Spirit-inspired Scriptures.

As we engage with Scripture and apply its teachings to our lives, we effectively tap into the Holy Spirit's guidance in discernment, enabling us to make God-centered choices. This understanding of the Spirit's role underscores the significance of Scripture in our discernment process and reaffirms our commitment to the authority, inerrancy, and sufficiency of the Spirit-inspired Scriptures.

Case Studies: Discernment in Action in the Bible

The Bible provides a wealth of examples demonstrating discernment in action. The stories of Joseph, Solomon, Daniel, and Paul all provide valuable insights into how discernment, as informed by the Holy Spirit-inspired Scriptures, shapes our choices and actions.

Joseph: Discernment Amidst Hardship

Joseph's story, found in Genesis 37-50, is one of discernment amidst hardship. Despite being sold into slavery by his brothers, Joseph did not allow his circumstances to govern his decisions. Instead, he made God-centered choices, guided by the principles he had learned from his forefathers.

Joseph's discernment shines when he resists the advances of Potipar's wife, saying, "How then can I do this great wickedness, and sin against God?" (Genesis 39:9, ASV). Joseph's clear recognition of God's law and his allegiance to it showcase his discernment, leading him to resist temptation even at the cost of being falsely accused.

Solomon: Request for Discernment

King Solomon's story in 1 Kings 3 highlights the importance of seeking discernment. When God appeared to Solomon in a dream and offered him anything he asked for, Solomon requested discernment. He prayed, "Give thy servant therefore an understanding heart to judge thy people, that I may discern between good and evil" (1 Kings 3:9, ASV). God was pleased with this request and granted Solomon extraordinary wisdom and discernment, which he used to rule God's people.

Daniel: Discernment and Conviction

In the book of Daniel, we see Daniel's discernment guiding his actions amidst a hostile foreign culture. When commanded to eat food from the king's table, which would have violated Jewish dietary laws, Daniel chose to obey God's law instead. He "resolved that he would not defile himself with the king's food, or with the wine that he drank" (Daniel 1:8, ESV). His discernment, rooted in Scripture, enabled him to make a God-centered choice that honored God and earned him favor with the Babylonian king.

Paul: Discernment in Ministry

The Apostle Paul's life offers another significant example of discernment in action. Guided by the Spirit-inspired Scriptures, Paul was able to discern when to speak and when to be silent, when to stay, and when to move on. He counseled the churches, corrected false teachings, and made strategic decisions about his missionary journeys based on his discernment of Scripture. For instance, his decision to go to Macedonia instead of Asia during his second missionary journey was informed by a vision (Acts 16:9-10, ESV), interpreted and applied in light of God's revealed Word.

Conclusion: Learning from Biblical Examples of Discernment

These biblical case studies exemplify how discernment, informed by the Holy Spirit-inspired Scriptures, influences our choices and actions. Joseph's, Solomon's, Daniel's, and Paul's decisions were not based on personal preference or circumstances, but on God's Word. Their stories underscore the importance of saturating our minds with Scripture and applying it correctly to make God-centered decisions.

In conclusion, practicing the art of discernment involves a commitment to Scripture, a heart for God's will, and the courage to apply God's Word to our lives. As we study these biblical examples and apply their lessons to our lives, we too can grow in our ability to make God-centered choices. This is the essence of discernment in action in the Bible, and it continues to be relevant for our Christian walk today.

Cultivating Discernment: Practical Steps for Developing this Skill

Discernment, as we've seen, is an essential aspect of the Christian life, enabling us to make God-centered decisions. The Bible is our primary source of wisdom, and through it, we learn to discern God's will. But how do we cultivate this vital skill? Here are some practical steps based on the teachings of the Holy Spirit-inspired Scriptures.

1. Immersing Ourselves in God's Word

The first and foremost step in cultivating discernment is immersing ourselves in the Scriptures. As the Psalmist declares, "Thy word is a lamp unto my feet, and light unto my path" (Psalm 119:105, ASV). The Word of God provides guidance, clarity, and illumination. It helps us discern between right and wrong, good and evil, truth and falsehood.

Therefore, we should strive to read, study, and meditate on the Bible regularly. We should also seek to understand its context, interpret it correctly, and apply it appropriately to our lives. Only by regularly engaging with the Scriptures can we develop and deepen our discernment.

2. Engaging in Constant Prayer

Prayer is an essential discipline in the Christian life. It is through prayer that we communicate with God, seek His wisdom, and express our desire to align our will with His. The Apostle Paul instructs us to "pray without ceasing" (1 Thessalonians 5:17, ESV). Continuous prayer helps us stay connected with God and remain receptive to His guidance. It also enables us to submit our decisions to God, seeking His discernment in all matters.

3. Cultivating a Humble and Teachable Spirit

Humility is crucial in cultivating discernment. Being humble means acknowledging our limitations and recognizing our dependence on God for wisdom. Solomon, when asked what he desired, humbly acknowledged his need for God's wisdom to lead the people of Israel (1 Kings 3:7-9, ASV). Similarly, we should approach God with humility, acknowledging our need for His wisdom and guidance.

Having a teachable spirit goes hand in hand with humility. It involves being open to correction and willing to learn from the Word of God and the wisdom of others. As Proverbs 12:15 (ESV) reminds us, "The way of a fool is right in his own eyes, but a wise man listens to advice."

4. Practicing Discernment in Community

The Christian life is not meant to be lived in isolation. We are part of the body of Christ, and we can benefit from the collective wisdom and discernment of our Christian community. Engaging in regular fellowship, participating in Bible study groups, and seeking counsel from mature believers can help us sharpen our discernment. As Proverbs 15:22 (ESV) states, "Without counsel plans fail, but with many advisers, they succeed."

5. Exercising Discernment in Everyday Decisions

Lastly, we cultivate discernment by exercising it in our everyday decisions. Each choice we make, no matter how small, is an opportunity to practice discernment. As we make a conscious effort to align our decisions with God's Word and submit them to Him in prayer, we will grow in our ability to discern His will.

Conclusion: A Lifelong Pursuit of Discernment

Cultivating discernment is a lifelong pursuit. It requires ongoing engagement with the Scriptures, continuous prayer, a humble and teachable spirit, the support of a Christian community, and the practice of making God-centered decisions. As we persist in these practices, we will grow in our ability to discern God's will and make choices that glorify Him.

Let us remember the words of Hebrews 5:14 (ESV), which state, "But solid food is for the mature, for those who have their powers of discernment trained by constant practice to distinguish good from evil." May we strive to be mature believers, ever growing in our ability to discern and always seeking to align our lives with God's Word.

Discernment and Modern Challenges: Navigating Today's World

Discernment, the ability to make God-centered choices, is an essential skill for the modern Christian. Our contemporary world presents us with myriad challenges, some unique to our time and others as old as humanity itself. This section will explore how discernment can help us navigate these challenges in a manner that aligns with God's Word.

Secularization and the Pluralism Challenge

We live in an increasingly secularized society, where religious perspectives often take a backseat to secular ideologies. Pluralism, the idea that all belief systems are equally valid, has become a defining characteristic of the contemporary world. However, the Scripture offers a different viewpoint. Jesus declared, "I am the way, and the truth, and the life. No one comes to the Father except through me" (John 14:6, ESV). As Christians, we are called to affirm this exclusivity of Christ amidst a pluralistic society. Discernment enables us to hold firm to our faith and navigate through secular ideologies while respecting others' beliefs.

Media Influence and the Truth Challenge

Our world is inundated with information from various media sources, which often present conflicting messages about truth and morality. With fake news, distorted narratives, and relativism, discerning truth can be challenging. However, the Scriptures provide us with a solid standard for truth. Jesus prayed to God the Father, "Sanctify them in the truth; your word is truth" (John 17:17, ESV). Through discernment, we can filter the information we consume, testing everything against the standard of God's Word and holding fast to what is good (1 Thessalonians 5:21, ESV).

Technological Advances and the Ethical Challenge

Technological advances, from bioengineering to artificial intelligence, pose complex ethical questions. Discernment is crucial in navigating these ethical quandaries. The Bible may not explicitly address every modern ethical issue, but its teachings provide a framework for ethical decision-making. For instance, the Scripture's affirmation of the inherent dignity of human life (Genesis 1:27, ASV) can guide our responses to bioethical challenges.

Relativism and the Moral Challenge

Relativism, the belief that moral truths are subjective and vary from person to person, is prevalent today. However, the Scriptures provide us with objective moral standards. Through discernment, we can uphold these standards amidst relativistic trends. As the Apostle Paul wrote, "Do not be conformed to this world, but be transformed by the renewal of your mind, that by testing you may discern what is the will of God, what is good and acceptable and perfect" (Romans 12:2, ESV).

Consumerism and the Contentment Challenge

Consumerism, with its emphasis on material acquisition, can lead us away from godly contentment. The Scriptures remind us that "godliness with contentment is great gain" (1 Timothy 6:6, ESV). Discernment helps us resist consumeristic temptations and find satisfaction in God.

Conclusion: Discernment for the Modern Christian

Our modern world, with its myriad challenges, makes the art of discernment more important than ever for Christians. Despite the complexities we face, the Bible, as the inspired, inerrant Word of God, remains our primary guide. Through consistent engagement with the Scriptures, prayer, humility, community, and practice, we can cultivate discernment to navigate today's world in a manner that glorifies God. The Holy Spirit-inspired words guide us when we have a correct understanding of them and apply them in a balanced manner. In this way, we can live out the command of Proverbs 3:5-6 (ASV), "Trust in Jehovah with all thy heart, And lean not upon thine own understanding: In all thy ways acknowledge him, And he will direct thy paths."

The Pitfalls: Avoiding Misinterpretation and Misdirection

The journey towards discernment, making God-centered choices, is fraught with potential pitfalls. These challenges often come in the form of misinterpretation of Scripture and misdirection in application. It is crucial to understand these challenges to safeguard ourselves and continue to walk on God's path.

Misinterpretation of Scripture

The Bible, as the inspired, inerrant Word of God, is our primary source of truth. However, the complexity and depth of Scripture, as well as our inherent limitations, can sometimes lead to misinterpretation.

A common misinterpretation error is proof-texting, the practice of using isolated, out-of-context Bible verses to support a particular viewpoint. For instance, Jeremiah 29:11 (ESV) is often cited to suggest a guaranteed life of prosperity: "For I know the plans I have for you, declares the Lord, plans for welfare and not for evil, to give you a future and a hope." However, in its historical and literary context, this verse speaks to Israel's deliverance from Babylonian captivity, not to personal prosperity.

To avoid this pitfall, we need to practice hermeneutics, the art and science of interpreting the Bible. Hermeneutics involves reading Bible passages in their context and considering their literary, historical, and cultural background. It also means understanding that the Bible, while having personal applications, is not primarily about us but about God and His redemption plan through Jesus Christ.

Misdirection in Application

The Holy Spirit-inspired words guide us in understanding the Bible and making God-centered decisions. However, this doesn't mean that the Spirit will miraculously direct our decisions. We don't receive divine revelation by simply praying for an answer. We must act on behalf of our prayers.

A misdirection error often occurs when we seek discernment apart from the counsel of the Christian community. God has given us fellow believers to provide wisdom, encouragement, and correction. The book of Proverbs repeatedly emphasizes the value of counsel in decision-making. For example, Proverbs 15:22 (ASV) declares, "Where no counsel is, the people fall; But in the multitude of counsellors there is safety."

To steer clear of this pitfall, we must value and seek the wisdom of mature, godly Christians. Their experiences and insights can help us avoid errors and see things from a broader, biblical perspective.

Conclusion: Guarding against Misinterpretation and Misdirection

As we navigate our journey of discernment, guarding against misinterpretation and misdirection is critical. By practicing good hermeneutics and seeking godly counsel, we can avoid these pitfalls and make decisions that honor God.

In the face of these potential pitfalls, the Apostle Paul's prayer for the Philippians remains our guide: "And it is my prayer that your love may abound more and more, with knowledge and all discernment, so that you may approve what is excellent, and so be pure and blameless for the day of Christ, filled with the fruit of righteousness that comes through Jesus Christ, to the glory and praise of God" (Philippians 1:9-11, ESV). As we rely on the Holy Spirit-inspired words and apply them in a balanced manner, we cultivate the art of discernment, making God-centered choices that bring glory to Him.

Discernment in Community: The Role of Fellowship

In the quest for spiritual discernment—making God-centered decisions—one cannot overlook the vital role that Christian fellowship plays. Throughout Scripture, we see that discernment is not an isolated activity but is significantly cultivated and enhanced within the community of believers. It is within this context of shared faith, wisdom, and experiences that discernment becomes a practiced skill.

Biblical Foundations of Fellowship and Discernment

The essence of Christian fellowship lies in shared commitment to Christ, mutual edification, and collective pursuit of understanding God's will. In the book of Acts, the early Christian community is described as devoting themselves to the apostles' teaching and fellowship, breaking of bread, and prayers (Acts 2:42, ESV). This passage illuminates the model of community where shared learning, mutual encouragement, and corporate prayer became the soil where discernment could thrive.

The Bible repeatedly emphasizes the importance of seeking wisdom from others. Proverbs 15:22 (ASV) says, "Where no counsel is, the people fall; But in the multitude of counselors there is safety." This counsel is sought not from any source but from those who fear the Lord and keep his commands, as Psalms 111:10 (ESV) advises, "The fear of the LORD is the beginning of wisdom; all those who practice it have a good understanding."

The Function of Fellowship in Enhancing Discernment

In a Christian community, members bring a diverse range of experiences, gifts, and perspectives. This diversity contributes to a collective wisdom that can aid in making sound, God-centered decisions. When we invite others into our decision-making process, we open ourselves to insights that we might otherwise miss.

Fellowship also provides a safety net against the pitfalls of misunderstanding Scripture and misapplying it. By discussing and studying the Bible collectively, we can better grasp its context, intended meaning, and application.

Moreover, fellowship cultivates accountability, which is crucial in developing discernment. When we make decisions within a community context, we expose our thoughts and intentions to the scrutiny of others. This encourages us to align our decisions with God's Word and maintain our commitment to live righteously.

Practical Steps for Cultivating Discernment in Fellowship

1. **Participate actively in a local church**: Regular involvement in a church community provides ample opportunities to learn from the collective wisdom of its members.

2. **Engage in small group Bible studies**: In these settings, you can dive deeper into Scripture and benefit from diverse insights, interpretations, and applications of the Word.

3. **Seek wise counsel**: When faced with important decisions, seek the advice of mature, godly Christians who have a track record of sound, biblically-based discernment.

4. **Pray with others**: Corporate prayer invites the collective wisdom of the community and acknowledges our dependence on God for discernment.

Conclusion: The Intersection of Discernment and Community

In summary, the journey towards discernment is not a solitary one. It requires active participation in a community of believers, drawing from collective wisdom, and upholding mutual accountability. As we navigate the complexities of life, the fellowship of believers provides a robust framework that nurtures our ability to make God-centered choices. As Proverbs 27:17 (ESV) reminds us, "Iron sharpens iron, and one man sharpens another." In our quest for discernment, we can rely on our Christian community to keep us sharp, focused, and grounded on the Word of God.

The Lifelong Practice of Discernment

Discernment is not a one-time event, a momentary insight, or a fleeting revelation. Rather, it is a lifelong journey, an ongoing process that deepens our understanding of God's will, sharpens our spiritual senses, and aligns our choices and actions with the divine plan. This chapter will explore the lifelong practice of discernment in depth, examining its progressive nature, the importance of consistent spiritual exercises, the role of growth and maturity, and the ultimate goal of this continuous endeavor.

The Progressive Nature of Discernment

Discernment, like any other spiritual discipline, is progressive in nature. The deeper we delve into the Word of God, the more we comprehend its truths, and the better we become at applying these truths in decision-making. Hebrews 5:14 (ESV) points out, "But solid food is for the mature, for those who have their powers of discernment trained by constant practice to distinguish good from evil."

This verse highlights two key elements in the lifelong practice of discernment. First, it emphasizes maturity, which comes with time, experience, and spiritual growth. Second, it underscores the role of "constant practice" in training our discernment. This leads us to the next important aspect: spiritual exercises.

Spiritual Exercises for Discerning

Just as physical fitness requires regular exercise, spiritual discernment needs consistent spiritual disciplines. These include:

1. **Daily Bible study and meditation**: Psalm 1:2 (ASV) says, "But his delight is in the law of Jehovah; And on his law doth he meditate day and night." Consistent engagement with the Scriptures enables us to understand God's will and align our choices with it.

2. **Prayer**: It is not a means of manipulating God but a way to align our will with His. Prayer fosters humility and dependence on God, which are crucial for discernment.

3. **Fellowship and accountability**: As discussed in the previous section, Christian community plays a significant role in honing our discernment. As we share, learn, and pray together, our collective wisdom grows.

The Role of Growth and Maturity

As Christians mature in their faith, their discernment should also grow. This growth process involves refining our understanding of God's Word, deepening our prayer life, and nurturing our relationship with fellow believers. It also requires humility to acknowledge when we err, the courage to correct our mistakes, and the willingness to learn from these experiences.

In Philippians 1:9-10 (ESV), Paul prays that the believers' love "may abound more and more, with knowledge and all discernment, so that you may approve what is excellent." This implies a growth and development in discernment, which comes with an increase in knowledge and deepening love.

The Ultimate Goal of Lifelong Discernment

The ultimate goal of our lifelong journey of discernment is to grow closer to God, to conform more and more to Christ's image, and to align our lives with His will. The practice of discernment is ultimately not about making the "right" decisions but about becoming the right kind of people—those who seek God's will above all and strive to live according to it.

Conclusion: Embracing the Journey

In conclusion, the art of discernment is a lifelong practice. It's a journey that takes us deeper into God's heart, reshapes our desires and decisions according to His will, and ultimately, transforms us into Christ's likeness. By understanding its progressive nature, maintaining consistent spiritual exercises, appreciating the role of growth and maturity, and focusing on the ultimate goal, we can embrace discernment as a vital part of our spiritual journey. As we do, we can look forward to the promise in Romans 12:2 (ESV), "Do not be conformed to this world, but be transformed by the renewal of your mind, that by testing you may discern what is the will of God, what is good and acceptable and perfect." This is the lifelong journey and the joy of discernment.

CHAPTER 10 Walking in Obedience: Following God's Will in Our Daily Lives

Introduction: Understanding Obedience in a Christian Context

Obedience, in the context of Christianity, is much more than adherence to a set of rules. It's about a relationship with God, expressed in living according to His will. It is about aligning our hearts, minds, and actions with His divine purpose and plan. This chapter explores obedience in depth, opening the door to a richer understanding of how obedience shapes our daily lives and molds us more closely into the image of Christ.

Obedience: Not a Burden, but a Blessing

In the broader culture, obedience may often be seen as a burden, a restriction on freedom. However, in a Christian context, obedience is a blessing. It's the path to true freedom, a profound expression of love, and a channel of divine blessing. As we read in John 14:15 (ESV), Jesus says, "If you love me, you will keep my commandments." This verse underscores that obedience is a heartfelt response to God's love, not a burdensome obligation.

In the book of Deuteronomy, we see a beautiful encapsulation of obedience as a channel of blessing. In Deuteronomy 28:1 (ASV), Moses communicates God's promise to Israel: "And it shall come to pass, if thou shalt hearken diligently unto the voice of Jehovah thy God, to observe to do all his commandments which I command thee this day, that Jehovah thy God will set thee on high above all the nations of the earth."

Obedience: Aligning with God's Will

Obedience is about aligning our will with God's will. This goes beyond mere compliance to His commands; it involves conforming our desires, attitudes, and values to His. As Romans 12:2 (ESV) instructs, "Do not be conformed to this world, but be transformed by the renewal of your mind, that by testing you may discern what is the will of God, what is good and acceptable and perfect."

When our will aligns with God's, obedience becomes a joy rather than a chore. It's not about what we "must" do, but what we "get" to do in response to His love and grace.

Obedience: An Outflow of Faith

True obedience springs from faith. It is a tangible demonstration of our trust in God's wisdom, goodness, and love. The author of Hebrews highlights this connection in Hebrews 11:8 (ESV): "By faith Abraham obeyed when he was called to go out to a place that he was to receive as an inheritance. And he went out, not knowing where he was going." Abraham's obedience was an act of faith, a trust in God's promises and plan.

Conclusion: Obedience as a Lifelong Journey

As we embark on this exploration of obedience, let's remember that it is a lifelong journey. It's about growth, transformation, and a deepening relationship with God. It's about learning to walk step by step, moment by moment, in alignment with His will. It's about experiencing the freedom and joy that come from living in sync with our Creator.

As we progress through this chapter, we will delve deeper into the practicalities of walking in obedience, the challenges that may arise, and how to navigate them. We will examine how obedience shapes our daily lives and how it molds us more closely into the image of Christ. Let us journey together in this exploration, and in doing so, draw closer to the heart of God.

Biblical Perspective on Obedience: Lessons from Scripture

To comprehend obedience in its fullness, we need to explore its biblical context. By studying the examples of obedience in the Bible, we can glean insights that help us understand what it means to live in obedience to God's will. Scripture does not shy away from showcasing both triumphs and failures in obedience, offering us profound lessons about its implications in our lives.

Lessons from the Old Testament

The Old Testament offers profound lessons on obedience through the narratives of individuals and the nation of Israel. Consider Abraham, a quintessential model of obedience. In Genesis 12:1-4 (ASV), God tells Abraham to leave his country, his people, and his father's household and go to the land God will show him. Abraham obeys without question, setting a benchmark for trust and obedience to God.

The Israelites' journey from Egypt to Canaan also offers several lessons. In Deuteronomy 28, God sets before them a clear choice: blessings for obedience and curses for disobedience. Sadly, the Israelites' history is marked by cycles of obedience, disobedience, punishment, repentance, and restoration. This pattern underscores that obedience brings blessings, while disobedience leads to adversity.

Abraham: Obedience Through Faith

Abraham's obedience to God, as shown in Genesis 22:1-19 (ASV), offers one of the most compelling examples in Scripture. Abraham's willingness to sacrifice his son Isaac demonstrated his faith and complete obedience to God. The account is not just about Abraham's willingness to give up his son, but also his unwavering faith in God's promises.

God had promised Abraham that Isaac would carry on his lineage, yet now God commanded Abraham to sacrifice this same son. Even in this seeming contradiction, Abraham trusted God, demonstrating obedience rooted in profound faith. This faith was rewarded, as the angel of the Lord stopped Abraham from sacrificing Isaac and reiterated the blessings God had promised him.

Jonah: The Consequences of Disobedience and the Blessings of Obedience

The story of Jonah, as detailed in the book of Jonah (ASV), showcases the consequences of disobedience and the blessings of obedience. Jonah initially fled from God's command to go to Nineveh, resulting in a storm and his being swallowed by a great fish. Yet, when Jonah repented and obeyed God, he was delivered from the fish, and his preaching led to the repentance of Nineveh, a city notorious for its wickedness.

Jonah's story serves as a stark reminder that while disobedience leads to unfavorable consequences, obedience, even after initial disobedience, can lead to forgiveness and God's blessing.

Lessons from the New Testament

In the New Testament, the theme of obedience reaches its zenith in the person and work of Jesus Christ. The most profound demonstration of obedience is found in Philippians 2:8 (ESV), "And being found in human form, he humbled himself by becoming obedient to the point of death, even death on a cross." Jesus' obedience to the Father, even unto death, epitomizes the sacrificial nature of obedience and establishes the basis for our salvation.

Paul's letters also emphasize obedience, tying it directly to faith. In Romans 1:5 (ESV), he mentions the "obedience that comes from faith" as a fundamental aspect of the Christian experience. Here, Paul establishes that true faith naturally results in obedience.

Jesus: Perfect Obedience and Sacrificial Love

Jesus Christ provides the perfect model of obedience. His life was a testimony of complete alignment with God's will. A critical point of Jesus' obedience is recorded in Matthew 26:39 (ESV) when he prayed, "My Father, if it be possible, let this cup pass from me; nevertheless, not as I will, but as you will."

In this agonizing moment, facing the prospect of the cross, Jesus chose obedience to God's will over His desire to avoid suffering. His obedience led to the ultimate sacrifice, opening the path for our redemption. Jesus' obedience is a model for us, a call to surrender our will to God, trusting His wisdom and goodness even in the midst of hardship and suffering.

The Early Church: Obedience in Community

The book of Acts showcases the obedience of the early Christian community. They devoted themselves to the apostles' teaching, fellowship, breaking of bread, and prayers (Acts 2:42, ESV). Despite facing severe persecution, they continued to obey God's command to spread the gospel, resulting in the growth of the church.

This obedience in community underscores the importance of mutual encouragement and accountability in living out God's commands. As we obey God collectively, we strengthen our resolve and extend God's kingdom.

Obedience and God's Law

Understanding obedience in a biblical context also requires considering God's Law. Psalm 119 is a remarkable celebration of God's Law, depicting it as a source of wisdom, guidance, and joy. The psalmist's delight in God's Law, reflected in verses like Psalm 119:97 (ASV), "Oh how love I thy law! It is my meditation all the day," portrays obedience as a joyful commitment, not a burdensome obligation.

Conclusion: Obedience as Response to God's Love

Across both Testaments, obedience is consistently presented as a response to God's love, grace, and covenant faithfulness. It is not a means to earn God's favor but a response to the favor He has already bestowed upon us in Christ. It is our loving response to His initiative of grace.

These lessons from Scripture offer a comprehensive view of obedience, highlighting its significance and implications in our Christian walk. Obedience, as revealed in the Bible, is an integral part of our relationship with God, shaping our character, guiding our decisions, and enabling us to experience the fullness of God's blessings. As we seek to walk in obedience, may we draw from these biblical insights, trusting that our journey will lead us closer to God's heart.

These biblical examples paint a vivid picture of obedience. They show us that obedience is a faith-driven, will-surrendering response to God's love and authority. It is not always easy or comfortable, but it is always rewarding. As we strive to walk in obedience, let's remember that it's a process, a journey. We will stumble, but we can find grace in our failures and strength in God's unchanging love for us.

The Link Between Love and Obedience: Understanding the Connection

As we navigate the journey of Christian life, a pivotal principle emerges from the teachings of Jesus Christ and His Apostles - the profound link between love and obedience. Unraveling this connection is critical for understanding and living out the Christian faith.

Christ's Teachings on Love and Obedience

Jesus emphasized the correlation between love for Him and obedience to His commandments. In John 14:15 (ESV), He declares, "If you love me, you will keep my commandments." He reiterates this in John 14:21 (ESV), "Whoever has my commandments and keeps them, he it is who loves me." From these passages, it is clear that love for Christ is manifest in obedience to His teachings. Our adherence to His commandments is not merely a sign of respect or compliance, but a profound demonstration of our love for Him.

Obedience as a Measure of Love

By linking love and obedience, Jesus presents the latter as a measure of the former. The extent of our obedience reflects the depth of our love for Him. It also emphasizes that love, in the Christian context, is not a passive feeling but an active commitment. It involves aligning our will with God's and consciously choosing to obey His commandments.

Love-Driven Obedience versus Legalism

A critical distinction must be made here - this call to obedience is not an endorsement of legalism. Legalism prioritizes strict adherence to the law over a relationship with God, often fostering self-righteousness and judgmental attitudes. Conversely, love-driven obedience springs from a heartfelt desire to please God, born out of our relationship with Him.

In contrast to legalism, love-driven obedience is not about earning God's favor but responding to His grace. Ephesians 2:8-9 (ESV) underscores that we are saved by grace, not by works, preventing anyone from boasting about their actions. Obedience, therefore, is not the means of our salvation but the evidence of it.

The Role of the Holy Spirit

While the Holy Spirit does not miraculously indwell us to guide our understanding of the Bible and decision-making, the Spirit-inspired words do serve as our guide. In John 14:26 (ESV), Jesus promised that the Holy Spirit would teach His disciples all things and remind them of everything He had said to them. When we have a correct understanding of the Bible and apply it in a balanced manner, these Spirit-inspired words lead us in love-driven obedience.

The Apostles on Love and Obedience

The Apostles, too, emphasized this connection between love and obedience. 1 John 5:3 (ESV) states, "For this is the love of God, that we keep his commandments. And his commandments are not burdensome." The Apostle John here confirms that obedience is a manifestation of our love for God and dismisses the notion that God's commandments are a burden. Instead, he suggests that love makes obedience a joy and a delight.

The Lifelong Journey of Love and Obedience

The link between love and obedience is not a one-time event but a lifelong journey. As our relationship with God deepens, our understanding of His love for us grows, and so should our commitment to obeying His commands. It's a dynamic, growing process where love fuels obedience, and obedience deepens love, bringing us closer to God and transforming us into the likeness of Christ.

In conclusion, understanding the connection between love and obedience is fundamental to our Christian walk. It shapes our perspective on God's commandments, informs our response to His grace, and defines our relationship with Him. By embracing this principle, we can better align ourselves with God's will and experience the joy and peace that come from walking in obedience out of love for Him.

Obedience in Practice: Applying God's Will in Daily Life

In the journey of faith, understanding the importance of obedience and its connection with love is one thing; translating it into practice is another. Practical application of obedience can appear challenging, but through a diligent and balanced understanding of the Holy Spirit-inspired words, we can navigate our daily lives by the guiding light of God's will.

Imbibing the Word of God

Central to obeying God is imbibing His Word, the Bible, into our daily lives. The Bible, the infallible, inerrant Word of God, should not merely be read; it should be studied, meditated upon, and applied. Psalm 119:105 (ASV) states, "Thy word is a lamp unto my feet, And light unto my path." The Word of God provides the much-needed wisdom and guidance for making decisions in line with God's will.

Prayer and God's Will

Prayer is another essential tool in our quest to align with God's will. It is not about requesting God to align with our will but rather, as seen in the Lord's Prayer, it is about aligning our will with God's: "Your will be done, on earth as it is in heaven" (Matthew 6:10, ESV). Prayer is not a spiritual slot machine to receive what we want but a means to seek guidance, strength, and peace as we navigate life's complexities.

Acting Out of Love, Not Legalism

As previously discussed, obedience out of love for God is entirely different from legalism. Our obedience should stem from our love for God, an outflow of our relationship with Him, rather than a means to earn His favor or avoid His wrath. John 14:15 (ESV) succinctly encapsulates this concept: "If you love me, you will keep my commandments."

Dealing with Life's Challenges

Inevitably, challenges will come our way, and the Bible does not promise a trouble-free life. In these moments, our obedience will be tested, and we must be steadfast. James 1:12 (ESV) encourages, "Blessed is the man who remains steadfast under trial, for when he has stood the test he will receive the crown of life, which God has promised to those who love him." Remember, we obey because we love God, and our love for Him helps us persevere during trials.

Interacting with Others

The concept of obedience also extends to how we interact with others. In Matthew 22:39 (ESV), Jesus instructs, "You shall love your neighbor as yourself." Obedience to this command manifests in our actions and attitudes toward others. We are called to exhibit Christlike love in all our relationships, whether with family, friends, colleagues, or strangers.

Walking the Path of Obedience

Walking the path of obedience is a continuous journey, not a destination. It involves regular self-examination, repentance, and realignment with God's will. We grow in obedience as we mature in our faith, understanding more deeply God's love for us and expressing our love for Him through our actions.

The Blessings of Obedience

Though obedience is not a means to earn God's favor or salvation, it is associated with blessings. As Deuteronomy 28:2 (ASV) promises, "And all these blessings shall come upon thee, and overtake thee, if thou shalt hearken unto the voice of Jehovah thy God." These blessings are not necessarily material but include peace, joy, fulfillment, and a deeper relationship with God.

In conclusion, applying God's will in daily life involves diligent study of His Word, prayer, loving obedience rather than legalistic compliance, perseverance in trials, love towards others, and continual growth in faith. Obedience in practice is a holistic concept that touches every aspect of our lives. It's a lifelong journey of walking in God's will, led by love, resulting in a blessed life rooted in the peace and joy of God.

Case Studies: Examples of Obedience in Biblical Characters

As we seek to walk in obedience to God, it's often helpful to study examples of those who've gone before us. In this section, we will examine the lives of three biblical figures: Noah, Daniel, and Mary, the mother of Jesus, who have modeled obedience in their daily lives.

Noah: Obedience in the Face of the Impossible

Noah stands as a towering figure of obedience in biblical history. In Genesis 6:9 (ASV), Noah is described as "a righteous man, blameless in his generation. Noah walked with God." Despite living in an exceedingly wicked generation, Noah maintained his righteousness by living in obedience to God.

God commanded Noah to build an ark, a task that seemed absurd and impossible. The dimensions of the ark were enormous, the task was daunting, and the ridicule from his contemporaries must have been immense, as rain had never been seen before. Yet, Noah obeyed. Genesis 6:22 (ASV) records, "Thus did Noah; according to all that God commanded him, so did he."

From Noah, we learn that obedience may sometimes require us to do things that seem impossible or are ridiculed by others. However, like Noah, we must remain steadfast and obey, trusting in God's plan and provision.

Daniel: Obedience Amid Adversity

The life of Daniel exemplifies obedience in the face of adversity. Daniel was a young Israelite taken captive to Babylon, a foreign land with a culture and practices vastly different from his own. Yet, he resolved not to defile himself with the king's food and wine, choosing to obey God's law above the king's command (Daniel 1:8, ESV).

Furthermore, when King Darius issued a decree that for thirty days, anyone who petitioned any god or man except him would be thrown into the lions' den, Daniel, aware of the decree, continued to pray to God as he had always done (Daniel 6:10, ESV). His obedience led him into the lions' den, but God delivered him.

Daniel's obedience teaches us that even in the face of adversity and potentially dire consequences, choosing to obey God over conforming to societal pressures or unjust laws is the path to true deliverance and victory.

Mary: Obedience to God's Calling

Mary, the mother of Jesus, displayed remarkable obedience when she accepted the call to become the mother of the Savior. Luke 1:38 (ESV) records her response to the angel Gabriel's announcement, "Behold, I am the servant of the Lord; let it be to me according to your word." Mary was a young, unmarried woman, and the consequences of becoming pregnant under such circumstances were severe. Yet, she obediently accepted God's will.

Mary's obedience underscores the importance of surrendering our plans to God, even when His plans seem inconvenient, difficult, or contrary to societal norms. True obedience means trusting God's plan and submitting to His will above our own.

In conclusion, the lives of Noah, Daniel, and Mary vividly demonstrate that obedience to God often challenges societal norms, personal convenience, and even logic. Yet, they also illustrate the extraordinary blessings that flow from obedience. By studying these examples, we can learn to walk in obedience, trusting God's sovereignty, and His perfect plan for our lives.

The Challenges of Obedience: Recognizing and Overcoming Obstacles

Walking in obedience to God's will is not always straightforward. It is a journey often marred with various challenges. This section explores these challenges and provides biblical guidance on how to overcome them.

Challenge 1: The Battle Against Self-Will

Perhaps the most pervasive obstacle to obedience is our self-will. This encompasses our personal desires, ambitions, and perceptions that often conflict with God's commands. In his epistle, James warns, "Each person is tempted when he is lured and enticed by his own desire" (James 1:14, ESV).

Overcoming the obstacle of self-will requires a heart of humility and submission. Just as Christ "humbled himself by becoming obedient to the point of death, even death on a cross" (Philippians 2:8, ESV), we are called to surrender our will to God's will. This surrender may entail giving up our personal desires, ambitions, or comforts for the sake of obeying God.

Challenge 2: The Lure of Worldly Values

We live in a world that often promotes values contrary to God's commandments. The apostle John cautions us, "Do not love the world or the things in the world. If anyone loves the world, the love of the Father is not in him" (1 John 2:15, ESV). Worldly values such as materialism, pride, self-reliance, and moral relativity can easily divert us from the path of obedience.

To overcome the lure of worldly values, we need to be transformed by the renewal of our minds (Romans 12:2, ESV), immersing ourselves in God's Word and aligning our values with His. The Psalmist declares, "I have stored up your word in my heart, that I might not sin against you" (Psalm 119:11, ESV). God's Word provides the moral compass to navigate the enticing allure of worldly values.

Challenge 3: Fear and Doubt

Fear and doubt are other significant barriers to obedience. We might fear the repercussions of obedience, or doubt whether we have accurately discerned God's will. When Moses was called by God to lead the Israelites out of Egypt, he expressed his doubts and fears, questioning his ability to carry out the task (Exodus 3:11, ASV).

To conquer fear and doubt, we must trust in God's sovereignty and His good purposes for us. The prophet Isaiah provides comforting assurance, "Fear not, for I am with you; be not dismayed, for I am your

God; I will strengthen you, I will help you, I will uphold you with my righteous right hand" (Isaiah 41:10, ESV).

Challenge 4: The Cost of Obedience

Obedience can be costly. It may entail losing friendships, facing persecution, or sacrificing personal comfort. Jesus made this clear when He said, "If anyone would come after me, let him deny himself and take up his cross daily and follow me" (Luke 9:23, ESV).

The cost of obedience can be overwhelming. Yet, we must remember the promise of Jesus, who said, "Everyone who has left houses or brothers or sisters or father or mother or children or lands, for my name's sake, will receive a hundredfold and will inherit eternal life" (Matthew 19:29, ESV). The temporal cost of obedience is far outweighed by the eternal reward that awaits us.

In conclusion, walking in obedience involves navigating various challenges, including self-will, worldly values, fear, doubt, and the cost of obedience. Yet, with humility, God's Word, trust in God, and the perspective of eternal rewards, we can overcome these obstacles and align our lives with God's will. As we do so, we come to experience the profound peace and joy that come from knowing we are walking in the path that our loving Father has set before us.

The Role of Discipline in Walking in Obedience

Discipline is paramount in our journey towards walking in obedience to God's will. In the context of spiritual obedience, discipline isn't punishment, but rather the practice of habitual behavior in accordance with God's teachings, a means of cultivating spiritual growth and character.

The Biblical Perspective on Discipline

Scripture holds several insights on the role and significance of discipline in a believer's life. In the book of Proverbs, it is written,

"Whoever loves discipline loves knowledge, but he who hates reproof is stupid" (Proverbs 12:1, ASV). This passage underscores the value of discipline as a way of gaining wisdom, showing its necessity for spiritual growth.

In the New Testament, the apostle Paul likens the Christian life to a race, emphasizing the importance of self-discipline: "Do you not know that in a race all the runners run, but only one receives the prize? So run that you may obtain it. Every athlete exercises self-control in all things. They do it to receive a perishable wreath, but we an imperishable" (1 Corinthians 9:24-25, ESV).

Discipline as a Means to Develop Spiritual Habits

One of the most direct applications of discipline is in the development of spiritual habits. These habits, including prayer, meditation on God's Word, and acts of service, are the building blocks of a life lived in obedience to God.

Prayer, for example, is a habit that requires discipline. Paul encourages us to "pray without ceasing" (1 Thessalonians 5:17, ESV), a command that requires discipline to integrate prayer into every facet of our lives.

Similarly, the regular study and application of God's Word demand discipline. The psalmist describes the blessed man as one who "meditates on [God's] law day and night" (Psalm 1:2, ASV). This meditation is not a sporadic engagement, but a disciplined daily practice.

Discipline and the Cultivation of Godly Character

Beyond fostering spiritual habits, discipline aids in the cultivation of godly character. As Paul points out, "discipline yourself for the purpose of godliness; for bodily discipline is only of little profit, but godliness is profitable for all things" (1 Timothy 4:7-8, ESV).

Discipline aids in the formation of virtues such as patience, kindness, humility, and self-control – qualities that reflect Christ's character. In practicing these virtues, we become more obedient to God's will, as these traits are in accordance with His teachings.

Discipline as a Form of God's Love

Discipline is also an expression of God's love, as seen in Hebrews 12:5-6 (ESV): "And have you forgotten the exhortation that addresses you as sons? 'My son, do not regard lightly the discipline of the Lord, nor be weary when reproved by him. For the Lord disciplines the one he loves, and chastises every son whom he receives.'"

Just as earthly parents correct their children out of love and a desire for their well-being, so too does God discipline His children. This divine discipline, while sometimes painful, is intended to correct and guide us towards the path of obedience.

Discipline and the Freedom of Obedience

Finally, discipline brings freedom. It might seem paradoxical that discipline, which involves adhering to rules, brings freedom. Yet, in the spiritual sense, it does.

Jesus states, "If you abide in my word, you are truly my disciples, and you will know the truth, and the truth will set you free" (John 8:31-32, ESV). Abiding in His word requires discipline, but it brings a freedom unknown to the world – freedom from sin, from the world's demands, and from the pursuit of self-satisfaction.

Discipline is instrumental in walking in obedience to God. It shapes our spiritual habits, refines our character, serves as an expression of God's love, and paves the way to true freedom. As we continually discipline ourselves in the light of God's Word, we align ourselves more with His will, leading to a life that glorifies Him and fulfills our purpose.

Yet, discipline is not a solitary pursuit. It's crucial to understand that it's by God's grace that we are empowered to be disciplined. Relying on our strength leads to legalism, but relying on God's grace leads to a life of joyful obedience.

It is by heeding the Spirit-inspired words in Scripture, understood correctly and applied in a balanced way, that we are guided towards disciplined obedience. As we pray and act in line with our prayers, we grow in discipline and obedience, ever maturing in our faith, living a life that's pleasing to God.

Navigating Times of Doubt: Trusting God's Plan

There's no denying that even the most faithful among us experience times of doubt. Life's trials and tribulations often lead us into a whirlwind of questions, and we may find ourselves grappling with uncertainty about God's plan. During such times, it's essential to remember that doubts do not equate to the absence of faith but can instead serve as catalysts for spiritual growth.

The Nature of Doubt

Doubt is a common human experience, one that does not exclude the realm of spiritual life. Biblical figures themselves, from Moses to Elijah, experienced doubt, showing us that it's not a sign of weak faith but a part of the human condition. It's crucial to remember that God, in His perfect foreknowledge, is aware of our doubts. However, this foreknowledge doesn't dictate our responses; rather, it anticipates what we will freely do.

The Presence of Doubt in Scripture

Doubt is a recurring theme in Scripture, offering reassurance that even those closest to God had their moments of uncertainty. Take Thomas, for example, who doubted the resurrection of Jesus. When told by the other disciples, "We have seen the Lord," he replied, "Unless I see in his hands the mark of the nails, and place my finger into the mark of the nails, and place my hand into his side, I will never believe" (John 20:25, ESV). Yet, when given the proof he needed, Thomas affirmed his faith with the profound declaration, "My Lord and my God!" (John 20:28, ESV).

This instance demonstrates that God can handle our doubts, and they can ultimately lead to deeper faith and understanding.

Understanding God's Plan

God's ways are beyond human understanding, as stated in Isaiah 55:8-9 (ASV), "For my thoughts are not your thoughts, neither are your ways my ways, saith Jehovah. For as the heavens are higher than the earth, so are my ways higher than your ways, and my thoughts than your thoughts." When we face doubts about God's plan, we must remind ourselves of this truth.

God's plan for our lives might not always align with our expectations or desires, but we can trust that it's always for our good and His glory. This is affirmed in Romans 8:28 (ESV), "And we know that for those who love God all things work together for good, for those who are called according to his purpose."

Trusting God Amid Doubt

Trusting God during times of doubt involves surrendering control and allowing God's plan to unfold. Proverbs 3:5-6 (ASV) advises us to "Trust in Jehovah with all thine heart, And lean not upon thine own understanding: In all thy ways acknowledge him, And he will direct thy paths." These verses guide us toward reliance on God, even when His plans appear unclear or confusing to our limited understanding.

Growing Through Doubt

Doubt can foster spiritual growth if handled correctly. When doubts arise, they should lead us back to God's Word, prayer, and the counsel of fellow believers. The Word of God is a reliable anchor during times of uncertainty. Reflecting on God's promises and past faithfulness can help to realign our hearts with trust in His plan.

Moreover, prayer serves as a lifeline in navigating doubt. Philippians 4:6-7 (ESV) encourages, "do not be anxious about anything, but in everything by prayer and supplication with thanksgiving let your requests be made known to God. And the peace of God, which surpasses all understanding, will guard your hearts and your minds in Christ Jesus."

Times of doubt can be challenging, but they also offer opportunities for spiritual growth and deeper understanding. By leaning into God's Word, utilizing prayer, and relying on the Holy Spirit inspired words in Scripture, we can navigate these seasons with resilience. We can grow in our trust of God's plan, finding comfort in His perfect foreknowledge and the truth that, even in doubt, we are loved and guided by an omniscient and gracious God.

The Fruit of Obedience: Blessings and Spiritual Growth

In the Christian life, obedience to God is not merely an obligation but an opportunity to receive blessings and foster spiritual growth. It involves heeding God's Word, pursuing His will, and responding affirmatively to His call on our lives. This section explores the fruit of obedience, highlighting the blessings it bestows and the spiritual growth it catalyzes.

Defining Obedience

Obedience in the Christian context means aligning our will and actions with God's will as revealed in the Bible. It is not a blind or forced compliance but a voluntary and loving response to God's love for us. Our obedience is a testament to our faith and an expression of our love for God.

Blessings of Obedience

Obedience is closely linked with blessings in the Scriptures. Deuteronomy 28:1-2 (ASV) makes it clear: "And it shall come to pass, if thou shalt hearken diligently unto the voice of Jehovah thy God, to observe to do all his commandments which I command thee this day, that Jehovah thy God will set thee on high above all the nations of the earth: and all these blessings shall come upon thee, and overtake thee, if thou shalt hearken unto the voice of Jehovah thy God."

Blessings here may not always be material or physical; instead, they often manifest as inner peace, joy, strength in trials, and a sense of purpose. They may also appear as divine favor, protection, and guidance. However, it's crucial to understand that these blessings are not transactional or contingent on our works alone. Instead, they flow from God's grace and His unconditional love for His children.

Obedience and Spiritual Growth

Spiritual growth is a journey that involves knowing God more deeply, conforming more to the likeness of Christ, and participating more in God's mission. Obedience plays a central role in this process. As we obey God's Word and follow His guidance, we become more attuned to His voice, cultivate deeper faith, and become more Christ-like in character.

In the book of John, Jesus connects obedience to love and a deeper relationship with Him. John 14:23 (ESV) states, "Jesus answered him, 'If anyone loves me, he will keep my word, and my Father will love him, and we will come to him and make our home with him.'" Here, obedience to God's commands is intertwined with a deeper love for God and a deeper communion with Him.

Moreover, spiritual growth is also evident in the fruit of the Spirit. Galatians 5:22-23 (ESV) enumerates these, "But the fruit of the Spirit is love, joy, peace, patience, kindness, goodness, faithfulness, gentleness, self-control; against such things there is no law." As we walk in obedience to God, these qualities become more prominent in our lives, demonstrating spiritual growth.

Living in Obedience

Living in obedience involves constant interaction with the Word of God, the Holy Spirit inspired words that guide us when we correctly understand and apply them. It requires daily surrender, a willingness to lay down our will and desires in favor of God's will. It also involves a heart of humility, recognizing that God's ways and thoughts are higher than ours (Isaiah 55:8-9, ASV).

The fruit of obedience—blessings and spiritual growth—are evident in the lives of those who choose to walk in God's ways. However, the journey of obedience is not always easy. It requires faith, humility, and a love for God that motivates us to align our lives with His Word. Yet, as we walk in obedience, we can expect to see a transformation in our lives, blessings that go beyond our understanding, and a spiritual maturity that brings us closer to the heart of God.

Misinterpretations of Obedience: Avoiding Extremes

In the Christian journey, the importance of obedience to God's will cannot be overstated. However, in our quest to follow God's commands, we often encounter misinterpretations and extremes that can distort the true nature of biblical obedience. This section explores some common misconceptions about obedience and provides insights on how to avoid these extremes.

Defining Obedience

Biblical obedience, at its core, is an expression of our faith in and love for God. It's a heartfelt response to God's love for us, demonstrated by aligning our thoughts, words, and actions with His commands as revealed in the Bible. It is not blind compliance, but rather a conscious decision to choose God's will over our own.

Misinterpretations of Obedience

Legalism: One extreme misinterpretation of obedience is legalism, a belief system that elevates the law above grace, implying that salvation is earned by obeying the law. In the book of Galatians, the apostle Paul addressed this misconception, emphasizing that we are justified by faith in Christ, not by the works of the law (Galatians 2:16,

241

ESV). We are called to obedience, not to earn salvation, but as a response to the grace we have already received.

Antinomianism: On the other end of the spectrum is antinomianism, the belief that grace frees us from any obligation to follow God's moral laws. Romans 6:1-2 (ESV) counters this, "What shall we say then? Are we to continue in sin that grace may abound? By no means! How can we who died to sin still live in it?" While we are saved by grace, it doesn't give us license to live in sin. Rather, we're called to live holy and obedient lives in response to God's mercy and love.

Avoiding Extremes

Understanding the role of grace and the law in our lives helps us avoid these extremes. We should remember that obedience is not a means to earn salvation but a response to God's saving grace. It is not a burdensome obligation but an act of love and gratitude towards God. While obedience can be challenging, God's grace empowers us to live in accordance with His will.

God's Word serves as our guide in navigating these misconceptions. Hebrews 4:12 (ESV) tells us, "For the word of God is living and active, sharper than any two-edged sword, piercing to the division of soul and of spirit, of joints and of marrow, and discerning the thoughts and intentions of the heart." When we approach the Scriptures with a humble and teachable heart, we can gain a balanced understanding of obedience that aligns with God's intentions.

Prayer also plays an essential role in avoiding misinterpretations. It opens the line of communication with God, allowing us to seek His wisdom and guidance. Though we do not believe in a miraculous indwelling of the Holy Spirit, we understand that God can guide us through His inspired words when we have a correct understanding of them.

Walking in obedience to God's will is a key aspect of our Christian journey. Avoiding extremes and misconceptions about obedience requires a balanced understanding of the role of grace, law, and faith in our lives. As we navigate this path of obedience, let us remember the words of the prophet Micah (Micah 6:8, ASV), "He hath showed thee, O man, what is good; and what doth Jehovah require of thee, but to do justly, and to love kindness, and to walk humbly with thy God?"

The Lifelong Commitment to Walk in Obedience

Christianity is often described as a journey, a lifelong commitment to walk in obedience to God. This walk requires consistent dedication and determination to live according to God's commands, always keeping our eyes focused on Jesus, our perfect example.

Understanding the Commitment

Walking in obedience is a continuous process that extends throughout our entire life. It's not a one-time event or an isolated series of events, but a continual commitment. 2 Chronicles 16:9a (ASV) provides an important perspective, "For the eyes of Jehovah run to and fro throughout the whole earth, to show himself strong in the behalf of them whose heart is perfect toward him." Our total commitment is an expression of our trust and faith in Him.

The Challenge of Perseverance

The Christian walk is fraught with challenges. There are moments of victory, but there are also trials and tribulations. It is essential, in these times, to remember Romans 5:3-4 (ESV), "Not only that, but we rejoice in our sufferings, knowing that suffering produces endurance, and endurance produces character, and character produces hope." The path to spiritual growth and maturity often runs through hardship, and it's our commitment to walking in obedience, even in adversity, that shapes our character and faith.

Living Out the Commitment

There are several key elements involved in living out our commitment to walk in obedience:

1. **Delve into God's Word**: Psalm 119:105 (ASV) beautifully expresses this, "Thy word is a lamp unto my feet, And light unto my path." Regularly engaging with Scripture helps us understand God's will and equips us to live obediently.

2. **Prayer**: Communication with God is crucial. Through prayer, we can seek His guidance, gain strength for the journey, and express our commitment to follow Him.

3. **Community**: Engaging with other believers allows us to be encouraged, corrected, and strengthened in our walk of obedience. Hebrews 10:24-25 (ESV) highlights the importance of community, "And let us consider how to stir up one another to love and good works, not neglecting to meet together, as is the habit of some, but encouraging one another, and all the more as you see the Day drawing near."

4. **Action**: James 2:26 (ESV) succinctly puts it, "For as the body apart from the spirit is dead, so also faith apart from works is dead." Our commitment is demonstrated not only by what we believe but also by what we do.

The Joy of the Commitment

Despite the challenges, there is great joy in committing to walk in obedience. John 15:11 (ESV) states, "These things I have spoken to you, that my joy may be in you, and that your joy may be full." When we walk in obedience, we experience a profound sense of fulfillment and joy that comes from being in a right relationship with God.

Our commitment to walk in obedience is a lifelong journey marked by a constant striving to align our will with God's. It's not without its challenges, but it's also not without its rewards. For every trial faced, there is growth in character, deepening of faith, and a joy that surpasses understanding. The path may be steep, but the destination is more than worth the journey. As we walk in obedience, may we echo the Psalmist's words in Psalm 119:10 (ASV), "With my whole heart have I sought thee: Oh let me not wander from thy commandments."

CHAPTER 11 God's Guidance in Troubled Times: Overcoming Life's Storms

Introduction: Facing Life's Storms with God's Guidance

Life is a journey that does not come without its share of storms. Some are mild and quickly passing, while others are turbulent, causing us to lose our footing and question our resolve. It's in these trying times that our need for God's guidance becomes clear. As believers, we have an unfailing source of wisdom and strength to call upon. The Lord, our Shepherd, is ever present, even in the darkest valleys.

The Reality of Life's Storms

Storms in life are inevitable. They come in various forms: illness, loss, relational breakdowns, financial hardship, and spiritual struggles, among others. These storms can leave us feeling fearful, disoriented, and alone. Yet, we are assured in Isaiah 43:2 (ASV) that, "When thou passest through the waters, I will be with thee; and through the rivers, they shall not overflow thee: when thou walkest through the fire, thou shalt not be burned, neither shall the flame kindle upon thee." It's a powerful promise that God is with us in the midst of our trials, guiding us through.

God's Guidance in the Storms

Understanding that God is with us in our trials is one thing; seeing His guidance and feeling His presence in the midst of a storm is another. But how do we recognize and receive God's guidance in troubled times?

Firstly, we must seek God's guidance in His Word. The Bible is the infallible, inspired Word of God that is useful for teaching, rebuking, correcting, and training in righteousness (2 Timothy 3:16, ESV). It provides counsel, wisdom, comfort, and encouragement in the face of adversity. Secondly, we must remain prayerful. God invites us to cast all our anxieties on Him because He cares for us (1 Peter 5:7, ESV). Through prayer, we can share our worries, fears, and desires with God, and in return, He offers peace that surpasses understanding.

The Purpose of Life's Storms

It's crucial to remember that God has a purpose in allowing storms into our lives. Romans 5:3-5 (ESV) teaches us that, "suffering produces endurance, and endurance produces character, and character produces hope, and hope does not put us to shame, because God's love has been poured into our hearts through the Holy Spirit who has been given to us." In the midst of our trials, God shapes us, molds us, and refines our faith. While we may not understand why we face certain storms, we can trust that God is working for our good and His glory.

As we navigate life's storms, we can take comfort in knowing that God is with us and guiding us every step of the way. His Word illuminates our path, His Spirit comforts us, and His love strengthens us. As we surrender our fears and doubts to Him and lean into His guidance, we can face life's storms with courage and hope, assured that our loving Father is working all things for our good and His glory. May Psalm 46:1-3 (ASV) be our confident declaration, "God is our refuge and strength, A very present help in trouble. Therefore will we not fear, though the earth do change, And though the mountains be shaken into the heart of the seas; Though the waters thereof roar and be troubled, Though the mountains tremble with the swelling thereof." Even in the midst of life's greatest storms, God is our steadfast refuge and guide.

Understanding Trials: The Biblical Perspective on Suffering

Life's trials can often seem arbitrary, cruel, or overwhelming. But when viewed through the lens of Scripture, a new understanding emerges, one that promises growth, refinement, and the opportunity to witness the remarkable power of God's guidance.

The Nature of Trials

Trials are a part of the human condition and they cut across every demographic. They are not a punishment or a sign of God's disfavor, but part and parcel of living in a fallen world. They range from the daily challenges we face to life-altering events such as the loss of a loved one or severe health crises. No one is exempted.

The Bible doesn't gloss over this reality. It candidly acknowledges that in this world we will have tribulation (John 16:33, ESV). But while acknowledging the reality of trials, the Bible also offers a radically different perspective on how we should view and respond to them.

The Purpose of Trials

James 1:2-4 (ESV) implores, "Count it all joy, my brothers, when you meet trials of various kinds, for you know that the testing of your faith produces steadfastness. And let steadfastness have its full effect, that you may be perfect and complete, lacking in nothing." This passage is not asking us to find joy in the trials themselves, but in the fruit they produce in our lives when we lean on God for strength and guidance.

Similarly, in Romans 5:3-5 (ESV), we are encouraged to rejoice in our sufferings, because they produce endurance, character, and hope. These passages underscore a key biblical teaching: trials, when approached with faith and patience, can be transformative. They can deepen our faith, refine our character, and draw us closer to God.

God's Role in Trials

It's crucial to note that while God allows trials, He does not abandon us in them. Instead, He promises to be with us in the midst of our hardships. Isaiah 43:2 (ASV) assures, "When thou passest through the waters, I will be with thee; and through the rivers, they shall not overflow thee: when thou walkest through the fire, thou shalt not be burned, neither shall the flame kindle upon thee."

Our Response to Trials

Understanding the biblical perspective on trials helps shape our response to them. Instead of despairing, we can trust in God's promise to be with us. Instead of questioning God's goodness, we can cling to the hope that He is working things out for our good (Romans 8:28, ESV).

Further, we're invited to bring our anxieties to God in prayer. Philippians 4:6-7 (ESV) urges us not to be anxious about anything, but in every situation, by prayer and petition, with thanksgiving, to present our requests to God. And the peace of God, which surpasses all understanding, will guard our hearts and minds in Christ Jesus.

The biblical perspective on suffering does not diminish the pain or difficulty of our trials. But it does offer a broader view, framing trials as opportunities for growth and a deeper relationship with God. When we grasp this understanding, we can navigate life's storms with resilience, faith, and a steadfast hope that our loving God is guiding us every step of the way.

God's Role in Our Trials: Comforter, Teacher, and Guide

As we navigate life's trials, it's essential to understand and draw strength from the multifaceted roles God plays in our lives during these times. Not merely a passive observer, God is an active participant, serving as our Comforter, Teacher, and Guide.

God as Comforter

The Bible portrays God as a source of comfort in times of distress. In 2 Corinthians 1:3-4 (ESV), Paul refers to Him as the "Father of mercies and God of all comfort, who comforts us in all our affliction." God's comfort transcends the soothing words or gestures of a friend; it's a profound, healing comfort that reaches the depths of our pain and offers genuine solace.

God's comfort isn't dependent on the removal of hardships but is available amidst them. As Isaiah 43:2 (ASV) assures us, "When thou passest through the waters, I will be with thee; and through the rivers, they shall not overflow thee: when thou walkest through the fire, thou shalt not be burned, neither shall the flame kindle upon thee." We can find solace in God's presence, knowing He walks with us through the fire and floods of life.

God as Teacher

Trials also provide a context for God to teach us vital spiritual lessons. Psalm 119:71 (ESV) candidly expresses, "It is good for me that I was afflicted, that I might learn your statutes." This verse isn't suggesting that suffering itself is good but that God can use it for our benefit, to deepen our understanding of His word and His ways.

Just as a teacher uses practical lessons to reinforce theoretical knowledge, God uses trials to shape and refine us. James 1:2-4 (ESV) echoes this sentiment, reminding us that the testing of our faith through trials produces steadfastness, and if allowed to have its full effect, it will render us "perfect and complete, lacking in nothing."

God as Guide

God doesn't merely comfort and teach us through our trials; He also guides us. He doesn't abandon us to navigate our hardships alone but provides guidance and direction. The Psalmist attests to this in Psalm 23:4 (ESV), stating, "Even though I walk through the valley of the shadow of death, I will fear no evil, for you are with me; your rod and your staff, they comfort me."

God's guidance is not about removing obstacles from our path but guiding us through them. He provides wisdom to discern the right steps, strength to face our challenges, and hope to sustain us.

Recognizing God as our Comforter, Teacher, and Guide during trials reshapes our perspective of these challenging seasons. It assures us that we're not abandoned in our pain, left to grapple with life's difficulties on our own. Instead, we have a Comforter who offers profound solace, a Teacher who uses these trials to teach us invaluable lessons, and a Guide who leads us every step of the way.

In comprehending these roles, we don't trivialize the pain of trials but rather find in them a means of experiencing God's comforting presence, transformative teaching, and guiding hand more deeply. As we do, we're empowered to navigate life's storms not with despair but with faith, resilience, and the assurance that our God is with us, comforting, teaching, and guiding us every step of the way.

Case Studies: How Biblical Figures Overcame Their Trials

The Bible provides rich narratives of individuals who faced intense trials, showing us how they overcame these through faith, obedience, and reliance on God's guidance. Let us delve into the lives of three such figures: Joseph, Hannah, and David.

Joseph: From Pit to Palace

The story of Joseph, one of Jacob's twelve sons, unfolds in Genesis 37-50. Joseph, favored by his father but despised by his brothers, faced a series of trials. Sold into slavery by his brothers, wrongfully accused by his master's wife, and imprisoned, Joseph might have seemed forgotten by God. Yet, he remained steadfast in his faith.

During these trials, Joseph chose to serve God faithfully, earning the favor of his masters, both in Potiphar's house and in prison

(Genesis 39:2-4, 21-23). Even when forgotten by the cupbearer whose dream he had interpreted, Joseph remained patient, trusting God's timing (Genesis 40:23). Finally, Pharaoh called for him and Joseph was promoted to a position of authority because of his God-given ability to interpret Pharaoh's dreams (Genesis 41:39-41).

Joseph's life is a profound testament to trusting God's sovereignty in times of suffering. Despite his circumstances, he continued to rely on God and act with integrity. When his brothers came to him in need, he forgave them, seeing God's hand in his trials: "And God sent me before you to preserve life" (Genesis 45:5 ESV).

Hannah: Sorrow to Song

In 1 Samuel 1, we meet Hannah, a woman anguished by her inability to have children. This trial was a source of deep distress and ridicule from her rival, Peninnah. Yet, in her pain, Hannah turned to God in fervent prayer, pouring out her heart before Him (1 Samuel 1:10-11).

God heard her plea and blessed her with a son, Samuel, who would become a significant prophet in Israel's history. Hannah's story teaches us that, in our trials, our first resort should be prayer. Her passionate plea to God wasn't merely a request for a child, but a vow of dedication that her child would serve God all his days (1 Samuel 1:11).

Upon receiving her blessing, Hannah praised God with a heartfelt song of gratitude (1 Samuel 2:1-10), teaching us to acknowledge God's deliverance and blessings. Her trial of barrenness led to a nation's blessing, proving that God can use our trials for greater purposes.

David: From Shepherd to King

David, Israel's second king, spent years in trials. As a shepherd boy, he fought off lions and bears to protect his flock (1 Samuel 17:34-36), demonstrating courage and faith in God. His most significant trial was facing Goliath, where David, despite his youth and inexperience, stood victorious because of his faith (1 Samuel 17:45-47).

David's trials didn't end there. King Saul's jealousy turned him against David, causing David to live as a fugitive. Despite Saul's pursuit, David refrained from killing Saul when he had the opportunity, choosing to respect God's anointed (1 Samuel 24:6).

David's life displays that even in trials, we can make choices that honor God. Though he later sinned grievously, he repented genuinely, showing us that we can turn back to God even after serious mistakes (2 Samuel 12:13).

These biblical figures faced daunting trials yet emerged stronger, their stories resounding with faith, obedience, and resilience. Joseph remained steadfast despite adversity, recognizing God's sovereignty. Hannah turned her sorrow into prayer, dedicating her blessing to God's service. David, in his trials, chose to honor God and repent when he faltered.

Their experiences teach us that trials are not to break us but to build us, shaping our character, deepening our faith, and drawing us closer to God. Through trials, we're given the opportunity to experience firsthand the comfort, guidance, and teaching of God, just as Joseph, Hannah, and David did. We learn that we're not alone in our trials, but under the watchful eye of a God who guides us, comfortingly walks with us, and instructively uses our trials for our good and His glory.

Seeking God in the Midst of Troubles: Prayer and Scripture

In the tumult of life's trials, two indispensable resources enable believers to discern God's guidance: prayer and Scripture. These powerful tools, rooted in the faith of generations of believers, offer us direct access to God's wisdom, comfort, and counsel, empowering us to navigate through our storms.

The Power of Prayer in Troubles

Prayer, in essence, is a conversation with God, an intimate dialogue that connects us with our Creator. It is the vehicle by which we express our innermost feelings, our fears, and our hopes. Prayer is not about using the right words or phrases, but about sincere communication with God.

In the face of troubles, prayer allows us to surrender our fears and anxieties to God. As the Apostle Peter encourages, "Cast all your anxieties on him, because he cares for you" (1 Peter 5:7 ESV). This casting involves a conscious decision to yield our worries to God, trusting His providence.

Jesus Himself, in the midst of His greatest trial—the prospect of the cross—sought solace in prayer. In the Garden of Gethsemane, he fervently prayed, "My Father, if it be possible, let this cup pass from me; nevertheless, not as I will, but as you will" (Matthew 26:39 ESV). Jesus' prayer exemplifies a profound submission to God's will, even in suffering.

Importantly, prayer is not merely about making requests. It is a time for listening, for seeking God's wisdom and guidance. In prayer, we align our hearts with God's, allowing His Spirit-inspired words to illuminate our understanding and guide our steps.

The Role of Scripture in Troubles

Scripture, the inspired and inerrant Word of God, is a reservoir of divine wisdom, guidance, and comfort. Its timeless truths provide the compass by which we can navigate through life's storms.

The psalmist declared, "Your word is a lamp to my feet and a light to my path" (Psalm 119:105 ESV). Scripture lights our way in the darkness of trials, revealing the path God has set for us. It reminds us of God's faithfulness and His promises, giving us hope when despair threatens to overwhelm us.

Moreover, Scripture teaches us about God's character—His love, justice, mercy, and sovereignty. Understanding who God is helps us trust His guidance in our trials. It reaffirms that He is in control, working all things out for our good and His glory (Romans 8:28).

However, to reap the benefits of Scripture, we must actively engage with it. This includes regular reading, deep study, meditation, and application of God's Word. The Holy Spirit does not miraculously indwell us to decipher Scripture. It is our responsibility to correctly understand it and apply it in a balanced manner. In doing so, we allow the Spirit-inspired words to renew our minds and guide our actions.

Prayer and Scripture: A Dynamic Duo

Prayer and Scripture are complementary practices. In prayer, we communicate with God, while in Scripture, God communicates with us. By prayer, we seek God's guidance; through Scripture, we receive it.

To overcome trials, believers should immerse themselves in prayer and Scripture. Praying without ceasing (1 Thessalonians 5:17) while meditating on God's Word day and night (Joshua 1:8) fortifies us against life's adversities. It enables us to recognize God's guiding hand, even in our darkest moments.

Life's storms are inevitable, but they are not insurmountable. With prayer and Scripture as our spiritual lifelines, we can withstand trials, secure in the knowledge that God is with us, guiding us, teaching us, and using our trials for our growth and His glory.

In the tumult of the storm, let us remember the words of the prophet Isaiah: "When you pass through the waters, I will be with you; and through the rivers, they shall not overwhelm you; when you walk through fire you shall not be burned, and the flame shall not consume you" (Isaiah 43:2 ESV).

This promise, like all God's promises, provides hope and comfort. It reminds us that we do not face our troubles alone. Guided by prayer and Scripture, and upheld by God's unchanging character, we can overcome life's storms, emerging stronger, wiser, and closer to our Creator.

Overcoming Fear: Trusting God's Sovereign Control

Fear is a common response to life's storms. The unknown, the unexpected, the uncontrollable—all can trigger deep-seated anxieties. Yet, in the midst of such storms, we are called to trust God's sovereign control. How do we overcome fear and embrace trust in God?

Understanding Fear and Trust

Fear arises when we feel threatened or out of control. It is a basic human emotion, signaling potential danger. Yet, unchecked fear can paralyze us, stifling faith and hindering growth.

Trust, on the other hand, is a firm belief in the reliability, truth, or ability of someone or something. Trusting God means recognizing His sovereignty, acknowledging His wisdom, and resting in His love.

The Sovereignty of God: A Bedrock for Trust

Sovereignty refers to God's supreme authority and control over the universe. Nothing happens without His knowledge or outside His domain. As the prophet Isaiah declares, "I am God, and there is none like me, declaring the end from the beginning and from ancient times things not yet done, saying, 'My counsel shall stand, and I will accomplish all my purpose,'" (Isaiah 46:9-10 ESV).

This does not mean God predetermines every human action—He does not violate human free will. Rather, God, in His omniscience, has perfect foreknowledge of all that will occur, yet this foreknowledge doesn't cause or determine human actions. Thus, even in the tumult of life's trials, God remains in sovereign control.

Overcoming Fear by Trusting God's Sovereign Control

How then do we overcome fear by trusting God's sovereign control?

Recognizing God's Sovereign Control

First, we must recognize God's sovereignty. This involves a conscious acknowledgment of His supreme authority, an admission that He is God, and we are not. Recognizing God's sovereignty means understanding that while we do not control the storms, God does.

Resting in God's Sovereign Love

Second, we must rest in God's sovereign love. God's sovereignty is not cold and impersonal; it is tempered by His love. God is a loving Father who cares for His children, even in their trials. As the Apostle Paul affirms, "For I am sure that neither death nor life, nor angels nor rulers, nor things present nor things to come, nor powers, nor height nor depth, nor anything else in all creation, will be able to separate us from the love of God in Christ Jesus our Lord" (Romans 8:38-39 ESV).

Trusting God's Sovereign Wisdom

Third, we must trust God's sovereign wisdom. God's ways are not our ways (Isaiah 55:8-9). What we perceive as calamity may be a refining fire, purging impurities and building character. Trusting God's wisdom means surrendering our limited perspective for His eternal one.

Applying God's Sovereign Word

Fourth, we must apply God's sovereign Word. The Holy Spirit-inspired Scriptures are our roadmap in the storm, providing guidance and comfort. It is essential, however, that we correctly understand and apply God's Word in a balanced manner. It's not a magic potion, but an instrument for renewal and transformation.

Overcoming fear by trusting God's sovereign control is not a passive resignation, but an active faith. It is a firm decision to lean on God's promises, rest in His love, trust in His wisdom, and apply His Word, even when the storms rage.

Remember, God is our refuge and strength, a very present help in trouble (Psalm 46:1 ESV). When fear strikes, let us hold fast to this truth, trusting His sovereign control, and find peace amidst life's storms.

The Role of Community in Weathering Storms

The human experience, according to biblical teaching, is not designed to be solitary. From the dawn of creation, community has been central to God's plan for His people. The role of community becomes even more pronounced during times of trouble, when shared faith and collective support can offer solace and strength.

Community in the Bible: God's Design for His People

The importance of community is underscored throughout the Bible. In Genesis, God declares that "It is not good that the man should be alone; I will make him a helper fit for him" (Genesis 2:18 ASV). This foundational principle is echoed throughout the scriptures, emphasizing the integral role of community in human life.

Community as a Support System in Troubled Times

One of the most significant roles of community in weathering life's storms is as a support system. The shared experiences, empathy, and encouragement found within a community can lighten individual burdens and foster resilience.

The Apostle Paul writes to the Galatians, "Bear one another's burdens, and so fulfill the law of Christ" (Galatians 6:2 ESV). In times of trouble, the collective strength of the community serves as a bulwark against the storm, and the members of the community are fortified by their mutual support.

Community as a Source of Wisdom and Guidance

Another key role of community in troubled times is the provision of wisdom and guidance. The community, especially a faith community rooted in the Word of God, can be a rich reservoir of knowledge, experience, and insight. This wisdom can be pivotal in helping individuals navigate the complexities of life's storms.

The book of Proverbs extols the virtues of communal wisdom, stating, "Without counsel plans fail, but with many advisers they succeed" (Proverbs 15:22 ESV). In the midst of life's tempests, the collective wisdom of the community can provide valuable guidance and direction.

Community as a Conduit of God's Comfort

In times of trouble, the community can also serve as a conduit of God's comfort. The Apostle Paul reminds the Corinthians, "Blessed be the God and Father of our Lord Jesus Christ, the Father of mercies and God of all comfort, who comforts us in all our affliction, so that we may be able to comfort those who are in any affliction, with the comfort with which we ourselves are comforted by God" (2 Corinthians 1:3-4 ESV).

This passage reveals a remarkable aspect of God's comfort—it is not solely a divine-human transaction, but often flows through the conduit of community. As individuals within the community experience God's comfort in their trials, they become channels of His comfort to others in their affliction.

Community as a Reflection of God's Love

Finally, community plays a vital role in reflecting God's love during troubled times. As individuals love and support each other, they embody the love of Christ, offering tangible expressions of God's love in the midst of the storm.

In John's gospel, Jesus declares, "A new commandment I give to you, that you love one another: just as I have loved you, you also are to love one another. By this all people will know that you are my disciples, if you have love for one another" (John 13:34-35 ESV).

Thus, in a time of crisis, the community, driven by love, becomes a beacon of hope and a testament to God's abiding presence.

In sum, community plays a crucial role in weathering life's storms. As a support system, a source of wisdom, a conduit of comfort, and a reflection of God's love, the community offers a collective strength that can bolster individuals during troubled times. However, it is crucial to remember that this community is most effective when it is firmly rooted in the Word of God, guided by His Spirit-inspired scriptures, and unified in its commitment to reflect His love. This divine foundation enables the community to provide enduring support, guidance, comfort, and love, empowering its members to overcome life's storms with faith and fortitude.

The Danger of Misinterpreting Trials: Balancing Faith and Action

Life's storms are inevitable, and often our first instinct is to question "Why?" As believers, we may be tempted to interpret our trials within the limited context of our understanding, which can lead to misguided assumptions and actions. It is important to strike a balance between faith and action, guided by God's Word, as we navigate these troubled times.

The Problem of Misinterpretation

Trials are part and parcel of life, a recurring theme in the Bible. They can serve as catalysts for spiritual growth and tools for refining our faith. However, our limited human perspective can sometimes lead to misinterpretation of these trials, and we may erroneously perceive them as punishment or as signs that God has forsaken us. This misinterpretation can be spiritually dangerous, leading to despair and discouragement.

The Bible repeatedly cautions against misinterpretation. For example, in John 9:1-3 (ESV), the disciples asked Jesus if a man was born blind because of his own sin or his parents'. Jesus responded, "It was not that this man sinned, or his parents, but that the works of God might be displayed in him." This passage underscores the danger of making hasty assumptions about the cause and purpose of trials.

The Necessity of Balance: Faith and Action

Balancing faith and action is crucial to interpreting and responding to trials accurately. Faith without action can lead to passivity, while action without faith can result in self-reliance and human efforts divorced from God's guidance.

The book of James stresses the importance of this balance. James writes, "What good is it, my brothers, if someone says he has faith but does not have works? Can that faith save him?...So also faith by itself, if it does not have works, is dead" (James 2:14, 17 ESV). Our faith should not be a dormant acceptance of circumstances, but an active trust in God that informs and prompts our actions.

Guided by God's Word

To navigate trials effectively, we must be guided by God's Word. The Psalmist declares, "Your word is a lamp to my feet and a light to my path" (Psalm 119:105 ASV). When faced with trials, we should seek guidance from the Bible to inform our understanding and shape our responses. Scripture, inspired by the Holy Spirit, provides divine perspective and wisdom, enabling us to interpret our trials within the larger framework of God's redemptive plan.

Responding to Trials: God-Dependent Action

When trials hit, our actions must be firmly rooted in faith and directed by God's Word. We should not passively endure trials or rush to "fix" situations in our strength. Rather, our responses should be characterized by God-dependent action.

Paul, in his letter to the Philippians, models this principle. He writes, "I can do all things through him who strengthens me"

(Philippians 4:13 ESV). This is not a call to autonomous action, but a recognition of the necessity of relying on God's strength in our actions.

In conclusion, navigating life's storms requires a careful balance of faith and action, guided by the truths of Scripture. Misinterpreting trials can lead to spiritual harm, but with a faith that prompts action, and action that is dependent on God, we can face trials with resilience and hope. Through this, we grow in spiritual maturity, deepen our reliance on God, and demonstrate our faith to a watching world. As we journey through trials, let us be mindful to maintain this balance, seeking always to honor God and align our lives with His Word.

Growth through Adversity: The Silver Lining of Life's Storms

Navigating through life's storms is an integral part of our human experience, often bringing periods of deep distress and uncertainty. However, these trials also carry a silver lining, providing unique opportunities for personal and spiritual growth. This perspective, rooted in biblical truths, invites us to look beyond the immediacy of our difficulties and recognize how adversity can be a catalyst for transformation and maturity in our faith journey.

Adversity and Spiritual Growth

The relationship between adversity and spiritual growth is consistently reflected in Scripture. In the midst of trials, our faith is tested and refined. The Apostle Peter metaphorically refers to this process as the refining of gold through fire, stating that "the tested genuineness of your faith—more precious than gold that perishes though it is tested by fire—may be found to result in praise and glory and honor at the revelation of Jesus Christ" (1 Peter 1:7, ESV). Adversity, much like the fire in Peter's metaphor, serves to purify and strengthen our faith, enhancing its value and resilience.

The Role of Perseverance

Perseverance plays a crucial role in the connection between adversity and growth. James writes, "Count it all joy, my brothers, when you meet trials of various kinds, for you know that the testing of your faith produces steadfastness. And let steadfastness have its full effect, that you may be perfect and complete, lacking in nothing" (James 1:2-4, ESV). Here, trials are not simply obstacles to be overcome; they are tools used by God to develop perseverance, leading to spiritual maturity.

Trust in God's Sovereignty and Wisdom

Our capacity to grow through adversity relies heavily on trust in God's sovereignty and wisdom. In times of trouble, we may not understand why we are undergoing certain trials, but we can find peace in knowing that God, in His wisdom, allows adversity for our ultimate good. The prophet Isaiah affirms this trust, stating, "For my thoughts are not your thoughts, neither are your ways my ways, declares the LORD. For as the heavens are higher than the earth, so are my ways higher than your ways and my thoughts than your thoughts" (Isaiah 55:8-9, ASV). Our faith grows as we learn to rely not on our understanding, but on God's sovereignty and wisdom.

Cultivating a Heavenly Perspective

Adopting a heavenly perspective is key to recognizing the silver lining in life's storms. Paul writes, "For this light momentary affliction is preparing for us an eternal weight of glory beyond all comparison" (2 Corinthians 4:17, ESV). This perspective shifts our focus from the temporal to the eternal, allowing us to see that the growth we experience through adversity contributes to our eternal reward.

Practical Steps: Prayer and Scripture

In navigating adversity, prayer and Scripture serve as our compass, guiding us and providing comfort. We are called to "pray without ceasing" (1 Thessalonians 5:17, ASV) and to meditate on God's Word day and night (Psalm 1:2, ASV). These practices root us in God's promises and equip us with spiritual fortitude to face and grow from our trials.

In conclusion, while life's storms can bring pain and confusion, they also offer unique opportunities for spiritual growth. As we navigate these trials, we are invited to lean into the refining process, trusting in God's sovereignty, adopting a heavenly perspective, and drawing on the resources of prayer and Scripture. Through this process, we not only weather life's storms but also emerge with a faith that is stronger, more resilient, and more deeply rooted in God's promises. The silver lining, then, is not just surviving adversity, but growing through it. This perspective is both the hope and the promise offered to us in Scripture, and it is the beacon that can guide us through even the darkest of storms.

Remaining Steadfast: The Importance of Perseverance

In the face of life's storms, remaining steadfast may seem like a daunting task. These tumultuous periods of adversity and hardship test our resolve, challenging our faith and resilience. Nevertheless, the Bible repeatedly emphasizes the importance of perseverance, presenting it as a critical characteristic of a robust and enduring faith.

The Biblical Mandate of Perseverance

Scripture is replete with exhortations to persevere. The Apostle Paul, in his epistle to the Romans, urged believers to rejoice in suffering, "knowing that suffering produces endurance, and endurance produces character, and character produces hope" (Romans 5:3-4, ESV). Here, Paul presents a sequential process in which perseverance is not just the outcome but also the catalyst for developing a hope-filled character.

In the book of Hebrews, perseverance is linked to the fulfillment of God's promises. The author writes, "For you have need of endurance, so that when you have done the will of God you may receive what is promised" (Hebrews 10:36, ESV). This verse underlines that perseverance is integral to experiencing God's faithfulness and the fruition of His promises.

Perseverance as an Act of Faith

Perseverance is inherently an act of faith. It demands an unwavering trust in God's sovereignty, even in the midst of adversity. This commitment is beautifully expressed in the book of Job. Despite severe trials, Job declares, "Though he slay me, I will hope in him" (Job 13:15, ESV). His perseverance was rooted in his unshakeable faith in God, a model for all believers navigating troubled times.

The Role of Perseverance in Spiritual Growth

Perseverance plays a vital role in spiritual growth. James emphasizes this, stating, "Blessed is the man who remains steadfast under trial, for when he has stood the test he will receive the crown of life, which God has promised to those who love him" (James 1:12, ESV). The metaphor of the 'crown of life' symbolizes the spiritual maturity and eternal rewards that stem from perseverance through trials.

The Power of Prayer in Perseverance

The discipline of prayer is crucial in bolstering perseverance. In his epistle to the Ephesians, Paul encourages believers to "pray at all times in the Spirit, with all prayer and supplication. To that end, keep alert with all perseverance, making supplication for all the saints" (Ephesians 6:18, ESV). Prayer serves as both a source of strength and a means of sustaining perseverance, fortifying the believer in times of adversity.

God's Faithfulness: The Groundwork of Perseverance

A steadfast perseverance is rooted in the recognition of God's unwavering faithfulness. The prophet Jeremiah, amid despair, finds hope by remembering God's steadfast love and faithfulness, stating, "The steadfast love of the LORD never ceases; his mercies never come to an end; they are new every morning; great is your faithfulness" (Lamentations 3:22-23, ESV). Trusting in God's faithfulness enables believers to persevere, knowing that God's mercies are ever-present.

Perseverance is not a passive endurance but an active, faith-filled steadiness that keeps us anchored in God, irrespective of life's storms. It is a divine mandate, a catalyst for spiritual growth, and a testament to our faith in God's sovereign control and unwavering faithfulness. In the face of trials, let us remember the words of Paul, who with unwavering perseverance declared, "I have fought the good fight, I have finished the race, I have kept the faith" (2 Timothy 4:7, ESV). This steadfastness, born of an enduring faith, is the lifeline we hold onto in navigating life's storms, fortified by God's word, guided by prayer, and anchored in His unwavering faithfulness.

Embracing God's Guidance in All Seasons of Life

Life is a dynamic journey filled with fluctuating seasons of joy, pain, growth, and struggle. In every season, the guidance of God remains a constant, an unwavering beacon leading us through calm waters and stormy seas alike. Embracing God's guidance, particularly in times of tribulation, is an integral part of a believer's journey.

God's Guidance: A Biblical Perspective

The Bible abounds with instances where God guides His people, assuring them of His constant presence. The psalmist celebrates this divine guidance, proclaiming, "You guide me with your counsel, and afterward you will receive me to glory" (Psalm 73:24, ESV). Here, the guidance of God is not merely temporal but culminates in the eternal glory of His presence.

God's Guidance in Times of Prosperity

God's guidance is not solely for periods of crisis; it is equally vital in times of prosperity. King Solomon, in his wisdom, cautioned, "Trust in the LORD with all your heart, and do not lean on your own understanding. In all your ways acknowledge him, and he will make straight your paths" (Proverbs 3:5-6, ESV). These verses serve as a reminder that self-reliance and prosperity should not diminish our dependency on God's guidance.

God's Guidance in Times of Adversity

The promise of God's guidance becomes most comforting in times of adversity. Isaiah, the prophet, assured God's people that, "When you pass through the waters, I will be with you; and through the rivers, they shall not overwhelm you; when you walk through fire you shall not be burned, and the flame shall not consume you" (Isaiah 43:2, ESV). This promise reinforces the unchanging nature of God's guidance, even amidst life's fiercest storms.

God's Word: The Ultimate Guide

God's Word serves as the ultimate guide for believers. The Psalmist affirms, "Your word is a lamp to my feet and a light to my path" (Psalm 119:105, ESV). Regular immersion in God's Word equips us to discern His guidance, illuminating our path and equipping us to navigate every season of life.

The Role of Prayer in Seeking Guidance

Prayer plays an essential role in seeking and discerning God's guidance. The Apostle Paul urges believers to "pray without ceasing" (1 Thessalonians 5:17, ESV), a directive that underscores the importance of continual communication with God. Through prayer, we express our reliance on God's guidance and open our hearts to discern His will.

Guidance through the Holy Spirit-Inspired Word

The Holy Spirit, who moved the authors of the Bible, has left us a trove of divinely inspired words to guide us. Paul acknowledged this when he wrote, "All Scripture is breathed out by God and profitable for teaching, for reproof, for correction, and for training in righteousness" (2 Timothy 3:16, ESV). These Spirit-inspired words provide the necessary guidance, correcting and training us to live righteously, irrespective of our circumstances.

Embracing God's guidance is an ongoing, dynamic process, integral to every season of our lives. His guidance, delivered through His Word and discerned through prayer, provides a constant, reliable compass, directing our paths in times of prosperity and steadying us in times of adversity. As we navigate the varying seasons of life, let us remain confident in God's unfailing guidance, ever-present and steadfast, leading us from temporal trials to eternal glory.

CHAPTER 12 Cultivating Virtues: The Role of Discipline in Christian Life

Introduction: Understanding Virtues in Christian Life

The Christian life is not merely about adhering to a set of beliefs or performing religious rituals. It is about a transformative relationship with God that manifests in the cultivation of virtues — the qualities that reflect Christ's character in us. Through the Holy Spirit-inspired words of the Bible, God provides us a framework for understanding and embodying these virtues.

The Biblical Definition of Virtues

Virtues in the Christian sense are moral and spiritual qualities that align with God's character and His will for humanity. They are traits that are commendable, admirable, and reflect the divine nature. The Apostle Paul provides a succinct list of these virtues in Galatians, known as the fruit of the Spirit: "But the fruit of the Spirit is love, joy, peace, patience, kindness, goodness, faithfulness, gentleness, self-control; against such things there is no law" (Galatians 5:22-23, ESV).

The Role of Discipline in Cultivating Virtues

Discipline is instrumental in the cultivation of virtues. It involves making conscious and consistent choices that align with God's Word, even when those choices are challenging or go against our human tendencies. The writer of Hebrews notes, "For the moment all discipline seems painful rather than pleasant, but later it yields the peaceful fruit of righteousness to those who have been trained by it"

(Hebrews 12:11, ESV). Discipline, while challenging, cultivates spiritual fruit that leads to righteousness and peace.

Discipline in the Study and Application of God's Word

Discipline in the Christian life extends to the diligent study and application of God's Word. "Do your best to present yourself to God as one approved, a worker who has no need to be ashamed, rightly handling the word of truth" (2 Timothy 2:15, ESV). Paul encourages Timothy, and by extension all believers, to be disciplined in their approach to Scripture, so they can correctly apply its truth in their lives.

Prayer as a Discipline

Prayer is another discipline that plays a vital role in the cultivation of virtues. Regular, intentional prayer is a discipline that connects us with God's heart, aligns our will with His, and strengthens us in our pursuit of virtue. "Pray without ceasing," Paul instructs in 1 Thessalonians 5:17 (ESV). This unending communion with God is the breath that sustains our spiritual lives.

The Importance of Community in Cultivating Virtues

The Christian community or the church plays an essential role in cultivating virtues. The Apostle Paul writes, "And let us consider how to stir up one another to love and good works" (Hebrews 10:24, ESV). The church provides a context where believers can encourage, correct, and spur each other towards the growth of virtues, making the community an indispensable aid in the disciplined pursuit of virtue.

Understanding and cultivating virtues is a fundamental aspect of Christian life, a reflection of Christ's character being formed in us. While the path of discipline can be challenging, the fruit it yields is of eternal value. Through the diligent study and application of God's Word, ceaseless prayer, and the supportive function of the Christian community, we can grow in the virtues that reflect God's character. As we commit to this disciplined pursuit, we become more like Christ, the ultimate embodiment of all virtues.

The Biblical Basis for Virtue: God's Expectations

In a world often plagued by moral relativism, the Bible provides a clear, consistent, and unchanging standard of virtue based on God's character and expectations. His desire for humans to reflect His image (Genesis 1:26-27, ASV) provides the foundational biblical basis for virtue.

God's Call to Holiness

One of the fundamental virtues in the Bible is holiness. "For I am the Lord your God. Consecrate yourselves therefore, and be holy, for I am holy" (Leviticus 11:44a, ASV). This call to holiness is not a recommendation but an expectation. It is a call to be set apart from moral corruption and to embody the purity of God's character in every aspect of life.

The Moral Law and Virtue

The Ten Commandments (Exodus 20:1-17, ASV) further elaborate God's expectations of virtue. These divine commands outline foundational moral virtues such as truthfulness, respect, fidelity, and contentment. They serve as the cornerstone of ethical conduct, providing a clear outline of how virtues should be lived out in daily life.

The Beatitudes: Christ's Exposition of Virtue

In the New Testament, Jesus provides a profound exposition of virtue in the Beatitudes (Matthew 5:3-12, ESV). These sayings highlight virtues like humility, righteousness, mercy, and peacemaking. They provide a portrait of the character traits that God values and expects His followers to embody.

The Fruit of the Spirit: Paul's List of Virtues

The Apostle Paul provides another comprehensive list of virtues in Galatians 5:22-23, ESV: "But the fruit of the Spirit is love, joy, peace, patience, kindness, goodness, faithfulness, gentleness, self-control." These virtues are the natural outcome of a life that is guided by God's Spirit through His inspired Word.

The Virtue of Love

Overarching all these virtues is the virtue of love. The Bible is unequivocal in asserting the primacy of love among all virtues. In 1 Corinthians 13:13, Paul states, "So now faith, hope, and love abide, these three; but the greatest of these is love" (ESV). God's love is the fountainhead from which all other virtues flow.

God's Grace and Virtue

While the Bible clearly outlines God's expectations of virtue, it equally emphasizes that these virtues are not attained by human effort alone. Ephesians 2:8-9 (ESV) states, "For by grace you have been saved through faith. And this is not your own doing; it is the gift of God, not a result of works, so that no one may boast." It is God's grace, accepted in faith, that empowers believers to cultivate and exhibit virtues.

The biblical basis for virtue is intrinsically linked to God's character and His expectations of those who seek to follow Him. Virtue, as reflected in holiness, moral obedience, humility, love, and the fruit of the Spirit, is the standard God has set for humanity. It is His design for the best possible life we can live. While the attainment of these virtues is a lifelong journey and a challenging task, God's grace provides the necessary empowerment to strive for and embody these virtues in our daily lives. Understanding and embracing God's expectations of virtue transforms our hearts, renews our minds, and influences our actions to reflect more accurately His divine image in us.

The Role of Discipline in Cultivating Virtues

Cultivating virtues in a Christian life is a transformative process that requires discipline. God's Word illustrates that discipline is a vital tool in shaping character, refining faith, and fostering virtues. Understanding the role of discipline in our spiritual journey helps us appreciate its significance in our pursuit of godliness.

Discipline as Spiritual Training

As with any form of training, discipline is the backbone of spiritual growth. The Apostle Paul makes this comparison in 1 Corinthians 9:24-27 (ESV), where he likens the Christian journey to a race that requires self-control and determination. He speaks of disciplining his body and keeping it under control, emphasizing the need for self-discipline in the pursuit of heavenly rewards.

God's Discipline: A Sign of Love and Adoption

The writer of Hebrews emphasizes that God disciplines those whom He loves (Hebrews 12:6, ESV). God's discipline is not punitive but corrective, aimed at steering us toward righteousness and spiritual maturity. This discipline is a testament to God's love and our status as His children. "For the Lord disciplines the one he loves, and chastises every son whom he receives" (Hebrews 12:6, ESV).

The Purpose of Discipline: Growth in Righteousness

Discipline serves to shape and refine our character. Proverbs 3:11-12 (ASV) confirms that God's discipline leads to wisdom and understanding. It yields the fruit of righteousness to those who have been trained by it (Hebrews 12:11, ESV). Therefore, discipline serves as a means through which we cultivate virtues and grow in holiness.

Discipline and the Cultivation of Virtues

Discipline plays a pivotal role in cultivating Christian virtues. Self-control, one of the fruits of the Spirit (Galatians 5:23, ESV), involves discipline in governing our desires and actions. Patience, another virtue, is developed as we discipline ourselves to trust in God's timing. Discipline in studying God's Word helps cultivate wisdom, while discipline in prayer fosters a relationship with God, building faith and dependence on Him.

Discipline: A Means to Overcoming Sin

Discipline also aids in the struggle against sin. Romans 6:12-14 (ESV) encourages believers not to let sin reign in their mortal bodies but to present themselves to God as instruments of righteousness. This active resistance against sin requires discipline. By disciplining our minds and bodies, we can resist temptations and live in a manner that honors God.

The Role of the Church in Discipline

The church also plays a vital role in discipline. Matthew 18:15-17 (ESV) outlines the process of church discipline, which aims at restoring erring believers to righteousness. While it is a challenging process, church discipline underscores the collective responsibility of the Christian community in fostering personal and communal holiness.

In summary, discipline is a key component in the cultivation of Christian virtues. It serves as spiritual training, a sign of God's love, a tool for growth in righteousness, a means to overcoming sin, and a mechanism for maintaining communal holiness. Through discipline, believers can effectively cultivate and exhibit virtues as they grow into the fullness of the character of Christ. The road of discipline may be tough and challenging, but it is necessary and rewarding in our journey of faith. Embracing discipline allows us to align our hearts, minds, and actions with God's Word, fostering a life marked by virtue and godliness.

Case Studies: Virtues Exemplified in Biblical Figures

Biblical figures provide invaluable lessons and insights into the practice and cultivation of virtues through discipline. In this section, we explore the lives of Daniel, Ruth, and Stephen, highlighting the virtues they exemplified.

Daniel: Wisdom and Integrity

Daniel's life is a prime example of virtues embodied through discipline, specifically the virtues of wisdom and integrity. Daniel was among the young Jewish men taken captive by King Nebuchadnezzar of Babylon (Daniel 1:1-6, ASV). Despite his circumstances, he resolved not to defile himself with the king's food or drink, which was against the dietary laws of his faith (Daniel 1:8, ASV). This act of self-discipline exemplifies integrity, a commitment to adhere to one's moral and ethical principles.

Furthermore, God gave Daniel the ability to interpret dreams and visions, a gift that he used with great wisdom (Daniel 1:17, ASV). His wise counsel and interpretation of King Nebuchadnezzar's dreams led to his rise to a high position in the Babylonian kingdom (Daniel 2:48, ASV). Daniel's life affirms that cultivating virtues through discipline, even in adversity, earns respect and honor.

Ruth: Loyalty and Love

The story of Ruth exemplifies the virtues of loyalty and love. Despite being a Moabite, Ruth chose to accompany her mother-in-law Naomi back to Bethlehem after the death of her husband (Ruth 1:16-17, ASV). Her loyalty to Naomi, expressed through her willingness to leave her homeland and adopt Naomi's people and God, is a powerful testimony of selfless love.

Ruth's discipline is also evident in her diligent work in the fields to provide for Naomi (Ruth 2:2-3, ASV). Ruth's steadfast loyalty and love eventually led to her marriage to Boaz, a wealthy and respected relative of Naomi (Ruth 4:13, ASV). Ruth's story highlights the virtues that can grow from disciplined choices grounded in loyalty and love.

Stephen: Faith and Courage

Stephen, one of the seven chosen to serve in the early Christian church (Acts 6:5, ESV), exemplifies the virtues of faith and courage. Stephen was full of grace and power, performing great wonders and signs among the people (Acts 6:8, ESV). He was deeply committed to spreading the message of Jesus, a task he undertook with unwavering discipline.

When brought before the council, Stephen courageously defended his faith, recounting the history of Israel and rebuking the people for their hard-heartedness (Acts 7:1-53, ESV). Despite the threat of death, Stephen stood firm, a testament to his disciplined commitment to his faith.

His faithfulness, even to the point of martyrdom, reveals a profound courage. As he was being stoned, Stephen prayed for his persecutors, a final act of disciplined faith and radical forgiveness (Acts 7:59-60, ESV). His life serves as an inspiration for cultivating faith and courage through discipline.

The lives of Daniel, Ruth, and Stephen provide profound examples of how discipline contributes to the cultivation of virtues. These biblical figures, through their wisdom, integrity, loyalty, love, faith, and courage, serve as reminders that disciplined adherence to God's teachings helps us grow spiritually and live virtuously. Their stories encourage us to pursue discipline in our Christian journey, fostering a life marked by virtue and godliness.

Virtues in Action: Practical Ways to Grow in Godliness

Growing in godliness requires conscious effort and discipline to cultivate virtues in our daily lives. This section provides practical ways to grow in godliness, allowing the virtues we've discussed to manifest in action.

Devotion to Scripture

The first step to cultivate godliness is nurturing a robust devotion to Scripture. The apostle Paul tells Timothy, "All Scripture is breathed out by God and profitable for teaching, for reproof, for correction, and for training in righteousness" (2 Timothy 3:16, ESV). The Word of God should serve as our primary guide in understanding and embodying godly virtues.

Therefore, we should endeavor to read and meditate on the Bible daily, seeking to understand its teachings and apply them to our lives. Daily devotional time allows us to reflect on the virtues displayed by biblical characters and how we can emulate them. It's also beneficial to engage in Bible studies with other believers to gain different perspectives and deepen our understanding of Scripture.

Prayer and Fasting

Prayer is a powerful discipline that nurtures a deep, intimate relationship with God. It's through prayer that we can seek God's wisdom and guidance in our journey of virtue cultivation (James 1:5, ESV). The Bible encourages us to "pray without ceasing" (1 Thessalonians 5:17, ESV), indicating that prayer should be a constant practice in our lives.

Fasting is also a crucial aspect of Christian discipline. Although often overlooked, fasting focuses our mind on God, denying physical desires to deepen our spiritual walk. Jesus, recognizing its importance, taught not if but "when you fast" (Matthew 6:16, ESV), suggesting it should be a normal part of Christian discipline.

Service and Generosity

True godliness manifests in our relationships with others. Jesus taught that the second greatest commandment, after loving God, is to "love your neighbor as yourself" (Mark 12:31, ESV). Service and generosity towards others are practical expressions of this commandment.

The early church provides an excellent example of such virtues in action. The believers were devoted to fellowship and shared their resources to meet each other's needs (Acts 2:44-46, ESV). Emulating this practice, we can engage in acts of service within our communities and churches and extend generosity to those in need.

Forgiveness and Reconciliation

Forgiveness and reconciliation are key virtues that Jesus emphasized. Jesus taught us to forgive others, for God has forgiven us (Matthew 6:14, ESV). We need to intentionally practice forgiveness when wronged, as difficult as it may be. This includes seeking reconciliation and restoring broken relationships, emulating God's reconciliatory work through Christ (2 Corinthians 5:18-19, ESV).

Pursuit of Holiness

Lastly, godliness entails a pursuit of holiness. Peter admonishes us to "be holy in all your conduct" because God, who called us, is holy (1 Peter 1:15, ESV). This pursuit involves abstaining from sin, seeking to live righteously, and allowing God's Spirit to refine us continually.

While the pursuit of holiness requires discipline and self-denial, it isn't a path of legalistic observance but a response of love and gratitude to God's saving grace in Christ. Remember, it's God's grace that trains us "to renounce ungodliness and worldly passions, and to live self-controlled, upright, and godly lives in the present age" (Titus 2:12, ESV).

In conclusion, the cultivation of virtues is a lifelong journey that requires discipline and commitment. Through devotion to Scripture, prayer, fasting, service, generosity, forgiveness, reconciliation, and the pursuit of holiness, we can grow in godliness. This path is not easy, but it's one that yields the fruit of a godly character, ultimately glorifying God and leading to a fulfilled, impactful Christian life.

The Power of Habit: Consistency in Cultivating Virtues

In our journey towards godliness, one essential yet often overlooked tool is the power of habit. Aristotle famously said, "We are what we repeatedly do. Excellence, then, is not an act but a habit." This wisdom applies perfectly to the cultivation of virtues in a Christian's life.

Habit Formation and Virtues

Every human action, from the mundane to the sublime, is guided by a complex network of habits that have been formed and strengthened over time. Habits are automatic responses to specific cues in our environment and they develop when we consistently choose to respond in a certain way.

In the Christian context, habit formation plays a critical role in cultivating virtues. If virtues are the characteristics we strive for, habits are the means by which we embody these virtues in our daily lives. They are the practical expressions of our virtues, the vehicles through which virtues become integrated into our character.

The Apostle Paul in Romans 12:2 (ESV) implores believers, "Do not be conformed to this world, but be transformed by the renewal of your mind." This transformation is a process that often involves the development of new, godly habits that align with God's will.

Consistency: The Key to Habit Formation

Consistency is the bedrock of habit formation. A single act does not establish a habit. It is the repeated, consistent performance of that act that engrains it into our behavioral repertoire.

The same principle applies to cultivating virtues. It isn't enough to act with kindness, humility, or patience sporadically or when it's convenient. We must strive to exhibit these virtues consistently, embedding them in our daily routines and responses.

279

Paul's exhortation to "pray without ceasing" in 1 Thessalonians 5:17 (ESV) underscores the importance of consistency. It's a call not just to persistent prayer, but also to consistency in all godly practices and habits.

Challenges to Consistency and Overcoming Them

Despite its importance, maintaining consistency can be challenging. Distractions, disruptions, and our inherent tendency towards comfort and ease can deter us from the disciplined practice needed to form godly habits.

However, there are several strategies we can employ to enhance our consistency.

First, we should start small. Major changes can be overwhelming and lead to burnout. Therefore, start with small, manageable actions that align with the virtue you're trying to cultivate. For instance, if you're cultivating the virtue of generosity, start by giving small amounts regularly to a cause you care about.

Second, establish clear, achievable goals. Goals provide direction and motivation, and they make our progress measurable. For example, if you're working on the habit of daily Bible reading, you could set a goal to read a specific number of chapters or pages each day.

Third, leverage accountability. Engaging a trustworthy friend or joining a group with similar goals can provide the necessary motivation to maintain consistency. A good example of this is joining a Bible study group when working on your Scripture reading habit.

Finally, remember that perfection is not the goal; progress is. There will be days when you falter. Don't let those days discourage you. Instead, use them as reminders of your reliance on God's grace and strength. In 2 Corinthians 12:9 (ESV), Paul recalls the Lord's assurance to him: "My grace is sufficient for you, for my power is made perfect in weakness."

In conclusion, the power of habit, fueled by consistency, is a transformative tool in our journey of cultivating virtues. Through regular, disciplined practice, virtues can move from being conscious efforts to ingrained responses, authentically reflected in our character and daily living. Our ultimate goal is not merely the formation of habits, but the transformation of our hearts and minds, bringing us ever closer to the likeness of Christ. In the words of Paul in Ephesians 4:22-24 (ESV), we are called "to put off your old self, which belongs to your former manner of life and is corrupt through deceitful desires, and to be renewed in the spirit of your minds, and to put on the new self, created after the likeness of God in true righteousness and holiness."

The Role of Community in Fostering Virtue

The Christian life was never meant to be lived in isolation. From the beginning, God deemed it not good for man to be alone (Genesis 2:18 ASV). While this verse is often used in the context of marriage, its broader application signifies our inherent need for community. Community is essential to fostering virtue, providing an environment where spiritual growth is encouraged, facilitated, and nourished.

Community as a Reflection of the Trinity

The concept of community is rooted in the nature of God Himself. The Holy Trinity, consisting of the Father, the Son, and the Holy Spirit, exemplifies perfect community - unity in diversity. The love and interdependence within the Trinity provide a blueprint for our human communities. As believers, we're called to reflect this divine community in our relationships with one another, helping each other grow in virtue and godliness.

Accountability and Encouragement

Within a community, believers have the opportunity to hold each other accountable. As written in Hebrews 10:24-25 (ESV), "And let us consider how to stir up one another to love and good works, not neglecting to meet together, as is the habit of some, but encouraging one another, and all the more as you see the Day drawing near." Community promotes the cultivation of virtue by providing an atmosphere of mutual accountability and encouragement. Through shared experiences and collective wisdom, we gain insights and learn from others' walks with God, spurring us on in our journey toward spiritual maturity.

Modeling and Mentoring

Community is also a space for modeling and mentoring. Older, more mature believers play a crucial role in nurturing the spiritual growth of younger ones. In Titus 2:3-5 (ESV), older women are exhorted to train younger women to love their husbands and children, to be self-controlled, pure, and submissive, among other virtues. This process of discipleship — a personal investment in the life of another believer — fosters the development of virtue, as these godly attributes are caught as much as they are taught.

Correction and Discipline

Another essential aspect of community in fostering virtue is its role in correction and discipline. Proverbs 27:17 (ASV) illustrates this well, "Iron sharpeneth iron; So a man sharpeneth the countenance of his friend." Through the community, we receive constructive criticism and correction that can sharpen us, refining our character and helping us mature in our faith. Discipline, though painful at the moment, yields the fruit of righteousness and is vital in cultivating virtues (Hebrews 12:11 ESV).

Service and Love

Community also offers opportunities for service and love — practical expressions of virtues. Jesus Himself affirmed that the greatest commandments are to love God and to love our neighbor as ourselves (Mark 12:30-31 ESV). In serving and loving one another within the community, we embody these commands and cultivate virtues such as kindness, humility, and patience.

In conclusion, community plays a pivotal role in fostering virtue. The mutual accountability, encouragement, mentoring, correction, and opportunities for service it provides serve to nourish and stimulate our growth in godliness. Yet, it's essential to remember that while community plays a critical role in our spiritual growth, the work of transformation is ultimately God's. As we strive to cultivate virtues within the context of community, we must continually rely on the power of God's Word and His grace, knowing that it's God who gives the increase (1 Corinthians 3:7 ESV).

The Danger of Legalism: Finding Balance in Discipline

While cultivating virtues plays an integral role in the Christian life, we must be mindful of the pitfalls that come with excessive rigidity in discipline, notably legalism. Legalism is an over-reliance on rules and regulations for moral guidance, often at the expense of grace and faith. As Christians, our aim is to cultivate a balanced approach to discipline that encourages spiritual growth without slipping into the trap of legalistic practices.

Understanding Legalism

Legalism manifests when we view our relationship with God as primarily law-based, hinging on strict adherence to rules and regulations for moral uprightness. It subverts the message of the Gospel, replacing God's grace with self-effort. Paul warns against this in his letter to the Galatians (Galatians 3:2-3 ESV), challenging them on whether they received the Spirit by the works of the law or by hearing with faith. The danger of legalism lies in its ability to divert our focus from a relationship with God to a religion about God.

Legalism and the Pharisees: A Biblical Case Study

A study of legalism wouldn't be complete without discussing the Pharisees, the religious leaders in the time of Jesus who epitomized legalism. Despite their strict adherence to the Mosaic Law and their self-imposed "oral laws," they missed the heart of God's commandments: love, justice, and mercy (Matthew 23:23 ESV). Jesus criticized them for their outward displays of piety, which concealed inner corruption, illustrating the futility of legalistic practices to effect genuine, inward change (Matthew 23:25-28 ESV).

Faith and Grace vs. Legalism

Contrary to legalism, the Bible teaches that we are justified by faith apart from the works of the law (Romans 3:28 ESV). It is by grace we have been saved, and this is not our own doing; it is the gift of God (Ephesians 2:8-9 ESV). While good works are an outcome of our faith, they are not the means of our salvation. This distinction is crucial. Our actions should flow from a heart transformed by God's grace, not from a legalistic desire to earn His favor.

Finding Balance in Discipline

Understanding the distinction between discipline and legalism is key to maintaining a balanced Christian life. Discipline is not about strict rule-keeping but about training and correction aimed at spiritual maturity (Hebrews 12:11 ESV). Discipline fosters a lifestyle conducive to godliness and virtue. Yet, it is always in the context of a grace-filled relationship with God, acknowledging our dependence on His Spirit for the power to live righteously.

The Role of the Holy Spirit

The Holy Spirit, through His inspired words, guides us in understanding the Bible and applying it in a balanced manner. While the Holy Spirit doesn't miraculously indwell in us to make decisions, His words serve as our guide. With a correct understanding of God's Word, we can discern the difference between a healthy, disciplined lifestyle and a legalistic, rule-centered one.

The Power of Love

As we strive to live disciplined lives, let's remember the greatest commandment: to love God and love others (Mark 12:30-31 ESV). This love is the fulfillment of the law (Romans 13:10 ESV). If love drives our actions, we move away from legalism and closer to the heart of God. In this way, love provides the balance we need in discipline.

Legalism poses a significant danger to our pursuit of virtue, as it replaces a relationship with God based on faith and grace with a system of rules and self-effort. As we seek to cultivate virtues, we must balance our discipline with an understanding of God's grace and love. Let us look to the Holy Spirit-inspired words of Scripture for guidance, maintaining a discipline that encourages spiritual growth without slipping into legalistic practices. Always remember, our ultimate goal is not rule-keeping, but becoming more Christlike in character and deed.

Virtues as Reflection of the Holy Spirit's Work

In our pursuit of a virtuous Christian life, understanding the role of the Holy Spirit is essential. The Holy Spirit, in this context, refers to the inspired words of Scripture, which serves as our guide. This chapter explores how virtues cultivated through disciplined adherence to the teachings of the Bible reflect the work of the Holy Spirit.

The Holy Spirit's Work

The Holy Spirit's work, as per our understanding, refers to the impact of the inspired words of the Bible. It involves guiding believers into understanding God's will and transforming their lives to reflect Christ-like character. In John 16:13 (ESV), Jesus refers to the Spirit of Truth (understood here as the teachings of Scripture), guiding us into all truth. This process of guidance and transformation primarily occurs through our disciplined study and application of the Bible.

Fruits of the Spirit: Virtues in Practice

One of the most poignant sections of Scripture that speaks to the outcome of the Holy Spirit's work is Galatians 5:22-23 (ESV): "But the fruit of the Spirit is love, joy, peace, patience, kindness, goodness, faithfulness, gentleness, self-control; against such things there is no law." These virtues, often referred to as the "fruits of the Spirit," represent the character traits that should develop in a believer's life as they align themselves with God's Word.

Love: The Supreme Virtue

The first and arguably most significant virtue listed in Galatians 5:22-23 (ESV) is love. The Bible continually underscores love's centrality in the Christian life. Jesus summarized all of God's commandments into two directives centered on love: love for God and love for our neighbor (Mark 12:30-31 ESV). The cultivation of love is a reflection of the transformative work of the Holy Spirit's inspired words in our lives.

Joy and Peace: Virtues of an Anchored Life

Joy and peace, the next two fruits, are not dependent on external circumstances. Instead, they are deeply rooted in our relationship with God. The Holy Spirit, through His inspired words, provides us with a perspective that sees beyond our immediate circumstances. This enables us to maintain joy and peace, regardless of life's trials.

Patience, Kindness, Goodness, and Faithfulness: Virtues of Character

These virtues are reflections of our character transformation as we align with the Holy Spirit's guidance through the Word. They affect our interactions with others, displaying God's character in our daily lives.

Gentleness and Self-Control: Virtues of Restraint

Gentleness and self-control are virtues that embody restraint and humility. They mirror the character of Jesus, as He exhibited these traits even when confronted with hostility and injustice. They represent a mature Christian life that is steeped in discipline.

Cultivating Virtues: A Continuous Journey

Cultivating these virtues is a continuous journey, one that requires discipline and dedication. It involves persistently engaging with the Scriptures and prayerfully seeking to apply God's teachings in our daily lives.

The Role of Free Will and Discipline

Understanding God's foreknowledge and human free will is crucial in cultivating virtues. God, being timeless and omniscient, knows what choices we will make. However, this foreknowledge doesn't determine our actions; it only reflects what we will freely do. Therefore, our disciplined efforts to cultivate virtues are not trivial but a necessary exercise of our free will.

Virtues are more than just moral standards; they are the manifestation of the Holy Spirit's work through the inspired words of Scripture in our lives. As we discipline ourselves to study and apply God's Word, we enable the cultivation of these virtues, reflecting the character of Christ in our daily lives. This process requires dedication, but it's a rewarding journey that anchors our lives in love, joy, peace, and the other fruits of the Spirit.

The Impact of Virtue: Personal and Communal Transformation

The disciplined cultivation of virtues carries significant implications, impacting both personal and communal lives. Rooted in the inspired words of the Holy Spirit, these virtues foster transformative changes that can resonate in our personal journeys and ripple across our communities. This chapter delves into the profound influence of virtuous living, highlighting the transformative power of virtues when rightly understood and applied.

Personal Transformation through Virtues

As believers engage with the Scriptures, they embark on a transformative journey. The Holy Spirit's inspired words guide and equip individuals to live in alignment with God's will. Each virtue cultivated is a step towards personal transformation, reflecting the character of Christ within us.

The virtues listed in Galatians 5:22-23 (ESV) such as love, joy, peace, patience, kindness, goodness, faithfulness, gentleness, and self-control, are signposts for this transformative journey. As believers embody these virtues, they experience a shift in their perspectives, attitudes, and behaviors. Love prompts selfless acts, joy fosters a grateful heart, peace instills a calm spirit, and so forth. The personal impact is profound as the disciplined cultivation of these virtues leads to a life that increasingly mirrors Christ's life.

Virtues and the Transformation of Relationships

Virtues not only transform us personally but also dramatically reshape our relationships. The virtue of love, for instance, directly affects how we relate to others. 1 Corinthians 13:4-7 (ESV) provides a detailed explanation of love's nature, outlining its patience, kindness, and absence of envy or boastfulness. When applied, this kind of love can dramatically improve relationships, promoting understanding, compassion, and harmony.

Similarly, virtues like patience and gentleness can de-escalate conflicts, fostering reconciliation and mutual respect. The ripple effect of these virtues extends beyond immediate relationships to influence broader social interactions.

Communal Transformation through Virtues

Beyond personal and relational transformation, virtues can profoundly impact our communities. Virtues promote actions and attitudes that contribute to societal harmony and justice. For instance, kindness and goodness foster acts of charity, contributing to communal welfare. Faithfulness and self-control build trust and reliability, strengthening the fabric of our communities.

Christians are called to be the "salt of the earth" and the "light of the world" (Matthew 5:13-14, ESV). This metaphorical language underscores the transformative influence believers are expected to have in their communities, an influence rooted in the virtues they cultivate.

The Role of Free Will and Discipline in Transformation

While God's foreknowledge is perfect, it doesn't determine human actions. The cultivation of virtues is a conscious choice, an exercise of our free will. This understanding accentuates the importance of discipline in fostering virtuous living. Without disciplined engagement with Scripture and intentional application of its teachings, personal and communal transformation would remain elusive.

The impact of virtues extends far beyond personal moral standards. The disciplined cultivation of virtues, guided by the Holy Spirit's inspired words, can catalyze personal, relational, and communal transformation. As believers embody the fruits of the Spirit, they engage in a continuous journey of transformation, progressively reflecting Christ's character. They become agents of change within their relationships and communities, illustrating the profound influence of a life rooted in virtues. It is a difficult journey, one that requires constant discipline and dedication, but the rewards are profound, ranging from personal growth to societal harmony.

The Lifelong Journey of Cultivating Virtues

The process of cultivating virtues is a lifelong journey, one that necessitates consistent discipline and dedication. It's not merely a quest to attain a set of moral standards, but an ongoing process of personal transformation rooted in the inspired words of the Holy Spirit, reflecting the character of Christ within us. This chapter delves into the process, stages, and significance of this lifelong journey, underlining the essential role of discipline in this transformative pursuit.

Beginning the Journey: Conversion and Commitment

The lifelong journey of cultivating virtues begins with conversion and commitment to the Christian faith. At conversion, individuals acknowledge their need for salvation and affirm their faith in Christ. This seminal moment initiates a new spiritual journey, marked by a commitment to live according to God's will as revealed in the Scriptures.

Yet, this initial commitment isn't the end but the beginning of a lifelong journey. As it is written in Philippians 2:12 (ESV), "work out your own salvation with fear and trembling." This charge underscores the necessity of continuous effort in nurturing our spiritual growth, an effort that prominently involves cultivating virtues.

Cultivating Virtues: A Lifelong Process

Cultivating virtues is not an instantaneous process; it's a lifelong endeavor that demands discipline, consistency, and patience. As Paul writes in Galatians 5:22-23 (ESV), the fruit of the Spirit includes virtues like love, joy, peace, patience, kindness, goodness, faithfulness, gentleness, and self-control. Cultivating these virtues involves constant engagement with the Word of God, leading to an increasingly Christ-like life.

Consider the virtue of patience. It's not simply a characteristic one acquires overnight but a virtue developed over time through various trials and tribulations. James 1:2-4 (ESV) states, "Count it all joy, my brothers, when you meet trials of various kinds, for you know that the testing of your faith produces steadfastness. And let steadfastness have its full effect, that you may be perfect and complete, lacking in nothing." This passage underscores how virtues are gradually cultivated through lived experiences, a process that requires time and discipline.

Stages of Spiritual Growth: From Milk to Solid Food

The lifelong journey of cultivating virtues also aligns with stages of spiritual growth. Just as physical growth necessitates a gradual shift from milk to solid food, spiritual growth involves progressing from basic understanding to deeper wisdom. The Apostle Peter, in 1 Peter 2:2 (ASV), encourages believers to "long for the pure milk of the word, that by it you may grow in respect to salvation." As believers mature in their faith, they delve deeper into the Word, fostering a more nuanced understanding and application of virtues.

Similarly, in Hebrews 5:12-14 (ESV), the author highlights the necessity of maturing in spiritual understanding, moving from "milk" to "solid food." This progression is crucial for the disciplined cultivation of virtues, demanding continuous engagement with the Word and its practical application.

The Significance of the Lifelong Journey

Why is this lifelong journey important? The process of cultivating virtues throughout life allows believers to continuously align themselves with the character of Christ. It enables them to become "salt of the earth" and "light of the world" (Matthew 5:13-14, ESV), positively influencing their surroundings.

Furthermore, it ensures that spiritual growth remains a dynamic, ongoing process, not a static state. It fosters a continuous deepening of faith, understanding, and application, reinforcing believers' commitment to live according to God's will.

Conclusion

The lifelong journey of cultivating virtues is a dynamic process of continuous spiritual growth and personal transformation. Initiated at conversion and fueled by commitment, this journey requires discipline, patience, and an ongoing engagement with the Word of God. As believers intentionally cultivate virtues, they progressively reflect Christ's character, positively influencing their personal lives and broader communities. Despite the challenges, the journey is rewarding, enriching both the individual and the community while glorifying God.

CHAPTER 13 The Journey Forward: Preparing for What God Has in Store

Introduction: Embracing the Journey with God

As Christians, we are called not only to a destination but to a journey – a lifelong journey that begins at the moment of our conversion and continues until we meet our Savior face to face. Embracing this journey means fully engaging in the cultivation of virtues, the deepening of faith, and preparing for what God has in store for us. The importance of readiness cannot be overstated. This chapter, therefore, focuses on preparing for the journey forward, to enable us to fully partake in God's divine plan.

Understanding the Journey: The Role of Discipline and Virtues

As we have explored in the preceding chapters, discipline plays an essential role in the Christian life, particularly in cultivating virtues. Disciplined engagement with the inspired words of the Holy Spirit enables us to develop Christ-like character, shaping us into the "salt of the earth" and the "light of the world" (Matthew 5:13-14, ESV). It is through this transformation that we prepare ourselves for the journey forward, for what God has in store.

The journey we undertake is not an aimless one. It is guided by God's Word and propelled by the virtues we cultivate. Through this journey, we continually transform, mirroring the character of Christ more closely. But this transformative journey does not happen in isolation. It involves engaging with our communities, influencing them positively through the virtues we embody.

Edward D. Andrews

God's Foreknowledge and Human Free Will

As we prepare for the journey forward, it's essential to understand the dynamic between God's foreknowledge and human free will. God, in His timeless and omniscient nature, knows what choices we will freely make. This foreknowledge, however, does not compromise or dictate our free will. It simply reflects what we, in our free will, choose to do.

God's foreknowledge provides a profound comfort as we navigate our journey. It assures us that our loving Creator, who knows the end from the beginning, has a divine plan for us. Yet, we are not passive participants in this journey. Our choices, actions, and the virtues we cultivate matter significantly. As we make decisions, take actions, and mold our character in line with God's Word, we actively participate in the unfolding of God's plan for our lives.

Embracing the Journey: From Passive Spectators to Active Participants

Embracing the journey means transitioning from passive spectators to active participants in God's divine plan. It involves aligning our lives with God's Word, making choices that reflect the virtues we cultivate, and taking actions that mirror Christ's character.

But how do we actively participate in this journey? First, we engage consistently with the Word, allowing it to shape our thoughts, decisions, and actions. As the Psalmist declares, "Your word is a lamp to my feet and a light to my path" (Psalm 119:105, ESV).

Second, we strive to live out the virtues we cultivate, reflecting Christ's character in our daily lives. As Paul exhorts in Philippians 2:12 (ESV), we are to "work out our salvation with fear and trembling," demonstrating the transformative power of our faith.

Lastly, we act upon our prayers, acknowledging that while we depend on God for guidance and provision, we also bear responsibility to act faithfully and courageously. As James reminds us, "faith without works is dead" (James 2:26, ESV).

The journey forward is a continuous process of transformation, guided by God's Word and shaped by the virtues we cultivate. It is a journey that requires readiness and active participation, moving beyond mere spectators to becoming vibrant, Christ-reflecting agents in God's divine plan. The road may be long and fraught with challenges, but the rewards of spiritual growth and a closer walk with God make every step worth it. Let us, therefore, embrace this journey, prepare for what God has in store, and look forward to the ultimate fulfillment of His divine plan.

Biblical Insights into God's Promises for the Future

As we look ahead on our journey as Christians, God's promises serve as an anchor, guiding us and giving us hope for the future. Throughout the Bible, we find numerous examples of God's faithfulness in fulfilling His promises, and these offer us insight into His unwavering commitment to His Word. This section aims to explore some of the key biblical insights into God's promises for the future, demonstrating how they prepare us for the journey ahead.

God's Promises: A Testament to His Faithfulness

God's promises are not merely abstract concepts; they are testaments to His faithfulness, rooted in His unchanging nature. As stated in Numbers 23:19 (ASV), "God is not a man, that he should lie; neither the son of man, that he should repent: hath he said, and will he not do it? Or hath he spoken, and will he not make it good?" This verse underscores the reliability of God's promises, providing us with the assurance that what He has promised, He will fulfill.

Throughout the biblical narrative, we see this promise-keeping nature of God on full display. From the Abrahamic Covenant, where God promised to make Abraham the father of many nations (Genesis 17:4-5, ASV), to the Davidic Covenant, where God promised to establish David's throne forever (2 Samuel 7:12-16, ASV), God's promises were fulfilled, affirming His faithfulness.

Promises and Prophecies: The Intersection of Past, Present, and Future

While the fulfillment of past promises offers assurance of God's faithfulness, biblical prophecies provide glimpses into God's future plans. Prophecy, as foretold by prophets moved by the Holy Spirit, serves as God's promises for the future.

One central promise is the second coming of Christ, a hope-filled event that all believers anticipate. As we find in John 14:3 (ESV), Jesus Himself promises, "And if I go and prepare a place for you, I will come again and will take you to myself, that where I am you may be also." This promise offers believers comfort and hope, assuring us that our journey on earth is part of a larger divine narrative that culminates in our eternal communion with God.

Another critical promise is the resurrection of the dead at Christ's return, a prophecy that redefines our understanding of life and death. In 1 Corinthians 15:52 (ESV), we read, "In a moment, in the twinkling of an eye, at the last trumpet. For the trumpet will sound, and the dead will be raised imperishable, and we shall be changed." This promise assures believers of eternal life, a future free from death, pain, and suffering.

The Role of Promises in Shaping Our Lives

Biblical promises have a transformative effect on our lives, influencing our decisions, actions, and attitudes. God's promises serve as a guide, directing us on the path of righteousness. They act as a lens through which we view our lives, influencing our choices in light of eternal realities.

Knowing that God promises eternal life to those who believe in Him affects how we live today. It encourages us to live righteously, to value spiritual over material wealth, and to invest in things with eternal significance. As stated in Colossians 3:2 (ESV), "Set your minds on things that are above, not on things that are on earth."

Moreover, the promises of God offer comfort in times of suffering and uncertainty. When facing trials, the promise of God's presence (Deuteronomy 31:6, ESV) and the assurance of His sovereign control over all things (Romans 8:28, ESV) give us the strength to persevere, knowing that our trials are part of God's larger plan for our good and His glory.

Preparing for the Fulfillment of God's Promises

As we anticipate the fulfillment of God's promises, it's essential that we prepare ourselves by aligning our lives with His Word. This preparation involves living out the virtues we've cultivated, such as faith, hope, love, and patience, which keep us grounded in the midst of life's trials and uncertainties. As we grow in these virtues, we become better prepared for the journey ahead, equipped to face whatever comes our way.

Prayer is another crucial part of our preparation. Through prayer, we express our dependence on God, acknowledging that He is the source of our strength and the fulfiller of His promises. As we bring our requests, praises, and thanksgivings to Him, we align our hearts with His, cultivating a posture of expectancy as we await the fulfillment of His promises.

In conclusion, God's promises for the future offer us insights that prepare us for the journey forward. Rooted in His faithfulness and conveyed through biblical prophecies, these promises guide our steps, shape our lives, and fill us with hope. As we await their fulfillment, may we continue to grow in virtue, grounded in prayer, and live in anticipation of the glorious future God has in store.

Case Studies: Biblical Figures Who Trusted God's Plan

The Bible is full of stories about individuals who demonstrated extraordinary trust in God's plan, despite facing daunting challenges, delays, and uncertainties. This chapter delves into some of these inspirational lives, seeking to draw lessons that can help us navigate our journey forward.

Abraham: The Father of Faith

Abraham, often called the father of faith, is a sterling example of trusting in God's plan. God promised Abraham that he would become the father of a great nation (Genesis 12:2, ASV), but years rolled on, and the promise remained unfulfilled. Yet Abraham held onto God's promise, even when circumstances seemed to belie its fulfillment.

Abraham's trust in God's plan culminated in the sacrifice of Isaac (Genesis 22:1-19, ASV). God asked Abraham to offer his long-awaited son Isaac as a burnt offering, which was a seemingly absurd demand, considering Isaac was the child of promise. Nonetheless, Abraham displayed remarkable trust in God's plan, willing to sacrifice Isaac because he believed God could raise him from the dead (Hebrews 11:17-19, ESV). Abraham's faith serves as an exemplar for believers, teaching us that trusting in God's plan often involves surrendering our most cherished blessings.

Joseph: Trust Amidst Adversity

Joseph's life was marked by a series of unfortunate events, from being sold into slavery by his brothers (Genesis 37:28, ASV) to being wrongfully imprisoned in Egypt (Genesis 39:20, ASV). Despite these challenges, Joseph never lost his trust in God's plan.

In retrospect, every hardship Joseph encountered was part of a grand plan to save many lives (Genesis 50:20, ASV). God raised Joseph to the position of governor in Egypt, where he stored up grain in anticipation of a severe famine. His position enabled him to provide for his family and the Egyptians during the famine. From Joseph's story, we learn that trusting God's plan involves recognizing His sovereignty over our adversities and believing He can use them for a greater good.

Esther: Courage and Conviction

Esther's story demonstrates how trust in God's plan is often intertwined with courage and conviction. As a Jewish queen in a Persian king's court, Esther risked her life to save her people from a plot to annihilate them (Esther 4:16, ASV). Esther could not see the future outcome, but she trusted in God's plan, saying, "if I perish, I perish" (Esther 4:16, ASV).

Her courage saved the Jewish people, illustrating how trust in God's plan can bring about significant outcomes. Esther's story teaches us that trusting God's plan often requires us to step out in faith, risking everything for the sake of what is right.

Paul: Transformative Trust

The apostle Paul's life was transformed by his trust in God's plan. Once a persecutor of the church (Acts 9:1, ESV), Paul became one of its most ardent missionaries after his encounter with Christ (Acts 9:15-16, ESV). His trust in God's plan led him to spread the Gospel throughout the Gentile world, facing numerous hardships (2 Corinthians 11:23-28, ESV).

Despite his trials, Paul remained undeterred, believing that his sufferings were part of God's plan for spreading the Gospel and preparing him for eternal glory (2 Corinthians 4:17, ESV). Paul's life underscores that trust in God's plan is transformative, turning trials into opportunities and adversaries into allies for the cause of the Gospel.

In conclusion, the lives of these biblical figures demonstrate that trusting in God's plan is a journey marked by faith, courage, conviction, and transformation. Despite the challenges they faced, they held onto God's promises, preparing for the future He had in store. Their stories inspire us to do the same, trusting in God's plan as we journey forward, preparing for what He has in store for us.

Understanding God's Timing: Trusting in His Perfect Plan

Understanding and trusting in God's timing forms an essential aspect of our spiritual journey. God's timing may not always align with our expectations, but it is always perfect, working towards His divine plan. This section will delve into the biblical perspective of God's timing and its significance in the life of a believer.

God's Timing: Beyond Human Understanding

God's timing, like His ways, is higher than our ways (Isaiah 55:8-9, ASV). It transcends human understanding and is not limited to earthly parameters of past, present, and future. As Peter writes, "with the Lord one day is as a thousand years, and a thousand years as one day" (2 Peter 3:8, ESV). Thus, God operates outside the constraints of time, and His timing is perfect in every sense. Recognizing this truth helps us trust God's plan even when His timing seems delayed or confusing from our limited human perspective.

God's Timing in Fulfilling His Promises

Biblical history is replete with instances where God fulfilled His promises at a time that may have seemed unexpected to human observers. Abraham and Sarah waited for many years before the birth of their son Isaac, the child of promise (Genesis 21:1-3, ASV). Similarly, the Israelites were in Egyptian bondage for over 400 years before God delivered them (Exodus 12:40-41, ASV). In both instances, God's timing was perfect, fulfilling His promises precisely at the right moment.

God's Timing in the Life of Jesus

The life of Jesus exemplifies the perfect timing of God. Galatians 4:4 (ESV) states, "But when the fullness of time had come, God sent forth his Son, born of woman, born under the law." Jesus's birth, ministry, crucifixion, and resurrection all happened in God's perfect timing, culminating in the provision of salvation for humanity.

Moreover, Jesus often referred to His timing during His earthly ministry. He told His brothers, "My time has not yet come, but your time is always here" (John 7:6, ESV), referring to His divine timetable, which was distinct from ordinary human timeframes. Even at the cross, Jesus yielded to God's timing, uttering, "Father, into your hands I commit my spirit!" (Luke 23:46, ESV). In every way, Jesus's life demonstrated complete submission to God's perfect timing.

Living in Alignment with God's Timing

Understanding and trusting in God's timing has profound implications for our lives. It means waiting patiently for God to act, even when circumstances seem dire. It involves trusting in His promises, even when their fulfillment seems delayed. It includes yielding our plans and desires to God's perfect plan and timing.

Just as a farmer waits for the harvest (James 5:7, ESV), we are to wait patiently for God's timing. This doesn't mean inactivity but rather active trust, continuing to do good and living in faithfulness (Galatians 6:9, ESV).

Embracing God's timing also necessitates trusting in His perfect plan. Jeremiah 29:11 (ESV) assures us, "For I know the plans I have for you, declares the LORD, plans for welfare and not for evil, to give you a future and a hope." Even when we don't understand His timing, we can rest in His good and perfect plan for us.

In conclusion, understanding and trusting in God's timing is a crucial aspect of our journey forward with Him. It teaches us to wait patiently, to trust in His promises, and to yield our plans to His. Although God's timing may not always align with our expectations, we can rest assured that it is always perfect, working towards His divine plan. As we prepare for what God has in store for us, may we always trust in His perfect timing, remembering the words of Ecclesiastes 3:11 (ASV), "He hath made everything beautiful in its time."

Preparing for the Future: Practical Strategies for Spiritual Growth

As we navigate our journey forward, preparing for what God has in store, it is critical that we strategically nurture our spiritual growth. This section outlines practical strategies that can guide us toward a deeper relationship with God and a more robust spiritual life, all gleaned from the rich tapestry of biblical teachings.

Engaging with God's Word

The Bible, being the inspired and inerrant Word of God, is the fundamental resource for our spiritual nourishment and growth. It is "living and active, sharper than any two-edged sword, piercing to the division of soul and of spirit, of joints and of marrow, and discerning the thoughts and intentions of the heart" (Hebrews 4:12, ESV). Regular, thoughtful engagement with the scriptures allows us to gain insight into God's character, understand His promises, and navigate our life's challenges with wisdom.

To maximize our interaction with God's Word, we should aim to make Bible reading and study a consistent part of our daily routine. Diverse methods can help maintain engagement, such as thematic studies, verse-by-verse expositions, or utilizing a systematic Bible reading plan. As we consistently interact with God's Word, we permit it to shape our thoughts, attitudes, and actions.

Prayer: Communicating with God

Prayer is our direct line of communication with God. It is not about convincing God to act according to our desires but is a means to align our will with His. In prayer, we acknowledge our dependence on God, express our gratitude, present our needs and concerns, and seek His guidance. The Apostle Paul encourages us to "pray without ceasing" (1 Thessalonians 5:17, ESV), highlighting the continuous and regular nature of our communion with God.

However, prayer is not merely about asking for our needs. It should be a balanced blend of adoration, confession, thanksgiving, and supplication. In modeling prayer, Jesus began by acknowledging God's holiness ("Our Father in heaven, hallowed be your name," Matthew 6:9, ESV) and ended with an affirmation of His power and glory. Such a model can shape our prayer life, enabling us to approach God with reverence, honesty, gratitude, and humility.

Building Fellowship and Community

The New Testament presents the Christian journey not as a solitary endeavor but a communal experience. The early believers "devoted themselves to the apostles' teaching and the fellowship, to the breaking of bread and the prayers" (Acts 2:42, ESV). Belonging to a community of believers fosters mutual encouragement, accountability, learning, and support. It provides an environment for practicing the 'one another' commands of the New Testament—love one another, encourage one another, bear one another's burdens, and so forth.

Service and Outreach

Serving others and sharing the Gospel are key aspects of our spiritual growth and preparedness for the future. Jesus modeled service in His ministry, stating, "even as the Son of Man came not to be served but to serve, and to give his life as a ransom for many" (Matthew 20:28, ESV). As we extend God's love to others through service, we become more like Christ.

Furthermore, sharing the Gospel is part of our commission as followers of Jesus. Whether locally or globally, we are called to make disciples (Matthew 28:19-20, ESV), sharing the good news of Christ with others. Such outreach efforts are not only a fulfillment of our calling but also a catalyst for our spiritual growth.

Fostering Personal Holiness

As we prepare for the future God has in store, striving for personal holiness is crucial. Peter's exhortation rings true: "But as he who called you is holy, you also be holy in all your conduct, since it is written, 'You shall be holy, for I am holy'" (1 Peter 1:15-16, ESV). Holiness is about aligning our thoughts, words, and actions with God's standards. It involves conscious decisions to resist sin and pursue righteousness, keeping our hearts and minds focused on God.

In conclusion, as we journey forward, we need to intentionally foster our spiritual growth. Engaging with God's Word, maintaining a vibrant prayer life, cultivating Christian fellowship, serving others, evangelizing, and striving for personal holiness are all practical strategies to guide us. As we make these practices a part of our life, we prepare ourselves for the future, aligning ourselves more closely with God's will, and equipping ourselves for whatever He has in store. Our journey may not be easy, but with God's guidance and our practical commitment, we can look forward to a future grounded in His promises.

The Role of Prayer and Scripture in Shaping Our Future

In our journey towards the future God has in store for us, two critical spiritual disciplines play a fundamental role: prayer and engagement with Scripture. These practices align our hearts and minds with God's will and illuminate our path forward. Let's delve into understanding how each of these contributes to shaping our future.

Prayer: A Dialogue with God

Prayer is our personal and direct communication with God. It's an acknowledgment of our dependence on Him, a means to express our adoration, confess our sins, express gratitude, and lay out our needs and concerns. But far beyond these, prayer is a divine dialogue designed to align our will with God's.

Paul's encouragement to "pray without ceasing" (1 Thessalonians 5:17, ESV) isn't a call to constant spoken prayers but an invitation to a lifestyle of ceaseless dependence on God, characterized by a prayerful attitude. It's about maintaining an ongoing dialogue with God as we navigate the daily ebb and flow of life.

Prayer plays a vital role in shaping our future because it aligns our hearts with God's will. As we express our desires, concerns, and fears in prayer, we also learn to listen and discern God's guidance and counsel. Our prayer lives thus become a platform for divine-human collaboration where our choices and actions can be influenced by God's wisdom.

However, prayer isn't a divine vending machine, where specific inputs guarantee desired outputs. Instead, it's a dynamic relationship where we express our desires, listen for God's guidance, and respond in faith and obedience. Our prayers, grounded in the awareness of God's wisdom and sovereignty, enable us to face our future with confidence and faith, regardless of the circumstances we encounter.

Scripture: God's Guidance for Our Journey

The Bible, as the inspired, inerrant Word of God, is a vital resource for shaping our future. It serves as our spiritual compass, providing direction and wisdom for our journey. "Your word is a lamp to my feet and a light to my path," declares the Psalmist (Psalm 119:105, ESV), emphasizing the Bible's role in illuminating our way forward.

Engagement with Scripture isn't merely an intellectual exercise. Instead, it's a transformative experience that molds our character, influences our choices, and shapes our future. The Bible equips us "for every good work" (2 Timothy 3:16-17, ESV), providing guidance for all aspects of life.

The Word of God carries the power to impact our future because it brings us into contact with God's thoughts, character, and plans. It reveals who God is, how He interacts with humanity, and His redemptive plan for the world. This divine revelation shapes our worldview, values, and actions, significantly influencing our life trajectory.

Furthermore, Scripture provides comfort and hope, especially in times of uncertainty. Biblical narratives reveal God's faithfulness and sovereignty, assuring us that He holds our future. Characters like Joseph, Moses, and Esther showcase God's ability to weave together even adverse circumstances for His purposes. Such insights anchor our faith, enabling us to face the future with hope and courage.

In conclusion, prayer and Scripture are indispensable practices in preparing for the future God has in store. As we converse with God in prayer and engage with His Word, we encounter divine wisdom that shapes our perspective, informs our decisions, and ultimately, influences our future. These spiritual disciplines don't provide a quick fix or a shortcut to a problem-free future. Instead, they offer a means to navigate our journey in alignment with God's will, equipped with divine wisdom, and fortified by faith. As we consistently engage in these practices, we can rest assured that we are well-prepared for whatever the future holds.

Community and the Church: Navigating Future Challenges Together

The journey forward towards what God has prepared for us is not intended to be a solitary endeavor. God created us to live in community, and He uses the church, the community of believers, to equip, strengthen, and support us in navigating future challenges. Our interconnectedness is designed to mirror the unity of the Trinity, the perfect divine community of the Father, Son, and Holy Spirit.

The Church: A Spiritual Family

The church, in essence, is not a building or a social institution. It is a spiritual family, an assembly of believers united by faith in Jesus Christ. As the apostle Paul wrote, "So then you are no longer strangers and aliens, but you are fellow citizens with the saints and members of the household of God" (Ephesians 2:19, ESV).

This spiritual family provides us with an environment for mutual edification and accountability. We can challenge and encourage each other to grow in faith and obedience, refining our character in the process. Just as iron sharpens iron (Proverbs 27:17, ASV), believers help each other become more Christ-like as they live and grow together.

Moreover, our spiritual family helps us shoulder our burdens, providing emotional and practical support. In Galatians 6:2, Paul exhorts, "Bear one another's burdens, and so fulfill the law of Christ" (ESV). As we navigate future challenges, our church community can be a source of comfort and strength, reminding us that we are not alone in our journey.

The Role of the Church in Preparing for the Future

God intends the church to be a central part of His plan for our future. As we assemble together, we can spur each other towards spiritual maturity, becoming thoroughly equipped for every good work (2 Timothy 3:16-17, ESV). The church's role includes teaching sound doctrine, correcting wrong beliefs, and encouraging consistent obedience to God's word. This equipping process prepares us to handle future challenges from a biblical perspective, applying God's wisdom to real-life situations.

Moreover, the church's collective witness serves as a beacon of hope in a world marked by uncertainty and despair. Jesus referred to His followers as the "light of the world" (Matthew 5:14, ESV). As we navigate the future together, our shared faith and hope can inspire those around us, pointing them to the eternal hope found in Jesus.

Navigating Future Challenges Together

As we face future challenges, our spiritual family – the church – becomes a stronghold. Not only do we find spiritual nourishment through the Word and worship, but we also experience practical help, emotional support, and communal resilience. Whether it's dealing with personal struggles or engaging in collective mission efforts, the church stands as a unified body, sharing joys, burdens, victories, and trials.

Importantly, while God's foreknowledge doesn't dictate our decisions, it reassures us that He is not surprised by our challenges. Being timeless and omniscient, God sees the end from the beginning, and His promise to work all things for the good of those who love Him (Romans 8:28, ESV) provides us with unshakeable confidence as we navigate the future.

In conclusion, community and the church play a critical role in preparing us for what God has in store. Through our spiritual family, we find encouragement, support, and a sense of purpose, enabling us to navigate future challenges with faith and resilience. As we move forward, may we continually seek to live out God's vision for our lives, supporting one another, growing in Christ-likeness, and shining as lights in a world that desperately needs the hope of the Gospel.

Misconceptions about God's Plan: Correcting Unbiblical Beliefs

As believers prepare for the journey that God has in store, it is essential to have a biblically accurate understanding of His plan. Misconceptions and misunderstandings can lead to confusion, frustration, and a distorted view of God's character and intentions. This chapter aims to clarify several common misconceptions about God's plan and provide biblical corrections.

Misconception 1: God's Plan is a Detailed Blueprint

One common misconception is that God's plan for our lives is like a detailed blueprint, outlining every step we should take and decision we should make. While it's true that God is omniscient and knows our every action before we take it (Psalm 139:16, ASV), this does not mean He dictates our every move. This misconception overlooks the significant role of human free will in God's design. God's sovereignty and human free will are both biblical truths that exist in tension with each other. As believers, we are called to make wise decisions based on God's Word and trust Him with the outcome.

Misconception 2: The Holy Spirit's Guidance is Mystical or Miraculous

Another common belief is that the Holy Spirit provides guidance through mystical or miraculous experiences. This misconception can lead people to seek dramatic revelations or signs as confirmation of God's will. However, it's crucial to understand that the primary way the Holy Spirit guides us is through God's Word. The Bible is inspired by the Holy Spirit (2 Timothy 3:16, ESV) and is sufficient to equip us for every good work (2 Timothy 3:17, ESV). Rather than seeking spectacular experiences, we should be devoted to studying and applying God's Word in our lives.

Misconception 3: God's Plan Always Leads to Prosperity and Ease

A prevalent misconception is the belief that if we're following God's plan, we will always experience prosperity, comfort, and ease. This belief, often propagated by prosperity gospel proponents, is fundamentally unbiblical. While God certainly blesses His children, He also uses trials and hardships for our growth and His glory (James 1:2-4, ESV). Jesus Himself told His followers that they would face tribulation in this world (John 16:33, ESV). Therefore, the presence of difficulties or suffering in our lives does not necessarily indicate that we're out of God's will.

Misconception 4: Prayer is a Means to Get What We Want

Some people view prayer as a tool to manipulate God into granting their desires. However, the purpose of prayer is not to get what we want, but to align our hearts with God's will. Jesus exemplified this in His prayer at Gethsemane, submitting His will to the Father's (Matthew 26:39, ESV). While we are encouraged to bring our requests to God (Philippians 4:6, ESV), we must do so with an attitude of trust and submission, recognizing that His wisdom far exceeds our own.

Misconception 5: God's Foreknowledge Equals Predestination

This misconception arises from misunderstanding the concept of God's foreknowledge. The Bible affirms that God knows in advance what individuals will freely choose. However, this foreknowledge doesn't compromise or dictate human free will. God's foreknowledge does not cause or determine human actions; rather, it only reflects what individuals will freely do. This refutes the views of extreme Calvinism that suggest God predestines some people to salvation and others to damnation.

Embracing Uncertainty: Finding Peace in God's Sovereignty

Life is fraught with uncertainty. We do not know what the next moment may hold for us, let alone the next month or year. As believers prepare for the journey God has in store, they must learn to embrace this uncertainty and find peace in God's sovereignty.

Understanding God's Sovereignty

God's sovereignty is a fundamental attribute of His character, denoting His supreme authority and control over all creation. In the Bible, God's sovereignty is often linked to His kingship. The psalmist declares, "The LORD has established his throne in the heavens, and his kingdom rules over all" (Psalm 103:19, ESV).

Despite the many uncertainties of life, believers can take comfort in knowing that God is not surprised or caught off guard by any situation. He is omniscient, knowing everything that will occur before it happens (Isaiah 46:9-10, ESV). Yet, His foreknowledge does not negate or compromise human free will; instead, it reflects what individuals will freely choose to do.

God's Sovereignty and Human Responsibility

While it's comforting to know that God is in control, it's essential to understand that this doesn't absolve us of our responsibility to make wise and godly decisions. The Bible teaches that God's sovereignty and human responsibility are not mutually exclusive but exist in tandem.

Even as the Apostle Paul recognized God's sovereignty in his life, he also understood his responsibility to "press on toward the goal for the prize of the upward call of God in Christ Jesus" (Philippians 3:14, ESV). As we seek God's guidance through prayer and the study of His Word, we must act on our understanding and apply it in our lives.

Embracing Uncertainty in Light of God's Sovereignty

As we face the unknown, we can find peace in God's sovereignty by cultivating a mindset of trust and submission. Instead of trying to control every aspect of our lives, we should learn to surrender our plans and desires to God, trusting that He will work all things for our good and His glory (Romans 8:28, ESV).

Embracing uncertainty does not mean living aimlessly or passively. It involves actively seeking God's will through His Word, making the best decisions we can based on our understanding, and leaving the outcomes in God's capable hands.

Finding Peace in God's Sovereignty

The knowledge of God's sovereignty provides believers with a deep sense of peace amid uncertainty. When we know that the God who created the universe is in control of our lives, we can face the future with confidence and courage.

Peace comes from understanding that God is not only sovereign but also good. His plans for us are for our welfare, not for calamity, to give us a future and a hope (Jeremiah 29:11, ESV). Even when our circumstances are challenging, we can trust that God is using them to shape us into the image of His Son (Romans 8:29, ESV).

In conclusion, as we prepare for the journey God has in store, we must learn to embrace uncertainty and find peace in His sovereignty. By understanding and accepting that God is in control, we can navigate life's uncertainties with faith and courage, knowing that our future is secure in His hands.

Stepping into the Future with Confidence in God

As we journey forward in life, preparing for what God has in store, it's crucial to step into the future with confidence in God. This chapter will discuss how our trust in God's promises, our commitment to prayer and Scripture, and our willingness to act on our faith can help us face the future with unwavering confidence.

Trusting in God's Promises

One of the primary ways to step into the future confidently is by trusting in the promises of God. Throughout the Bible, God has made numerous promises to His people. For instance, in Jeremiah 29:11 (ESV), God promises to provide a future filled with hope: "For I know the plans I have for you, declares the LORD, plans for welfare and not for evil, to give you a future and a hope."

While the context of this promise was initially directed to the people of Israel, the principle stands for all believers today. God's promises reveal His character: He is faithful, good, and trustworthy. When we trust in His promises, we can be sure that He will fulfill them in His perfect timing and according to His perfect will.

Prayer and Scripture: Our Tools for the Journey

To prepare for the journey ahead, believers need to rely on the tools God has given them. Among these tools are prayer and Scripture. Prayer allows us to communicate with God, express our desires, seek His will, and invite His guidance in our lives. As we commune with God through prayer, we should remember that prayer is not a means of manipulating God into giving us what we want. Instead, it's an act of surrender where we yield our plans to His will.

The Bible, God's inspired and inerrant Word, is our roadmap for life. It provides instruction, encouragement, and wisdom. As we faithfully study and meditate on Scripture, the Holy Spirit-inspired words guide us. These words help us understand God's will, learn His ways, and make wise decisions as we step into the future.

Acting on Our Faith

Faith is not a passive stance but an active engagement with God's truth. To step into the future with confidence, we must be willing to act on our faith. This means not just hearing God's Word but applying it in our lives, a principle emphasized by James when he wrote, "But be doers of the word, and not hearers only, deceiving yourselves" (James 1:22, ESV).

Acting on faith may involve stepping out of our comfort zones or taking risks for God's kingdom. It may mean making difficult decisions or standing firm in our convictions, even when the world opposes us. Yet, it is through such actions that our faith grows stronger, and our confidence in God deepens.

The Role of Community in Building Confidence

Stepping into the future with confidence in God is not a solitary endeavor. The Christian life is designed to be lived in community. Fellow believers can offer encouragement, accountability, and support as we face the uncertainties of the future together. The early Christian community set a strong example for us in this, devoting themselves to the apostles' teaching and the fellowship, to the breaking of bread and the prayers (Acts 2:42, ESV).

Finding Confidence in God's Sovereignty and Foreknowledge

Ultimately, our confidence rests not in our own abilities, understanding, or circumstances but in the sovereignty and foreknowledge of God. God is sovereign, meaning He has ultimate control over everything. Nothing happens without His knowledge or outside of His authority.

God's foreknowledge, His ability to know what will happen before it occurs, is comforting as well. Although He knows in advance what we will choose, His foreknowledge doesn't compromise our free will. It reflects what we will freely do, providing a sense of certainty in our unpredictable world.

Stepping into the future with confidence in God is a vital aspect of the Christian journey. As we trust in God's promises, immerse ourselves in prayer and Scripture, act on our faith, lean on our community, and find rest in God's sovereignty and foreknowledge, we can face the future with unwavering confidence. The journey forward may be filled with unknowns, but we know the One who holds the future, and in Him, we have every reason to be confident.

BIBLIOGRAPHY

Andrews, Edward D. "FAITHFUL MINDS: A Biblical and Cognitive Behavioral Therapy Approach to Mental Health and Wellness." Christian Publishing House, 2023.

Andrews, Edward D. "MERE CHRISTIANITY REIMAGINED: Rediscovering the Faith for the 21st Century." Christian Publishing House, 2023.

Andrews, Edward D. "UNSHAKABLE BELIEFS: Strategies for Strengthening and Defending Your Faith." Christian Publishing House, 2023.

Andrews, Edward D. "YOU CAN MAKE A DIFFERENCE: Why and How Your Christian Life Makes a Difference." Christian Publishing House, 2017.

Andrews, Edward D. "GOD WILL GET YOU THROUGH THIS: Hope and Help for Your Difficult Times." Christian Publishing House, 2017.

Andrews, Edward D. "THE POWER OF GOD: The Word That Will Change Your Life Today." Christian Publishing House, 2018.

Boice, James Montgomery. "Foundations of the Christian Faith." InterVarsity Press, 1986.

Carson, D. A. "The Cross and Christian Ministry: Leadership Lessons from 1 Corinthians." Baker Books, 2004.

Chan, Francis. "Crazy Love: Overwhelmed by a Relentless God." David C. Cook, 2008.

Frame, John M. "Systematic Theology: An Introduction to Christian Belief." P&R Publishing, 2013.

Grudem, Wayne. "Systematic Theology: An Introduction to Biblical Doctrine." Zondervan, 1994.

Henry, Matthew. "Matthew Henry's Commentary on the Whole Bible." Hendrickson Publishers, 2006.

Keller, Timothy. "The Reason for God: Belief in an Age of Skepticism." Penguin Books, 2008.

Lewis, C.S. "Mere Christianity." HarperOne, 2001.

MacArthur, John F. "Twelve Ordinary Men: How the Master Shaped His Disciples for Greatness, and What He Wants to Do with You." Thomas Nelson, 2006.

Piper, John. "Desiring God: Meditations of a Christian Hedonist." Multnomah Books, 2011.

Sproul, R.C. "Knowing Scripture." InterVarsity Press, 2009.

Stott, John R.W. "Basic Christianity." InterVarsity Press, 2008.

Swindoll, Charles R. "Improving Your Serve: The Art of Unselfish Living." Thomas Nelson, 2004.

Tozer, A.W. "The Knowledge of the Holy: The Attributes of God: Their Meaning in the Christian Life." HarperOne, 2009.

Willard, Dallas. "The Divine Conspiracy: Rediscovering Our Hidden Life in God." HarperOne, 1998.